the legacy of
Ida Lillbroända

"Is it the metaphysical, genetic, spiritual, metaphoric bridge to a new world, Ida being the link from the Old World to the new?"

arlene sundquist empie

the legacy of
Ida Lillbroända

finnish emigrant to america 1893

boulder house publishers

la conner, washington

The Legacy of Ida Lillbroända was informed by generations of Ida's kin in Finland and America, including my daughters Lauren Lindskog Blanc, Kristen Lindskog Jarvis, Leslie Lindskog Burrows and my grandchildren for whom this book originated as a gift of their heritage and to whom it is dedicated: the youngest generation who carry in their blood Nordic genes, values, and strong connection to Nature from our unique *finlandssvensk* heritage:

Kristen Burrows, Lilly Burrows, Cole Burrows, Jack Jarvis, Jessica Jarvis, Blake Jarvis, Julien Blanc, Marielle Blanc, Cedric Blanc.

With immense gratitude to all the people who shape our lives and inspire our future and for the inspiration, encouragement, and unconditional love of my extended family and friends in Finland.

A toast to all our relations—past, present, and future. Skål!

—Arlene Sundquist Empie

The Legacy of Ida Lillbroända: Finnish Emigrant to America 1893
Copyright © 2010 by Arlene Sundquist Empie
First published in the United States of America by Boulder House Publishers

Library of Congress Control Number: 2010911060
The Legacy of Ida Lillbroända: Finnish Emigrant to America 1893
/ by Arlene Sundquist Empie — lst. ed.
p. cm.
Includes bibliographical references and index

ISBN 978-1-931025-05-8 Clothbound

FIRST EDITION

10 9 8 7 6 5 4 3 2 1

Book and jacket design by David Alcorn
Cover photo: Birch Forest in Finland by Kristen Burrows
    Insert: Ida, Vivian, Leona and Daniel Sundquist (ca. 1920)
    Back flap: Arlene Sundquist Empie in Finland by Kristen Burrows
Endsheets: Birch forest in Finland   Photograph by Kristen Burrows
Frontispiece: The little bridge at Lillbroända (ca. 1930) Photograph by Leona M. Sundquist (1896–1988)
Published in the United States of America

Content

Illustrations

Photographs by Leona M. Sundquist (1896–1988)
unless otherwise noted.

Acknowledgments

If words alone could sustain us, I honor those authors and lyricists who provide nourishment with special appreciation to Finnish author Juhani Pallasmaa for his inspiring and poetic writings. A deep bow to those who tell the stories and write them down for future generations. Through words and imagery, the life story of an extraordinary woman unfolds in *The Legacy of Ida Lillbroända*. Descriptive excerpts from letters and unpublished manuscript by Leona M. Sundquist (1896-1988) Professor Emeritus, Western Washington University, provide insight into the activities and mindset of first and second generation Swedish-speaking Finns in early 20th century America. Sundquist documented life in America through the lens of her Leica and snapshot views of the places the immigrants left behind in Finland. She emphasized the ordinary and captured the beauty of the moment. "The Family" written in 1932 at the University of Washington by Esther Sundquist (1912–2004) is a further source of information.

As I sort through images of generations past, I contemplate the lasting and significant importance of photographs in recording personal history. Each photograph tells us more about people and place than a thousand words. I look into their faces with wonder; they silently stare back at me. I bow to the photographers who made these lasting impressions. Notably, identifying people in the photographs is a simple task often overlooked. Photographs of people and places not identified become lost to history.

I express gratitude to astute Finnish researcher Staffan Storteir who would not let drop the matter of Ida's elusive passage to North America. Our lengthy journey was fraught with misspelled passenger lists and incorrect dates, but his determination and perseverance brought results. Thanks to Sue Swiggum, TheShipList.com and Harry Dodsworth who offered 1893 newspaper announcement of SS Oregon's arrival.

I am grateful to historians and genealogists: Ed Schnebele, family historian and archivist, Swedish Finn Historical Society; Vincent O. Erickson, Ph.D., retired anthropology professor, for his in-depth knowledge of our family history in North America and Finland; Nancy Sundquist Euken and Norma Sundquist Gilbertson who provided familial information; author K G Olin, Jakobstad; Alf Blomqvist, Jakobstad, competent and exacting genealogist who assisted with Nykarleby records; Hasse Nygård, Swedish Finn Historical Society's Finlander and Talko Project; Hasse and Helena Andtbacka whose expertise includes Kronoby; Vidar Liljekvist, who is knowledgeable about Larsmo records; Börje Vestö, Cronoby database; and Sven-Erik Wiik, Kronoby.

Special thanks to text editor Gunnar Damstrom, Editor, *The Quarterly* Swedish Finn Historical Society, for his astute assistance regarding Finland-Swedish historical and cultural matters. Sincere thanks to Author Susanne Österlund-Pötzsch for her inspiration and pertinent information in "Swedish Finn Descendants in North America: Creating Cultural Identity—'American Plus.'" And Pernilla Holmgård for sharing her relevant thesis "The Finland-Swedish Heritage: And its Influence on Third Generation Descendants in the Northwest of the USA." My appreciation to *småkusin* Inger Sandvik and many newly found relatives and friends in Finland who shared information. My thanks to book designer David Alcorn and to the keen eye of copy editor Heidi Thomas. Kudos to David Hall, HKP Architects, for my award-winning writer's Studio by the Sea and Robert Maxwell for Macintosh support.

Foreword

The Storyteller

Brilliant afternoon sunlight reflected off Bellingham Bay and spilled into Aunt Leona's small kitchen, highlighting one side of her beautiful, but lined face. On her head sat her usual toque, as she called it, a brimless dusty blue knitted cap that she wore even inside the house. I was seated at her kitchen table when my 90-year-old aunt, then matriarch of the Sundquist family in America interrupted her story, leaned forward, and looked intently at me. She handed me a sturdy brown envelope chock full of large negatives of black and white photographs she had taken in the early decades of the 20th century and the original manuscript of *The Life and Times of the Sundquist Family* handwritten on a roll of continuous computer paper.

"Someday you may want to write about our family history. You should have these."

I ponder if it were at that moment when she handed me the envelope, the torch was passed. I was destined to be a family storyteller, as the eldest daughter of the second generation born in the United States, although it would be some years later that I would undertake writing this story. It seems that in most families, tribal people or clans, there is one who receives the mixed blessing of becoming the storyteller. Every family needs one; not every family is so fortunate to have one— The Storyteller, the gatherer of life stories, anecdotes, and keeper of the family flame.

A gift from my Aunt Esther further reinforced my new position as Storyteller: When I began writing, Ida Maria's daughter Esther Sundquist Schnebele, then 92 years old, presented me with her treasured antique Kalevala Koru necklace from Finland. The large striking bronze piece with the double bird motif replicates the end piece of the Lady of Häme festal chain (700–800 A.D.) found in Janakkala, Häme region in southern Finland.

"This is a storyteller's necklace," she said. "You must have this."

Storytelling is not something we necessarily choose to do. It might be a self-imposed task, an assignment by divine guidance or as in my Aunt Esther's case, a required paper assigned in University of Washington Sociology class 1932 that is a richly documented family history. In 1975, Leona Marie Sundquist wrote a rich and compelling story *The Life and Times of the Family of John Leonard and Ida Marie Vikstrom Sundquist: As recalled by their Eldest Daughter Leona Marie Sundquist.*

What is it that compels at least one member of a family, if not two in my generation including cousin Ed (Sundquist) Schnebele, to devote themselves to copious research, exploration and the time it takes to fit all the pieces of the family puzzle together? Consider for a moment that perhaps one is chosen. Or consider also that stories find us. My first book *Minding a Sacred Place* tells an ancient story that had been waiting for millennia to reveal itself. My husband and I did not anticipate the adventure that awaited us when we built a vacation home in 1978 known as "Boulder House" in the arid Upper Sonoran Desert of Arizona that provided for us a respite from the rainy winter weather in the Pacific Northwest and for spiritual catharsis as well. Indeed, we had unknowingly been directed to a sacred place, a place that holds clues to the cosmology of the first people in the American Southwest, therefore the title of our story *Minding a Sacred Place.*

It became apparent that we were brought there for a reason when we were stunned to witness a ray of sunlight at equinox touch the edge of a spiral petroglyph carved perhaps millennia ago by the first inhabitants. Four ceramic vessels dating before 700 AD were uncovered as excavation began for our firepit that unbeknownst to Architect Charles F. Johnson, he had designed in the exact place of an ancient firepit. We were the chosen ones to hear a story sequestered for millennia within an immense outcrop of Precambrian boulders in the North American Southwest. Revelations continued to be unveiled as we lived within the same boulders that sheltered the First People long ago.

It seemed that living within the outcrop of granitic stone and personally participating in celebrating winter solstice, summer solstice and equinox— cyclical events commemorated by petroglyphs patiently carved in granitic stone, I regained a forgotten memory as deep emotions bubbled to the surface of my being.

Mythologist Mircea Eliade wrote of a time:

"All men were less aware of belonging to the human species than of a kind of cosmic-biologic participation in the life of their landscape."

We were experiencing that kind of sentient living among the magnificent outcrop of living stone. There, an ancient story was revealed through the sun's interaction with rock imagery about living in harmony with Nature and celebrating calendric cycles as part of their cosmological belief system. This revelation, coupled with my own unique experiences, planted the seed of wonder about my heritage and ancestors. I came from generations of people who farmed in Finland and in America, and I too was raised on a farm, lived closely with Nature, keenly aware of seasonal cycles.

Juhani Pallasmaa, Finland's distinguished contemporary architect, whose early childhood years were spent at his grandfather's farm in Finland, wrote:

"I believe now that even one's sense of beauty and ethical judgment are firmly grounded in the early experience of the integrated nature of the human life world."

His words were as if my own when he wrote:

"With age I have become increasingly aware of how indebted I am to the richness of this farmer's life sphere in the late 1930s and 1940s for providing an understanding of my own embodied existence, and of the essential interdependences of the mental and physical aspects of daily life. Beauty is not a detached aesthetic quality; the experience of beauty arises from grasping the unquestionable causalities and inter-dependences of life."

Writing is a gift, and I don't doubt that it was for me a gift from a sacred place, as Boulder House is where I began writing my first essays about the dastardly destructive effects on the arid desert environment by overly zealous land developers in Arizona. Publication of my stories and public response were validation that indeed it was a fine gift. Storytelling, too, is a gift received, just as writing is a gift. In any case, once anointed with the responsibility of family storyteller, the task became all consuming and the pleasure and rewards commensurate with the task. It is the storyteller who stirs the passion of the journey, both the storyteller's and the historical portion. Consider that in writing family history, the names themselves, who begat who, are only relevant to my family and can likely be replaced with other family names as the Nordic emigrant story becomes 'our' story.

Ida Maria Andersdotter Lillbroända was a private person protected by the embrace of family. She did not discuss her past. I am inherently grateful to my aunts Leona and Esther Sundquist who wrote informative essays in the early 1900s. Their voices complement my story with historical information and first-person accounts about the lives and times of the Sundquist family in early twentieth-century America. Curiously, neither wrote but scant information about their parents' lives in the Old Country. Ida Maria's life before she emigrated from Finland is confined to four concise paragraphs in Leona's descriptive manuscript, but I discovered the brevity of information was typical of that which most Scandinavian immigrants offered in the late 1800s and early 20th century. Their time was consumed by the tasks at hand; they "kept their nose to the grindstone" and dedicated themselves and their families to a quick assimilation into the American culture and education as preparation for success in the New World. They did not talk about the Old Country. They did not look back.

The first genealogy chart I received from Finland simply said: Ida Maria Anders.dr. Lillbroända, *född* 1876-02-09 i Överbråtö, Kronoby, *död i Amerika*. Emigrant. USA & 1893-...-*livsöde, inte känt*. The last three Swedish words: Life story, not known. Those few words were the extent of what was written about my grandmother in Finland. Did it mean no one had any interest in her life story since she had left her home country? Certainly, among other names, I was aware of information about marriage, where they moved, children, and date of death. I was deeply moved by such scant information about a woman who left her mark, who made a difference in America. It appeared in print as if she had died when she left Finland. Emigrant. Did one word finalize her existence? Emigrant. "Life story, not known" prompted me to define her life for my family, for those who come after us, and for succeeding generations of her relations in Finland—the story of her life in America.

With the little information that I had about her young life, myriad questions arose that initiated my journey of finding the girl my grandmother once was and a personal journey of finding my roots. I never dreamed what I was getting into when I launched my search to find Ida Maria. I didn't know her name in her homeland; I knew little about Finland. What a gathering of the dead! And the living. An unexpected reward was meeting over 100 *småkusiner* in Finland that I did not know I had and falling in love with a contemporary Finland that has a deep national compassion toward Nature and sensitivity to their cultural arts and music. I share their pride in Finland's leadership in the world in education and environmental sustainability, and a woman president.

My ancestors were Finns—Swedish-speaking Finns. Does being of Finnish heritage in America matter in this humongous American mosaic in the 21st century? Yes, culture matters; traditions matter. Connections to the past are necessary and requisite for personal grounding in these tumultuous times; perhaps as contrast, rapidly developing technologies prompt us to hang onto and guard those values instilled by our heritage and our cultural traditions. Culture matters to humanity. Anthropologist Wade Davis writes about a cultural and spiritual web of life: "An 'ethnosphere,' the sum total of all the thoughts, beliefs, myths, and institutions brought into being by the human imagination that is as vital to our collective well-being as the biosphere."

Finding our roots is to know our heritage, to know who we are as a people, and our roots provide the foundation for the future. I realized the importance of my being—I was the vessel carrying forward the blood of my maternal ancestors, the same blood and cumulative blood memory that will go forward in future generations. Our Finnish ancestors will live on in our American lives, as long as they are remembered.

   With the beauty of love from parents and grandparents and the values they instilled, I patterned my lifeway with dignity, grace and self-determination as the women before me had done, and I have passed on to my daughters and to my grandchildren Ida Maria's "American Dream" of individuality and education. My grandmother emigrated from Finland over 100 years ago at the end of the nineteenth century because of opportunities in America for women and education for her children. Now my daughters carry on their great grandmother's dream of education for her progeny, as the third generation born in America earned their university degrees and the fourth generation moves on to universities.

   Chance and synchronicity have on many occasions entered into my personal life of seven decades; sometimes I wish I had journaled these seemingly amazing lifetime occurrences, but I accept metaphysical intervention more as a natural happening, and I give thanks. I relate a story relative to a serendipitous happening:

   A book that was shelved in Ida Maria's handcrafted oak library cabinet came into my possession quite recently. Flipping through the pages in *The Arts,* Written and Illustrated by Henrik Willem Van Loon (New York: Simon and Schuster 1937), I quite by chance stopped at page 64, Chapter Five entitled "Heinrich Schliemann" which the author explains:

   "For the greater part is devoted to an explanation of the word 'serendipity,' as it relates to Schliemann's career, and for which he mildly apologizes. I hope you won't mind a slight detour . . . I want to say something about my old friend and strange-looking word 'serendipity.' The word occurred originally in a story mentioned by Horace Walpole, the English wit and connoisseur, who died in 1797. The title of the novel was *The Three Princes of Serendip*, which was the old name for Ceylon. These three young men were forever making discoveries by 'accidents and sagacity' of things for which they were really not looking at all. Since then, serendipity came to mean 'the faculty of making happy and unexpected discoveries by accident.'"

I hope that making happy and unexpected discoveries shall always be the criteria for my often-visiting old friend 'serendipity'. One of many serendipitous occurrences in my life occurred at the Swedish Finn Historical Society's annual banquet in 2002. There was random seating for attendees, so I found an empty chair. The subject of ethnic identity arose at the table. I was well into my manuscript, and I had found during my research a well-written manuscript posted online by a student at Åbo Akademi University, Finland: "Swedish Finn Descendants in North America: Creating Cultural Identity – 'American Plus'." I suggested this would be an informative paper for everyone to read. An attractive girl seated next to me on my left inquired, "Who wrote the paper?" I searched my memory for the name, and I replied, "I can only remember that her first name is Susanne." The lovely blonde visitor from Finland looked at me, and she said, "I wrote that paper. I am Susanne Österlund-Pötzsch."

Karma continues, although more than likely Finnish magic: My esteemed copy editor Gunnar Damstrom discovered, while perusing my manuscript comfortably seated in his summer house in the Finnish Archipelago, that the name *hustrun Lisa Mattsdotter, Finne*, one of the *Faddrar* sponsors for Ida Maria Andersdotter Björnvik baptism at Larsmo, likely inhabited the same dwelling in 1876 where the house was then located and known to be the Finne house prior to being moved to its present location. And another incident when Damstrom noted that his great grandfather Edvin Hjelt was Master of the SS Polaris in 1902, the ship on which Ida Maria and John Sundquist departed Finland February 1902 on their final return to America.

The Legacy of Ida Lillbroända includes myriad discoveries by chance and synchronicity, seemingly uncanny encounters as I look back upon events. By chance, was it all by chance? I ponder the chain of events, people, and information gathering that occurred over a five-year period. By chance I connected with Staffan Storteir through the Finngen internet talk site when I submitted an inquiry about Ida Maria's passage to North America. The highest credit is due this astute Finnish researcher whose dogged determination led through a maze of errors in passenger data transcriptions to finding Ida's passage to North America arriving Quebec in 1893 aboard the SS Oregon. And then by chance on a Canadian website, I came across the hospital register where Ida and her travel partner were quarantined. The journey to finding Ida was circuitous and the discoveries exciting, which makes an interesting story.

Livsöde, inte känt life story not known motivated me to tell the story about this woman who left her homeland, traveled West and made a difference—a life story filled with rewards and accomplishments. Who or what directs our actions that ultimately lead to results? Or conversely, did Ida find us? It seemed that Ida finally appeared, in her own good time. All the pieces of the puzzle fell in place with the rhythmic force that topples a row of dominoes. For me, the culmination of the experience of putting this story on paper and her appearance meant that she approved my telling her story in the 21st century.

The Legacy of Ida Lillbroända took on a life of its own, and I found that my mission to tell Ida Maria's story held greater meaning beyond documenting her life for my children and grandchildren and her extended family in America and Finland—it was every emigrant's story.

Sun thoughts,
Arlene Sundquist Empie

the legacy of
Ida Lillbroända

Chapter *1*

On Wednesdays

On Wednesdays, I jumped off the yellow school bus, ran down the gravel road to our grand multi-gabled, early twentieth century farmhouse in Cedardale and quickly changed from my pleated wool plaid skirt and red sweater into faded blue jeans and a warm grey pullover sweatshirt. I pedaled my blue Schwinn bicycle down the rough country road, stood upright and pumped strenuously over the railroad embankment, coasted down the other side, and swerved onto the worn dirt path next to the drainage ditch alongside the road. My parents commanded that I wasn't allowed to ride on Highway 99, the roadway to nearby Mount Vernon and the main road between the United States/Canadian border and Seattle. But sometimes, when I was certain there was no oncoming traffic on the highway, I would escape the narrow path. I firmly grasped the handlebars, jumped the fat-tired front wheel onto the concrete pavement, and reveled in the smooth, fast ride on a straight, paved road, the wind streaking through my long blonde hair, the color of wheat stalks in autumn. Out on the open road, traveling alone the one-mile distance to my grandmother's house, my chest swelled and my heart pounded with a sense of freedom and discovery. As I sped down the open road, my mouth wide open, I inhaled the pungent odor of rich farmland, tall grass, moist earth, and manure that together is the smell of rural country.

On Wednesdays, Grandma Sundquist and I always listened to the exciting detective melodrama "Mr. Keen, Tracer of Lost Persons" broadcast on the radio at four o'clock. Mr. Keen, the sage old tracer of missing persons and his sidekick, Mike Clancy, carried our imaginations to another time and place. The polished mahogany Gothic-style console radio sat atop a white handwoven cloth that hung down, partially concealing the spindly golden oak legs of the nightstand next to Grandma Sundquist's bed.

Her devoted caregiver, Mrs. Maude Kyle, always had fresh flowers from the garden or sprigs of fern or greenery arranged in a small hand-painted porcelain bud vase on her bedside table—a vase that daughter Ida Elvira had handpainted. Grandma was in bed—almost every day now. No one told me why, except that her health was declining, and Grandma never complained about whatever ailment she had.

On this Wednesday, she lay in her immaculate white bed, propped up amid thick down pillows, the white muslin sheet carefully folded over her handwoven coverlet. When I entered the room, her head was turned away from the door; she was looking out through the slightly raised, double-sash window, her gaze fixed on something in the distance. From her bed, she could look to the west over the farmland to the first farmhouse that she and her husband John created—a home far from their Finnish homeland, the farmhouse that had been passed down to the next generation, to my father, the eldest son. From this vantage point, weathered grey hand-split cedar posts strung with barbed wire defined the cropland. Wheat, potatoes, oats—each colorful crop fenced in like border stitching outlining the squares of a patchwork quilt. In the original farmhouse, hope rose with the sun each morning as the sun's first rays penetrated her east-facing upstairs bedroom; now she looked to the west where the sky held a hint of the red glow of a waning winter sunset.

The lace around the pillowcase framed her face and wavy grey hair, lace that my mother crocheted. The olive tone of my grandmother's skin deepened against the whiteness of the freshly laundered linen. I scanned her relaxed face. The deep lines of seventy-one years receded in the midst of soft mounds of a goose-down pillow. I looked at her hands gently folded one over the other on the creamy coverlet she had woven. Her thin parchment-like skin, blotched with brown "liver spots," as my mother called them, revealed her bony hand structure. Her hands, once as strong as a man's, bespoke decades of hard work in the fields and in the farmhouse; protruding veins appeared like giant earthworms on her skin, ambling from forearm to fingers.

These were the same quick, demonstrative hands that waved flour in the air while explaining to me the art of fashioning buns from cardamom-scented bread dough. In her hands were the artistic traditions of her Finnish ancestors. I thought of the rhythmic click of her long wooden knitting needles from which, as if by magic, wool mittens, sweaters, and caps took form, issuing forth from her once-nimble fingers. Who else could knit without looking at the yarn and needles in their hands? Or knit faster than my grandmother? As the knitting took on form, the ball of yarn in the handcrafted wooden bowl spun and bounced as if it were propelling the yarn upward to meet her fingers.

I remember when I would sit for hours, or so it seemed, with my elbows firmly propped on my bent knees to hold the stretched out skein of wool yarn between my extended arms and straight hands while she wound the strand of yarn into a ball bigger than a softball. Grandma introduced me to the sense of working with wool: "Keep the yarn loose and free as you wind; let it slip through your fingers. Think of it like the ball itself gently seizing the strand of wool yarn," she instructed me. "If you wind the ball too tight, yarn will lose its resiliency. The secret is to keep turning the ball with one hand while at the same time you wind with the other hand." I was mesmerized watching the strand of yarn criss-cross around the ball creating a stunning design. Together we would fill the wooden bowl with soft pliant balls of wool yarn, a bowl that a neighbor, Mr. Holmquist, fashioned for my grandmother.

Grandma would often hand card her own wool for yarn and for the filling in quilts. Carding is the process that prepares raw wool for spinning. She would obtain a fleece from farmers at the riverfront who raised sheep. The fleece had to be washed and washed and finally rinsed in soft rainwater from the rain barrel. I would pick out burrs, seeds, and other foreign materials. After the fleece was washed and dried, I would pluck at it to loosen it for carding. She didn't approve of the American cards; her wood carding tools came from the Old Country. The crimped steel wires were mounted on leather backing, ready to be tacked onto the convex "working" side of the curved wood-handled paddles. I tried carding, too, as Grandma processed the fluffy pile of wool, but never quite got the knack of wielding the pair of wood-backed hand cards. The last cards were mailed from Finland in a wood box to Ida Sundquist, RFD No. 5, Mt. Vernon, Washington with holiday wishes: *God Jul Önskas av Familjes Vikstrom.*

I recall, too, the swoosh of the long wood shuttle as Grandma threw it confidently over the taut warp threads on her loom, caught it on the other side, and then, the firm clack-clack of the beater as she pressed thread into cloth like a magician. A firm downward push with her feet on the wood pedals of the floor loom that Grandpa had constructed for her and the harnesses would separate the threads and create a shed for the next entry of the shuttle carrying weft yarn. Weaving was also her opportunity for creative expression, exemplified by her skillful blending of colorful yarns and threads and the various traditional Finnish patterns that she wove into cotton and linen coverlets, table-cloths, and napkins.

A soft breeze nudged the bedroom curtains that she created from fabric woven on her loom and brought me back into the moment. Grandma opened her eyes and softly gazed at me. I had interrupted her silent reverie. Her hand rose and slowly brushed her long silver-grey hair away from her face. She turned toward me and placed her fingers against her cheek in a pensive pose as she studied my face.

Grandma told me to pull up a chair by the edge of her bed, and without fail, her first question was: "Would you like milk in your coffee and a sugar cookie?"

I learned very early in life that *kaffedags* coffeetime is a near-ritual ceremony observed among Finland Swede families in America. In the Nordic tradition, coffeetime would be mid-morning and again around four o'clock in the afternoon, a social setting when everyone is seated around a table to enjoy cardamom-flavored bread and cookies with their coffee. Grandma would don a fresh apron over her "house dress." It seemed her house dress didn't vary much from church dress, except for the fabric. I was always offered coffee at *kaffedags*, albeit more milk than coffee, ever since I was a small child sitting at the break-fast table in the nook, banging my feet against the storage box under the window seat, and Grandpa admonishing me for kicking his hand-crafted furniture. Grandma, however, did not approve when I poured a little coffee from my cup into the saucer, puckered my lips, and blew on the coffee before sipping from the saucer—just like Grandpa— with a cube of sugar tucked in my cheek.

"It's time for 'Mr. Keen, Tracer of Lost Persons,'" I said, stumbling on the words, as I was accustomed to doing.

I stuttered so badly that I had sent fifty cents for a pamphlet *How to Stop Stuttering in 30 Days*—mailed in a plain brown wrapper—but despite the deep breathing, facial and oral exercises that they proposed to cure this perplexing speech impediment, I continued to struggle with the mysterious malady. Later I would discover that stuttering may be a genetically transmitted nervous disorder. It seems that I inherited this trait from my grandmother's side of our family, as we would later find that my great aunt Hilda Sofia Andersdotter's "stammar" affliction was entered by the pastor in the *kommunionbok* in the 1880s at Kronoby church in Finland. Although painful episodes of humiliation in my younger years remain imprinted on my mind, at least they were not recorded in church records.

"Mr. Keen, T-t-t-tracer of L-l-l-lost Persons," I repeated, as my face winced, and I once again stumbled over the words.

I reached for the radio dial. Mr. Keen's partner, Mike Clancy, played the dumb Irishman. Case after case, following Mr. Keen's lengthy dissertation outlining the story, he would always remark: "Saints preserve us, Mr. Keen, do you mean . . . ?" The two characters didn't have official positions; they were simply summoned to help solve the mystery. They ignored procedure and barged into homes without search warrants. Their dialogue was clear and simple, and when Mr. Keen confronted the suspect, his sturdy, persuasive voice took on a mean edge.

Just as Mr. Keen's faithful and strong-armed assistant and companion Mike Clancy always seemed to jump ahead with his oft-misguided clue, Grandma and I interjected our conclusions in between their heavy dialogue and were pleased with ourselves when we solved the mystery first.

I am reasonably certain that we never engaged in any philosophical conversations. Considering my speech impediment, I rarely initiated a conversation, and Grandma had slowed down during our last years together. Her past cheerful and enthusiastic nature was now subdued. She was soft and serious, seemingly preoccupied with her own thoughts, a faint hint of a smile on her face. Her questions were generally about my well-being: "How are things going at school?" What did I think of Mrs. Minnie Gerriets, the Home Economics teacher? "She was in school with your aunts," Grandma reminded me. "Is she still thin as a rail?"

Our visits now were mostly just listening quietly to our favorite radio program. This day was a short visit as I still had chores to do on the farm before it got dark, feeding the calves, hosing down the milk house.

This day was also our last visit.

⚬⚬

When you are a youngster, it is difficult to accept death in our active lives; death comes to others, not to those close to us. The one thing I vividly recall about her memorial service is that I walked alone in the misty rain down the long steps of Salem Lutheran Church at the end of the funeral processional following Grandma's casket, and that I publicly wept while the crowd of people below with their upturned faces watched our silent procession.

I was fortunate that my grandmother was part of my life for thirteen years. She influenced my life and my values long after she left this world. She not only blessed me with her artistic skills, she fulfilled her American Dream that her children and grandchildren pursue educational opportunities to fully develop their abilities. I would in turn face the world as my grandmother did, with a strong, but quiet presence, with grace, style, and inner beauty, carrying with me that particular Finnish characteristic summed up in the Finnish word *Sisu*—the inherent determination and power to persevere, to do whatever it takes—and more, if needed. *Sisu* also has its other side when the combination of determination, perseverance, and obstinacy translates to hardheadedness.

Grandpa Sundquist had left us two and a half years earlier. (In the Forties, we children always used surnames when referencing our grandparents.) After Grandma Sundquist's death, the family gathered for four days to grieve, to give support to each other, and to remember my grandmother's life. Aunts and uncles cried and laughed. I watched. The Sundquist family had dealt with grief before: Ten-year-old Johan Vincent drowned in the Skagit River nearby; college graduate Ida Elvira was killed in a train crash near Centralia, Washington.

In the farmhouse kitchen, my father silently settled his grief near the warmth of the wood-burning stove and the rhythm of the old rocking chair. Neighbors and friends stopped by to pay their respects, bringing with them offerings of casseroles, cakes, and cookies, while my mother continued to cook and bake copious amounts of food. She made cardamom bread for coffeetime and rye bread for open-face tuna and egg sandwiches, deviled eggs, Swedish meatballs and baked cured ham, lemon chiffon and angel food cakes that called for a dozen eggs, and eggs were plentiful on the farm. And the ubiquitous Jell-O: pans of orange Jell-O with diced canned fruit, lime Jell-O with chopped celery and grated

carrots, strawberry Jell-O whipped with heavy cream, Jell-O ad infini-
tum. Assuredly, we would not go hungry.

Ida Maria Sundquist left an indelible impression on all who loved
her. Her wisdom, integrity, and direction were invaluable to those
around her. I watched grown-up sorrow from afar. I hurt. We children
were left alone to speak in whispers, not really understanding any part
of this—except that Grandma was not coming home.

For me, there would be no more Wednesdays with Grandma. I sat
on the woodbox next to the kitchen stove and from a partially curtained window, I looked westward through the barren branches of the
cherry tree silhouetted against the sunset and pondered her passing.

> In the early morning fog that creeps across rich
> moist earth reclaimed from the sea
> her breath now mingles with Earth's breath
> drifts lazily through green pastures
> hovers over lily pads on the slough, finally rises upward
> through pale green leaves of weeping birch trees
> to mingle wispily amidst graceful branches of tall cedars
> and disappear into the endless blue-grey sky beyond.

Ida Maria

Chapter 2

The Search for Ida Maria – What's in a Name?

Decades slipped away after my grandparents had passed on. I too had moved away from the Sundquist family farm where I was raised, the same farm established in 1903 by Ida Maria and her husband John Sundquist and conveyed in 1930 to their eldest son, my father Daniel Sundquist. I had been swept away in the tide of an American lifeway, appreciative of my family, but not necessarily delving into the family's past history. Now my daughters wanted to know about our heritage and our family traditions. And I realized I did not have good answers.

When my grandmother and I were together, she never talked about her life as a young girl in the "Old Country" nor did she mention any relatives in Finland. While some people have the privilege of also knowing their great-grandparents, I was stunned when I realized that I didn't even know my great-grandparents' names. John and Ida Maria Sundquist, typical of most first-generation Nordic immigrants in America, kept to the tasks at hand and dedicated themselves and their families to assimilation into the American culture and education as preparation for their success in the New World. They did not talk about the Old Country. They did not look back. But the larger question that confronted me was—Why didn't I ask?

I chided myself: If only I had had the presence to ask. I searched for excuses: Perhaps, it is our inherent Nordic reticence that we stand back, out of respect or parental upbringing or that one doesn't pry or question family matters. But, as I have discovered, there comes a time when those who could answer the questions are gone. And now I lament: There is no longer someone to ask.

By chance, about the same time that my thoughts turned to learning more about my heritage, the eldest Sundquist daughter and matriarch of the family, Leona Marie Sundquist, Professor Emeritus, Western Washington University, presented me with a copy of her manuscript *The Life and Times of the Family of John Leonard and Ida Maria Vikstrom Sundquist.* In this extraordinary document, she portrays the lives of the Sundquist family during the early decades of the twentieth century and provides invaluable, informative insights into the activities and mindset of the first and second generation Finland Swedes in America. The first page of Leona Sundquist's manuscript is notably remarkable because of its brevity. It left me wanting to know more.

John Leonard Sundquist met Ida Maria Vikstrom in the small iron-mining town of Ely, Minnesota in the early years of the 1890s. They were both immigrants from Finland. Father was born in Soklot, Nykarleby, Finland. Mother grew up in Kronoby at Lillbroända on the bank of a small stream. One of three daughters born to Mr. and Mr. Anders Vikstrom, she had had three years of schooling. At the age of 16 or 17 with a girlfriend, she decided to find her fortune in "Amerika."

They landed in Quebec, Canada, and were promptly quarantined for weeks, as an infectious disease had spread among the passengers. Mother was very miserable there, unhappy and homesick. Once in recalling the experience, she said that if she had had the money she would have taken the next boat back home. But fortunately for us, her children, she had to end her journey in Ely, Minnesota, where an uncle found work for her as a domestic.

Father, the oldest son in a family of seven children, found himself at the age of ten a breadwinner for his mother, sisters and brothers, his father having drowned while fishing. Father had no schooling. I do not know the year Father decided to go to America, the land of opportunity, nor do I know why and how he went to Ely, Minnesota. But I do know that the panic of 1893 found him among the unemployed. He, along with some friends, batched in a cabin on the shores of a lake. They fished, hunted, trapped and somehow survived. When he found work, the going wage was $1.00 a day. He considered himself fortunate. However, it seemed an inadequate

return for his efforts after leaving his homeland for the promised land of America. The gold mining boom in the West
beckoned.

Father left Ely to explore the possibilities for the good life
in Telluride, Colorado. He apparently found it to his liking,
and he sent for Mother to join him there. They were married
in March 1895.

Four concise paragraphs is the extent of information in her manuscript about her parents' lives in Finland, their emigration, and their
arrival in America. I wanted to know about my grandmother's life
before she was married. I wanted to know about her life in Finland. She
spoke Swedish; therefore, I thought she had emigrated from Sweden.
And what might have prompted a young girl in the 1890s to leave her
parents, siblings, and her homeland to travel halfway around the globe
to a new country—the New World?

Through oral tradition passed down by the elders, our extended
family knew that it was grandmother who insisted on returning to
America after a visit to the homeland in 1901. She had seen firsthand the
opportunities for women and for her children's education. Ida Maria
was unwavering in her goal: "*Till Amerika vi gå.*" I was compelled to
know more about this remarkable woman whose strong determination
and Finnish *sisu* carries on through generations of women.

The manuscript reads: "They landed in Quebec and were promptly
quarantined." Who was her travel companion? Was it inappropriate for girls to be traveling unchaperoned? And by what route did one
journey from Finland to North America in the early 1890s? Quebec?
Quarantine? Under what circumstances might passengers be quarantined? What year did they land in Quebec? And why Canada, rather
than New York's Ellis Island?

A few sentences later in the manuscript, Ida Maria is in Minnesota.
Was there a family chain of migration that she followed? Who was the
uncle who helped her to find work as a domestic? Then she is summoned to Colorado where she married John Sundquist. Where did they
meet? In those four scant paragraphs, I was overwhelmed with more
questions than answers: Who were Ida Maria's two sisters, and where

were they? Had Ida Maria left Finland to seek a better life? Had she fled? Worse, was she banished from her native home?

There were so many unanswered nagging questions hovering over the story as it was written: Why were important details left out? Why wasn't the whole story revealed? Were there family secrets? Skeletons in the closet? Why did a portion of history remain unspoken?

Leona Marie Sundquist, author of the manuscript, was the family historian or at least, one of the family's storytellers. She was awarded the title Distinguished Service Professor Emeritus of Western Washington University; her research and honors in her chosen field were extensive. Her documentation of the lives of the Sundquist family in early twentieth-century America was expounded upon in great detail throughout her manuscript, as one might expect from her professorial credentials. Only the beginning of the story was scanty. I pondered why she did not elaborate more on John and Ida's families, especially since she visited Finland in 1901-02 as a precocious child and again in 1931 while she was in the East at Columbia University. While I was intrigued by what might have been left out, I yearned to know more about the girl my grandmother once was and eagerly began the search for Ida Maria.

From the few documents our family possessed, and as far as we knew, my grandmother's maiden surname was Wikstrom:

Ida Wikström, Kronoby, is written in ink in nineteenth-century cursive on the back of an ecru-colored photograph and in another handwriting, a lightly penciled date—(ca. 1893.) The frame of the portrait bears the photographer's logo artistically composed from the initials C.W.H., the name Howorth, and the studio address 1627 Superior Street W., Duluth, Minn. Like many young emigrant girls following their arrival in America, she sat for a formal studio portrait to send home to assure her family that she was doing well in America. Ida Maria's hair was beautifully coifed with tight curls on her forehead; the bodice of her dress that appears in the photograph has double edging around the wide triangular neckpiece with a narrow upright collar divided in the front. A delicate bow with a floral applique is anchored at her neckline with a gold pin.

Ida Maria Wikstrom is the name written on the certificate when she married John L. Sundquist in Telluride, County of San Miguel, Colorado, 16 March 1895. Another document in our possession is a letter from Finland edged in black, which signifies a death. Printed in black ink on white paper with a wide black border around the edges, the folded letter had been addressed in script with black ink and mailed in 1923 to Mrs. Ida Sundquist in *Amerika* announcing her father Anders Vikströms funeral at Kronoby Church in Finland. A yellowed newspaper clipping from the *Finnish American* with a black cross at the top tells of the death of Anders Wikström.

Wikstrom, Wikström, and Vikströms. I was wallowing in confusion about the various spellings. I learned that the addition of an "s" at the end of the name signifies the possessive "s" in the Swedish language and does not require the apostrophe as when written in English. And the letters W and V are often interchanged in the Swedish language. In America, Ida Maria dropped the diacritic mark above the Swedish letter "ö" that indicates it is an additional vowel pronounced differently from the way the vowel "o" is pronounced; therefore, the name Wikstrom.

I contacted Syrene Forsman at the Swedish Finn Historical Society in Seattle. I knew little about Finland; I had not traveled there, nor did I understand the naming system or that place names could reference a parish, farm, village, or town. Forsman explained that Kronoby is a village in the northern central region of *Österbotten* Ostrobothnia on the West Coast of Finland. She initiated the first inquiry to a Finnish genealogist about Ida Maria Wikström or Vikström. There was no record to be found in Kronoby.

I attempted to locate Ida Maria Wikstrom in Finnish emigration records at www.migrationinstitute.fi. Again, no record of that name.

Serendipitously, the postman delivered a letter at the same time, handwritten in pen and ink from a second cousin on my paternal side with whom I had not been in contact for forty years. His letter informed me of his aunt's passing in Seattle, a cousin to my father. I wrote him and also inquired if we had any living relatives in Finland. I found that Dr. Vincent Erickson, anthropologist and retired professor, University of New Brunswick, was well versed on matters relating to our common ancestry in Finland. His awaited response finally arrived, and I noted his elegant penmanship on fine stationery:

"Your dad still has three first cousins in Finland, daughters of your grandfather's youngest brother, Henrik Sundquist. You have many cousins living in the same area where our great-grandparents were born, and several would like to make contact with you."

It was more than I had hoped for. Vincent's communiqué had set the direction; the seed had been planted. Not long after Vincent's letter had arrived by post, an e-mail appeared that evoked a strange sensation in me.

"My name is Inger Sandvik, and I am your second cousin," she wrote from Jakobstad, Finland. "My grandfather Henrik Sundqvist and your grandfather John were brothers."

Although Inger's letter was clearly written in perfect English, I was compelled to read it several times. I was astounded to find that I have a cousin whom I didn't know existed. We communicated each week, sometimes more often, as if we were renewing personal contact after a short hiatus—discussing cultural affairs, relatives, and matters of personal interest like work, children, and music. Our alikeness was startling, such as our interests in cultural anthropology, our love of Nature and open spaces, and our desires for world peace. Each morning, I eagerly scanned the plethora of incoming email messages hoping to find Inger's name.

Rather than the American way of identifying cousins as "second or third cousins or cousins once or twice removed," Inger taught me the Swedish word *småkusin* that translates as "small cousin," a word that fairly well identifies relationships beyond first cousin and simplifies verbose explanations about family connections.

I explained my plight to Inger: I could not locate any information about my grandmother Ida Maria Wikström from Kronoby. While Inger and I are related through our grandfathers who were brothers, my *småkusin* enthusiastically offered her assistance in finding my *farmor*, my father's mother. Inger said she lived near the town of Kronoby, and she knew people from there. I told Inger I had learned from my aunt's manuscript that Ida Maria had lived at the end of a little bridge—Lillbroända—by the Kronoby River. Leona wrote in her manuscript:

> I was consistently introduced as "Ida Lillbroändas äldsta flicka," Ida End of the Little Bridge's oldest girl. No question as to where I belonged, to whom I belonged, and where I occurred in the family hierarchy. Grandfather Anders' house, red with white trim, stood on the bank of a small stream. A small bridge invited you to the front yard and the entryway to the home called "Lillbroända."

The place name Lillbroända was the key.

"The Ida Maria mystery goes on," Inger wrote:

> "One of my colleagues Alf Blomqvist at work (in Jakobstad) just came in and said he had heard I was searching for information about Anders Vikstrom."

Alf Blomqvist, who is employed at the same company in Finland as Inger, had done research and agreed to help Inger locate information about my grandmother. Blomqvist went to Börje Vestös Cronoby database and found a list of Ida Maria's ancestors. Inger attached brief information to her email and said she would mail the ancestor list to me.

> "It's in Swedish," she wrote. "I will translate it for you later on, but I wanted to send it right away so you can read the names and dates. *Född*=born and *död*=died. More Later."

Terse words described the life of my grandmother Ida Maria in Finland:

> Ida Maria Anders.dr. Lillbroända, *fôdd* 1876-02-09 i Överbråtö, Kronoby,*död i Amerika.* Emigrant. USA & 1893-..-*livsöde, inte känt.*

Ida Maria Andersdotter Lillbroända, born 1876, February 9 in Överbråtö, Kronoby, died in America. Emigrant. USA 1893. Life story not known.

At first sight I was stunned, then overjoyed to learn that the woman whose maiden name we thought to be Ida Maria *Wikstrom* in America was known as Ida Maria Andersdotter Lillbroända in Finland. But then, a peculiar sadness permeated my being as I reread the last words: Life story not known.

Were those few words the extent of what was known about my grandmother in Finland? Did it mean that no one had an interest in her life story because she had left her homeland? Was there no one to go to the parish registrar and enter the date of her marriage in America—or her date of death? Her position in life, her children? Keeping in mind that some 50,000 people left from the Swedish-language parishes of Ostrobothnia, tracking emigrants became a near impossible task for the clergy, but the dearth of recorded information for Ida Maria Andersdotter Lillbroända made it appear, at least to this granddaughter, as if she no longer existed when she left Finland. One word finalized her life in the country of her birth—Emigrant.

Inger wrote, "Half the village of Kronoby is on alert now trying to find out about Ida Maria's life."

Within days, I received Ida Maria's *antavla* table of ancestors that Inger had mailed. I was ecstatic to learn her ancestral lineage. But where did the name Wikström come from? There were important pieces missing to this genealogical puzzle. Then another email from Inger:

"I got a phone call from Kronoby yesterday. It was from Rolf Törnqvist and if I got it right, his grandfather was Viktor Vikstrom, the brother of Anders Lillbroända—Ida's father. Ida's father is named Anders Andersson Björnvik Lillbroända. No one seems to understand why Ida used the name Vikstrom. According to Rolf Törnqvist the Vikstrom brothers came from a place called Björnvik (Bear Bay) in Larsmo, north of Jakobstad. He said that his grandfather Viktor always went by the name Vikström. He said Anders did not change his name to Lillbroända, but I phoned your second cousin Berit Backnäs, Anders niece, to check and she verified that Anders did take the name Lillbroända when he moved to Kronoby and bought the house in Kronoby called Lillbroända."

This information explained the surname Vikström, but I still did not know when or why Ida Maria took the name Vikström or Wikström. And I needed to know more about the place called Björnvik.

Word about my search continued to spread among relations in Finland, and no sooner said than the answer arrived via another letter sent by *småkusin* Patrik Hansell on the maternal Hästö side of my grandmother's family:

> "For more information, turn to Vidar Liljekvist who knows a lot about people who have lived at Björnvik in Larsmo. He is familiar with the Larsmo church book."

Anders Vidar Liljekvist has in-depth knowledge of the area and the people at Björnvik back to 1600. He found in the Larsmo church records that Ida's father Anders was born in Björnvik and also recorded were the births of Ida Maria and her two sisters. The Larsmo church book listed Ida Maria as born 9 February 1876 at Björnvik in Eugmo village, Larsmo Parish—not Kronoby as our family had thought and that had been incorrectly recorded in one of the Kronoby genealogical records. Björnvik was where Ida Maria's paternal ancestors had lived for generations. Ida's father, *Bonde* Farmer Anders Andersson Björnvik married Kajsa Greta Simonsdotter Hästö from Hästöby village, Kronoby. Three children were born while the couple lived at Björnvik—Hilda Sofia, Ida Maria, and Wilhelmina.

When Ida Maria was five years old, the family moved to Kronoby. Each member of the family was granted *Flyttningsbetyg* on 12 March 1881, the certificate that was carried to the new parish when moving within Finland. Anders Andersson Björnvik, his wife Kajsa Greta, and their three daughters, along with Anders' brother Viktor and their mother, Maria Kristoffersdotter Knif, moved a few miles south to Kronoby to the house that Anders purchased from Jacob Simonsson at the end of the little bridge. While at Björnvik, Ida's father Anders from

Björnvik had used the place name Björnvik following his patronymic Andersson. At the new location, Anders Andersson Björnvik and his family all took the farm name Lillbroända, as was commonly done at that time when a family moved to a new place. Adults most often would take the name of the place they moved to after about one year; children born on the farm would take that name upon birth. Since the person didn't take on the destination name immediately, the new parish might record their previous farm surname, which helps provide genealogists with a link.

Ida Maria's father was now known as Anders Andersson Björnvik-.Ändr. Lillbroända. (Ändr. is Swedish abbreviation for *Ändrat till* "changed to"). His brother Victor did not change his place name. The name change was apparently of one's choosing as the records reveal that when Viktor later moved to Lybäck, the name of another farm, where he would normally have changed to Viktor Andersson Lybäck, he continues to be recorded in the church communion books as Viktor Andersson Vikström.

Anders Andersson Lillbroända died in 1923. The first time his name appears in Kronoby church records as Anders Andersson Vikström is not until years later when a letter dated 9 September 1931 signed by K.J. Berg, *Kyrkoherde* Pastor, attests to the family of Anders Andersson Vikström and the family of Ida Maria's sister Wilhelmina Sabel. The date of the letter coincides with Leona Sundquist's visit to Finland in 1931 and may have been written at her behest.

What's In a Name?

The customary manner of naming children in Finland in earlier time periods was by a patronymic system, distinctly different from other countries. It is imperative that one understands this Finnish naming system before undertaking genealogical research in Finland. A Finnish name not only encompasses patronymics but could also include place names, farm names, and surnames.

Finland is divided into several distinct cultural areas and there are cultural differences in patronymics within those areas: In the Swedish-speaking regions of Western Finland and where my ancestors lived, a patronymic is formed by attaching *son* or *dotter* to the father's given name. The patronymic, derived from the name of the father, clearly defines the lineage of a son or daughter, thus Anders' children carry patronymic names—Andersson or Andersdotter. In areas where Finnish language is predominant, a patronymic would be formed by adding *poika* (son) or *tytär* (daughter).

Within my grandmother's maternal ancestral line, the patronymic naming system extends back nineteen generations to 1485, the date of the earliest records in the church books. To graphically explain the succession of patronymic names, the following exemplifies four generations in Ida's paternal line:

> Beginning with Ida's great-great grandfather Anders Andersson Björnvik: her great-grandfather is Johan Andersson Björnvik, son of Anders; her grandfather: Anders Johansson Björnvik, son of Johan.
> Ida's father: Anders Andersson Björnvik-Ändr. Lillbroända, son of Anders.

In this cultural patronymic naming tradition, it must be understood: Andersson and Johansson are *not* family names, but patronymics; the names are *not* inherited from one generation to another. Daughters carried the name of their father. Ida Maria Andersdotter was Anders daughter; Ida's mother: Kajsa Greta Simonsdotter Hästö was Simon's daughter.

There are occasional exceptions when a child might have a matronymic, the mother's name. For example, Lisasson, the son of Lisa, an unmarried woman, indicating a child born out of wedlock. There are also children born of families where the mother's line was the most important, then the child's name would be matronymic.

Swedish-speaking Finns might add the name of a place or the farm where they reside in addition to the patronymic, i.e. Ida Maria Andersdotter Lillbroända, but the only way of tracing familial identity is by the patronymic, which sometimes logistically becomes the name in the middle, but should never be considered as a "middle name."

Genealogist Hans-Erik Andtbacka explained, "The whole Kronoby Parish was divided into farms. The name after the patronymic was, for ordinary people, more or less an address—the name of the farm they lived on."

Adding the farm name to the patronymic does not indicate ownership of land or buildings, nor does it identify familial relationship. There could be several families not related but residing on the same farm who carry the farm name, which was the case at Lillbroända. Traditionally, if a man moved to a new farm to work or to a farm he may have purchased, he would then take the new farm name as his surname, i.e. Anders Andersson Björnvik- Ändr. Lillbroända. Yet another name variation might be used in conversation: The place name and given name might be reversed to Björnvik Anders, indicating that he is the Anders from Björnvik.

A name search for an ancestor can become a complicated process, often plagued by human error in recording. Confusion surmounts because of the number of given names in use during that time in Finland's history was limited in comparison to the number of names that are in use today. If an infant daughter died, her name might be given to a girl born later into the same family. I found the same given names among cousins in the same generation, as well as repeated in the next generation. It became apparent in my search for Ida Maria's ancestors that birthdates are of the utmost importance to verify that you have the right person. Vidar Liljekvist brought to my attention that one ancestor chart in America listed the wrong Anders, a cousin to Ida Maria's father, who also carried the name Anders, but he was born in 1850; her father Anders, born a year earlier in 1849. An error such as this would seriously impact any search of one's ancestral lineage.

"What's in a name" has other possibilities—the surname. The use of surnames had been part of the aristocracy. Only noble people, clerics, and the bourgeois class used surnames and generally in the Swedish language, as Finland had been under Swedish rule for centuries. Among the common folk, surnames were not used before 1850 in Western Finland. A surname might be derived from the person's occupation or topographical characteristic of the landscape. As the surname system was modernized, Nature names became popular. For example, my father's name Sundquist is one of the Finland Swede Nature names, a combination of *Sund* meaning strait; *qvist*, a branch. My paternal great-grandfather Daniel Mattsson Nabb-Pörkenäs Sundqvist was the first generation to take the surname Sundqvist in the mid-1800s.

Prior to the 1920s, you could simply change your surname if you grew tired of the old one, but in 1922 a new law went into effect in Finland that everyone must take a surname; otherwise, one would be assigned. The name of Ida Maria's father, Anders Vikström, on the 1923 death announcement suggests that Anders had taken the surname Vikström. All that was necessary to make the change was a letter to the governor of the county to ask permission. The applicant was required to announce the new name in one newspaper where he was living. If there were no objections, he then informed the parish registrar's office about the change of surname. The 1922 law requiring a surname further complicates genealogy research when attempting to understand familial relationships as when brothers, for example, would choose different surnames or spellings, such as Ödal and Ådahl.

The easy manner of changing surnames in Finland prior to 1920 may in part explain why Finland Swede emigrants who arrived in America in the late nineteenth and early twentieth centuries occasionally changed their surnames. More often than not, the name change was implemented in order to have a surname that could easily be understood by neighbors and officials in the new country. The Swedish language includes letters that do not exist in the English alphabet: *å*, *ä*, and *ö*. These letters had to be replaced in the English language. For example, Hästö in Swedish changed in America to Hesto. Regrettably, some of the centuries-old *Österbotten* farm names, such as Lillbroända, were abandoned for an anglicized name.

There were other reasons, too, that name changes might occur on the journey to America. Ship passenger arrival manifests compiled in Liverpool, England, where emigrants embarked on the ocean-going segment of their journey to North America, were rife with spelling errors. The change may have occurred when the immigrant purchased his ticket from the steamship company representative, and his/her name was misspelled (assuming there was a "correct spelling.") Or it may have been the person who copied the names to the passenger manifest for the ocean-going vessel. English-speaking persons in Liverpool were notorious for misspellings of names unfamiliar to them. The name they wrote might take a strange twist, as from Lillbroända to Albranda.

The New World became a place for mankind to begin again, a place where every man can be re-born and re-create himself. In such circumstances, the adoption of a new name is therefore not surprising. Once in their new country, the immigrant might keep the changed name, as in this legendary story about a new arrival in America: A travel-weary and frightened emigrant from Germany, confronted by the demanding United States Immigration Officer at the port of entry, was asked his name. He forgot. He responded in his native tongue, that he couldn't remember: "*Ich vergesse.*" The stoic English-speaking immigration official wrote on the register what he thought he had heard— Ferguson— which, as the story goes, explains why there are so many Fergusons in America.

The Ellis-Island-name-change story is as American as apple pie. The report that the clerk at the Port of Immigration "wrote down" the immigrant's surname is suspect, as passenger lists were not created at Ellis Island. During immigration inspection at Ellis Island, the inspector had a passenger list created abroad. However, the information was transferred to a handwritten card that opens the possibility for error.

Ida Wikstrom's name written on the back of her photograph taken in Duluth is the first time that we see Ida Maria using the surname Wikstrom. Was it her intention to facilitate her assimilation into the new culture with an easily pronounced name? Perhaps there are other reasons. But there is nothing formally recorded in the Finnish church records to indicate that Ida Maria used the name Wikstrom in Finland. Liljekvist elucidated about the name Vikström:

> "The name comes from (Björn)vik-ström and may utilize a V or W in the spelling, but a W would be pronounced as V. Other Vik-names also used V or W, such as: Vikman or Wikman, Viklund or Wiklund and other Vik, Wik, or Wiik. All of these names are used in the village of Björnvik today."

But it was the translation of Wikstrom that grabbed my attention, notwithstanding that the W and V are the same in Swedish. The English language translation of the Swedish word Vikstrom means: *vik* (bay) and *ström* (stream or current.) From my own perspective, as somewhat of a dreamer, I mused that perhaps my grandmother dreamed of being carried away by the current into the vast sea beyond the shores of the Gulf of Bothnia and to places unknown. I imagined her as a young girl standing on granitic stone at water's edge looking westward, her mouth wide open breathing in sea air, the vast sky above and freedom beyond.

Ostrobothnian coastline

Anders Andersson Björnvik
| Född 05-05-1771   #60308
| Kronoby
|
| Margareta Olofsdr Kass
| Född 1772   #60309

Johan Andersson Björnvik
| Född 08-05-1797   #60306
| Larsmo
| Död 08-11-1843

Anders Johansson Björnvik
| Född 03-07-1823   #60304
| Larsmo
| Död 28-08-1872

| Hans Andersson Kackur
| Född 07-07-1777   #89247
| Larsmo
|
| Greta Michelsdr Murmästar
| Född 30-09-1777   #89248
| Larsmo

Greta Lisa Hansdr Kackur
| Född 24-10-1800   #60307
| Larsmo

Anders Andersson Björnvik
| Född 11-08-1849   #60219
| Larsmo
| Gift 04-03-1874
| Kronoby
| Död 27-01-1923

| Matts C. Knif
| Född 18-01-1761   #60313
| Gift 01-07-1784
| Död 19-03-1838
| Maria Andersdr Knif Haga
| Född 01-01-1759   #46354
| Död 12-12-1821

Kristoffer Mattsson Knif
| Född 16-03-1794   #60312
| Öja
| Gift 05-06-1819
| Karleby
| Död 04-12-1852

Maria Kristoffersdr Knif
| Född 19-03-1820   #60305
| Öja
| Död 21-01-1902
| Kronoby

| Anders Andersson Tjäru
| Född 29-10-1770   #48236
| Gift 11-06-1795
| Död 14-11-1841
| Maria Hansdr Kort
| Född 17-05-1777   #48237
| Död 08-03-1824

Brita Andersdr Tjäru
| Född 16-03-1800   #48238
| Öja
| Död 21-03-1860

Ida Maria A. Lillbroända
| Född 09-02-1876   #60221
| Larsmo

| Anders Simonsson Broända
| Född 23-09-1753   #32141
| Kronoby
|
| Lisa Johansdr Tuomisalo
| Född 19-06-1757   #76381
| Död 1789

Michel Andersson Broända
| Född 10-04-1786   #59201
| Kronoby
| Gift 01-11-1812
| Kronoby
| Död 20-04-1851

Simon Michelsson Hästö
| Född 23-01-1819   #59199
| Kronoby
| Gift 07-02-1841
| Död 15-01-1877

| Matts Mattsson Bjong
| Född 21-09-1735   #76383
| Gift 13-10-1757
| Död 08-08-1808
| Maria Jacobsdr Lyttare
| Född 14-02-1738   #76382
| Död 21-12-1778
| Kronoby

Brita Mattsdr Bjong
| Född 16-07-1773   #57798
| Kronoby
| Död 05-04-1836

Kajsa Greta S. Hästö
| Född 20-07-1848   #60218
| Kronoby
| Död 27-10-1910
| Kronoby

| Simon Hansson Storvikar
| Född 11-02-1744   #56928
|Gift 12-12-1771

Simon Simonsson Andtbacka
| Född 02-09-1788   #59202
| Kronoby
| Gift 27-08-1809
| Död 15-01-1859

| Död 28-04-1802
| Lisa Jacobsdr Andtbacka
| Född 17-10-1754   #56929
| Kronoby

Greta Simonsdr Andtbacka
| Född 17-07-1818   #59200
| Kronoby
| Död 21-12-1858

| Johan Bertilsson Cronlund
| Född 04-11-1754   #89238
| Kronoby
| Gift 07-10-1784
| Margeta Mattsdr Lybäck
| Född 18-04-1768   #89239
| Kronoby

Brita Caisa J. Cronlund
| Född 17-06-1788   #59203
| Kronoby

Antavla ancestor chart

```
                                                              Hans Larsson Lybeck
                                                            | Född 1672        #45083
                                        Lars Hansson Lybeck | Kronoby
                                      | Född 18-01-1693#44960 |
                                      | Kronoby              | Karin Mattsdr Finnilä
                                      | Gift 1712             Född 1665        #49942
                 Anders Larsson Lybäck | Död 07-07-1763      Kronoby
               | Född 17-04-1714#44962 |
               | Kronoby              |                      Anders A. Merijärvi
               | Död 01-12-1777       |                    | Född 1675        #56326
                                      |                    | Död 16-08-1740
                                      | Anna Andersdr Björk |
                                        Född 1691     #44961 |
                                        Påras, Kronoby      | Anna Cnutsdr Slotte
                                        Död 1736             Död 24-05-1754   #56327

 Matts Andersson Lybäck   |
| Född 03-09-1744  #54910 |
| Kronoby                 |                                  |                        #0
| Gift 24-10-1766         |                                  |
| Död 13-01-1784          |                                 _____
                          |                                  |          #0 |
                          |                                  |              |          #0
                          | Margareta Mattsdr      |
                            Född 12-08-1716#57809  |
                            Död 12-03-1805         |
                          |                                  |                        #0
                          |                                 _____
                          |                                  |          #0 |
                          |                                                           #0

| Margeta Mattsdr Lybäck
| Född 18-04-1768   #89239
| Kronoby                                                    Anders Mattsson Näse
|                                                          | Född 1645        #45039
|                                       Anders Andersson Näse | Gift (gm
|                                     | Född 1679     #44924 | Död 1716
|                                     | Bråtö, Kronoby      | Margareta S. Skrubbacka
|                                     | Gift 1699            Född 1645        #45040
|                  Anders Andersson Näse | Kronoby           Död 1703
|                | Född 06-01-1710#44831 |         Död 1733
|                | Ytterbråtö, Kronoby  |                    Matts Jönsson Lyttare
|                | Gift .. Okt 1729     |                  | Född 1648        #56276
|                | Kronoby              | Elsa Mattdr Lyttare | Gift 1670
|                | Död 11-07-1767       | Född .. Sep 1672#44925 |
|                                        Bråtö, Kronoby      | Margareta Jacobsdr
|                                        Död 08-10-1752       Född 1651        #56277
| Malin Andersdr Näse      |            Död i slag
  Född 12-10-1747 #44840   |
  Kronoby                  |                                  Per Jacobsson Andtbacka
  Död 09-02-1832           |                                | Född             #45043
  Lönnbäck, Kronoby        |             Per Persson Andtbacka | Gift (gm)
                           |           | Född 29-04-1675#44931 |                Död ....
                           |           | Bråtö, Kronoby      | Lisbeth Ersdr A. gift
                           |           | Gift (gm)            Född             #45044
                           | Margeta Persdr Andtbacka | Kronoby Död ....
                             Född 20-11-1706#44832 |     Död 21-01-1751
                             Ytterbråtö, Kronoby   |
                             Död 09-07-1776        |                            #0
                             Död i lungsot.        | Brita Mattsdr Andtbacka |
                                                     Född 1678     #44932 |
                                                     Kronoby              |
                                                     Död 1718                          #0
 13/13
```

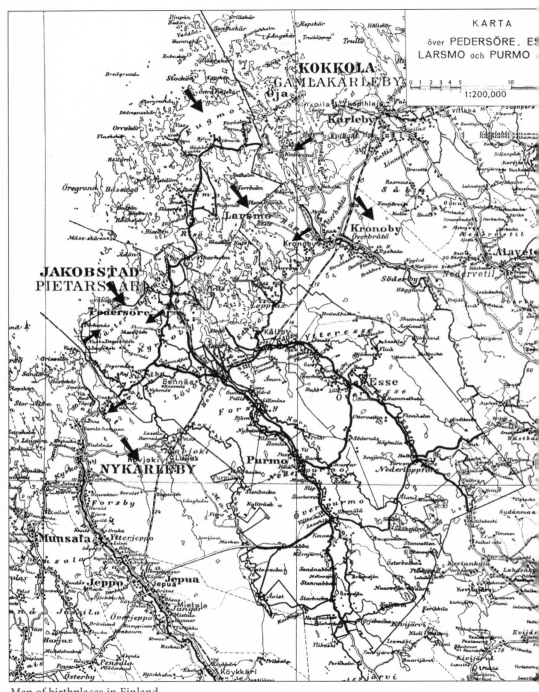

Map of birthplaces in Finland

Chapter 3

Finland Swede Heritage

O n the path to finding Ida Maria, I uncovered place names relevant to her life in Finland: her birthplace in Larsmo, the
Hästöby and Björnvik birthplaces of her mother and father,
and the place called Lillbroända where she lived as a young girl. Each
discovery presented another challenge and opportunity for learning.
To find answers to myriad questions and to embrace the sense of place
that is Finland, it became apparent that I should go to the source, to the
places where my grandmother was born and lived. I could not ignore
that inner beckoning to know my roots, perhaps more so because of my
own family of three daughters and nine grandchildren, so that they may
carry forward the ancestral information on their path into the future. It
was essential to my being to know about my ancestors, to honor them,
to thank them.

When I proposed to my family that we should make a pilgrimage to
Finland to find the girl my grandmother once was, my suggestion was
met with surprise.

"I thought we were Swedish!" my daughter exclaimed.

Admittedly, I was one who had reinforced that impression. I had
thought, as did others in our family, that my Sundquist grandparents
were of Swedish heritage. While I knew that they had emigrated from
Finland, I simply assumed they were Swedish: They spoke the Swedish
language; the family attended a Swedish Lutheran Church. The concept
of a unique group of Finland Swedes or Swedish-speaking Finns had
never been introduced.

I consulted my elder Sundquist aunts and their cousin Agnes Sunnell.
Am I of Finnish heritage or Swedish? Our family carries on Swedish
cultural traditions in this country. If Finnish, why did my grandparents speak Swedish? Having asked the questions, my American relatives were adamant in explaining that we are *Finlandssvenskar* Finland

Swedes. I offered that I recently read that the Swedish-speaking Finns were a minority ethnic group in Finland. They would accept none of that kind of thinking, although it is true that presently in numbers Finland Swedes represent less than six percent of Finland's population. The Swedish-speaking community does possess characteristics that are considered inherent in the concept of minority considering its size that is numerically smaller with respect to the rest of the population, its distinct features, and its determination to preserve its special identity and further its long-standing and formal ties since the land was under Swedish rule.

Some Swedish-speaking Finns may have a certain reluctance to consider a minority status due to the fact that the Finnish Constitution guarantees Swedish language official status on equal terms with Finnish. The official Finnish position is that Finland Swedes are not considered a minority but rather a de facto linguistic minority. The size of the Swedish-speaking community relative to the whole population has continued to decrease: in 1880 it was 14.3%, in 1910 11.6%, and at present less than 6%. In absolute numbers, the Swedish-speaking Finns have remained at about 360,000 over the last 100 years. The main concentrations of Swedish-speaking Finns in Finland live in the coastal area of the provinces of Pohjanmaa (Österbotten), Uusimaa (Nyland) and Varsinais Suomi (Egentliga Finland). The Åland Islands are entirely Swedish speaking. It was from the western and southern parts of Finland that the greatest waves of Finland Swedish migration to North America occurred in the late nineteenth and early twentieth centuries.

The interesting and not minor detail about the Swedish language relative to this unique linguistic and cultural group known as Finland Swedes can be understood by knowing the geography and the common history of Sweden and Finland for over 700 years.

The Gulf of Bothnia separates the East Coast of Sweden and the West Coast of Finland. In archaic times, there were settlements along the coasts; however, for the purpose of discussing Swedish-speaking folk, the Viking expeditions during 9th–11th centuries were the earliest to arrive to parts of Finland's coastlines and archipelagos setting up Swedish-speaking trading posts toward the East as far as present-day Russia. People from coastal Sweden migrated and settled in the uninhabited coastlands of western and southern Finland prior to and during the period of the crusaders followed by Christian missionaries. Swedes colonized the Ostrobothnian coast in the late 1200s and 1300s; Finnish-speaking people had lived further inland for centuries. In Finnish history, the Middle Ages began in the 1150s when King Erik of Sweden and Bishop Henry, according to legend, undertook a crusade to the southwestern part of Finland to establish Swedish dominion and organize a bishopric there, although there is archaeological evidence that Christianity had reached the Finns in the 11th century. Until the middle of the 12th century, the geographical area that is now Finland was of interest to both its western neighbor Sweden and the Catholic Church, and its eastern neighbor Novgorod (Russia) and its Greek Orthodox Church. The Swedes made two more crusades, one in 1239 to the district of Hämeenmaa (Tavastland) in central Finland and in 1293 to Karelia in the east. This was not taken lightly by the people of Novgorod who then conducted raids into Finnish territory, burning the city of Åbo as late as 1318. The conflicts did not end until the 1323 peace treaty of Pähkinäsaari (Nöteborg) between Sweden and Novgorod that established Finland as part of the kingdom of Sweden. Swedish settlers continued to arrive throughout the period 1400–1800.

In the Peace of Westphalia in 1648, a collection of treaties that brought to an end the Thirty Years' War on the European continent, the Swedish kingdom became a European great power (1617–1721) and extended its realm around the Baltic, but in the period that followed, Sweden found itself at war with several countries and finally to suffer defeat after the long war with Russia in the early 18th century.

With consolidation of the administration in Stockholm, Swedish rule was extended to Finland in the 17th century. Swedes were appointed to high offices in Finland, which strengthened the position of the Swedish language in Finland. The Swedish kingdom had slowly gained control over the whole of the northern territory. As a consequence of Swedish domination, the Swedish legal and social systems took root in Finland.

The Swedish King Gustavus Adolphus IV (1792–1809) joined the armed neutrality with Denmark and Russia in 1800 during the Napoleonic Wars, but when Gustavus refused to come to terms with France, Napoleon prompted Russia to invade the Swedish territory in February 1808 without a declaration of war. This coalition proved to be too much for Sweden's meager resources; the war was lost. When the Treaty of Hamina (Fredrikshamn) was signed in 1809, a third of the area under the Swedish realm was handed over to the Russians.

Following the Russian conquest of mainland Finland and Åland, Finland was officially made an autonomous Grand Duchy under Russian rule. Czar Alexander I, Grand Duke of Finland from 1809 to 1825, convened the Finnish representative body and promised to uphold the Lutheran faith and basic constitutional laws and rights that were in force in the country giving Finland extensive autonomy, thereby creating the Finnish state with its own Senate and Diet. The Grand Duchy was exempted from military service for a period of 50 years, a gesture which was highly popular with the population which had suffered terribly during the Swedish military adventures. Swedish remained the official language in Finland, but calls for official recognition of the Finnish language in the Grand Duchy of Finland were increasingly heard. The Czar supported the desire among Finnish speakers to find their own culture and use their own language, albeit his motive was to break the populace of their emotional ties to Sweden.

The influence of Swedish language and culture within Finland was at its peak in the 18th century at a time when the Finnish language and culture existed principally among the peasantry. Swedish, not Finnish, was the language of jurisdiction, administration and higher education in Finland. Socially ambitious Finnish families often raised their children with the Swedish language during the 17th-19th centuries, ultimately leading to a situation where the administrative elite had limited knowledge of the popular language, Finnish. Until the 19th century, few publications were in Finnish except for religious works: Bishop of Turku Mikael Agricola (1510–1557) translated The New Testament into Finnish in 1548 and is known as creator of Finnish written language as Finnish had not been previously used as a literary language. The Reformation started by Martin Luther in the early 16th century reached Sweden and Finland and set in motion a rise in Finnish language culture. In 1642 the entire Bible appeared in Finnish, also at the time of the country's first printing press.

When the Swedish kingdom lost the area of Finland to Russia in 1808, that event set the stage for a Finnish nationalistic movement. In Europe, the late 19th century era of national romanticism followed the

Napoleonic upheavals on that continent, a social reform manifest in the arts of regions that once had been subjected to foreign artistic or political domination. In Finland, a movement toward awakening the national consciousness found its roots and gained momentum led by academic youth and their leaders.

A celebrated individual Johan Vilhelm Snellman (1806–1881) felt that the Finnish language was key in promoting a sense of national identity. He was one of the figureheads of the nationalist movement who worked to promote the Finnish language, to make it an official language alongside Swedish. Snellman returned to Helsingfors University shortly after the death in 1855 of Czar Nikolai I. He sensed that under the protection of the more liberal Czar Alexander II, who had ascended the throne of all Russia, Finland could develop its national character. In 1863 as a senator, he achieved an ordinance placing Finnish on equal footing with Swedish as the official language of the Grand Duchy. Snellman belonged to a debating society *Lauantaiseura* or Saturday Society, which was of central importance in developing the national culture of Finland and the status of Finnish language as early as 1830s and 1840s. He stressed the importance of literature in fostering national consciousness. The Saturday Society gave rise to the Finnish Literature Society, which became one of the strongest institutional champions of Finnish culture.

Fennomans, a political movement, intensified the effort to raise Finnish language and culture from peasant status to the position of a national language and a national culture. Many members of the Fennoman movement were of the Swedish-speaking upper class who chose to promote Finnish culture and language as a means of nation building. Some Swedish-speakers learned Finnish and spoke Finnish in the society and at home; some were from Finnish or bilingual homes. Many people fennicized their previously Swedish family names. Some had previously changed their Finnish names to Swedish names after climbing society's ladder, understandably as official positions were only open to those speaking Swedish, and a Finnish name would have perhaps prevented their success in finding employment.

The Fennomans motto coined by Adolf Ivar Arwidsson, one of the early leaders of the Finnish national movement:

Svenskar äro vi icke, ryssar vilje vi icke bliva, låtom oss alltså vara finnar.

Swedes we are no longer, Russians we have no desire to become, so let us be Finns!

During this era of national romanticism in Finland, many important and talented artists contributed greatly to the national awakening. Of particular importance to the enrichment of the Finnish literary language was the first publication in 1835 of the Finnish national folk epic *The Kalevala*, a collection of ancient poems and verses gathered by Elias Lönnrot as he traveled the countryside of eastern Finland and Karelia. While getting his master's degree at Academy of Turku 1827, Lönnrot became acquainted with a small circle of nationalistic minded teachers and students who wanted to promote the Finnish language, which awakened his interest in Finnish folk poetry. Rune songs with different stories had been sung all over Finland from 1000 B.C. until the 16th century when, following the Reformation, the Lutheran Church banned them as pagan. The tradition disappeared from western parts of Finland, but songs and singers remained in Karelia where Lönnrot recorded rune songs from the last generation of singers. Later, he traveled into Sami land where rune songs could still be heard. Publication of the "old" *Kalevala* in 1835 with 32 poems and 12,000 verses gave the Finnish people their own history and ancient culture and became a source of great satisfaction and pride to the national consciousness that was fast developing among the Finns. The later 1849 publication has 50 poems and 22,795 lines of verses in a pattern of rhythm known as the Kalevala meter.

Alexis Stenvall, later known by the name of Aleksis Kivi (1834–1872), wrote *Seven Brothers*, a classic Finnish novel that played a role in Finns' understanding of themselves, and the author Johannes Brofeldt, who descended from Swedish family Brofeldt and later changed his name to Juhani Aho (1861–1921), is known for his classic novel *Juha* in Finnish literature. Aho was a member of the Young Finland circle of artists that also included composer Jean Sibelius (1865–1957). Sibelius was born to a Finland Swedish family and graduated from the Finnish-language lyceum in Hämeenlinna (Tavastehus). Sibelius' starting point lay in romanticism and partly in Finnish folk music. He created a national musical tradition inspired by the national awakening, and most noteworthy his symphonic poem Finlandia (1899) which became a symbol of protest against oppression and censorship during the period of Russification 1899–1905.

Zacharias Topelius (1818–1898), professor of Finnish history, was a great influence on the shaping of the Finns' conception of history and their national self-understanding. His writing style was dominated by romantic idealism and moralism and a strong patriotic fervor and belief in a fate that directs human activities. He wrote his literary work in Swedish, although he had a command of the Finnish language. He envisioned one nation with two languages. National poet and writer Johan Ludvig Runeberg (1804–1877) was born into a Swedish-speaking family. He authored a collection of poetry *Fänrik Ståls sägner* I-II Tales of Ensign Stål that includes the poem that became Finland's national anthem *Vårt land (Maamme* Our Country), a patriotic song that expresses a proud passionate response to the people's love of Nature and their native land.

The Language Decree issued in 1863 by Czar Alexander II marked the beginning when Finnish and Swedish were both declared to be official languages of administration and legal proceedings. From 1883 onward, civil servants were obliged to use Finnish language and issue documents in Finnish. In 1892, Finnish finally became an official language on an equal footing with Swedish. Finland declared independence from Russia 6 December 1917. The Constitution adopted 1919 reinforced Finland as officially a bilingual country with Finnish and Swedish as the national languages. Later Language Acts have been passed to protect the linguistic rights of the Finnish-speaking and Swedish-speaking populations.

Within a generation's time, the Finnish language clearly dominated in government and society. This was met by the populace with differing reactions, since for centuries Swedish had been the language of those of higher status, the clergy, education and public administration, as well as the population of Ostrobothnia on the West Coast of Finland, southern areas, and Åland Islands. A Swedish language movement arose in the 1860s among the Swedish-speaking population as a counter reaction to the Finns language movement. They claimed the same right as the Fennomans to maintain their cultural foundation.

Authors Susanne Österlund-Pötzsch and Carola Ekrem point out in their book *Swedish Folklore Studies in Finland 1828–1918* that a similar national/ethnic project took place among Swedish-speaking Finns in developing a national identity. "In many cases, the overriding concern was to save Swedish-speaking folk culture from disappearing under the perceived threats of fennicisation and modernity." Folklore research was of immense importance in the development of Finnish national identity, and the first edition of the *Kalevala* in 1835–1836 appeared at an opportune time. The work was a triumph for the promotion of Finnish culture as the epic offered evidence of Finland's heroic past and national character.

The aforementioned authors attest that part of the reason as to why Swedish folklore had been disregarded as an object of study can be discerned from the social and political situation of 19th century Finland. Swedish had long been the dominant language of the leading classes in Finland, cultural expressions in Swedish were not deemed to require any protective action.

The emergence of Swedish folklore studies as a means to promote a common Finland Swedish identity began with Johan Oskar Immanuel Rancken (1824–1895) who advocated the immense importance of collecting the folklore of the Swedish-speaking Finns on a par with Finnish folklore in developing a national identity.

Svenska Litteratursällskapt i Finland The Society of Swedish Literature in Finland was founded in 1885. Its mission statement emphasizes collection work, specifically evidence of the origins and development of Swedish culture in Finland. The first of 23 volumes known as *Finlands svenska folkdiktning* Swedish Folk Poetry of Finland was not published until 1917. Ernst Lagus, who pioneered the publication of *Finlands svenska folkdiktning*, poetically affirmed in the preface to the first in the series:

> "The commenced publication series stem from a population, few in numbers, but strong in spiritual activity through the tradition and poetry which has been cultivated amongst them ... and shall bear witness of how the Swedish population on the eastern shore of the sea have embraced the message which was already carried here in ancient times on the wings of

thought and memory. It will give an insight into the soul of the people, and it will help answer the question of what Finland's Swedes have given — perhaps also received —from their Finnish brothers. December 1916 Ernst Lagus, chief editor."

Considering the international interest in *The Kalevala,* translated into 49 languages, we can only hope that someday, people will be able to read The Swedish Folk Poetry of Finland in many languages.

The emergence of a new national identity amidst two official national languages was not without some trepidation among the populace. The politics of the day and the public discourse regarding Finnish becoming an official language within such a short period after centuries of Swedish rule were subjects of discussion among Finland Swedish households. Accusations of betrayal by diehard Fennomans were directed toward those who wished to maintain their Swedish language. The language strife even caused the breakup of families. For a young Ida Maria Lillbroända in Finland, the issues surrounding language and culture must have been confusing and unpleasant.

When her daughter Leona visited relatives in Ostrobothnia in 1931, the conversations a generation later in the agrarian society from which Ida Maria emigrated in 1893 were still focused around language and cultural differences that left Leona in a perplexed state of wonder about the Swedish element and its future existence in the new Finnish Republic. Letters Leona wrote in 1931 to her parents and siblings in America only recently uncovered in 2009 reflect her impressions and concern about the possible loss of Swedish cultural customs and traditions and the Swedish language. From her conversational style of writing, we get a sense of the underlying emotions and attitudes that still prevailed in the rural settlements decades after Ida Maria's departure.

Leona wrote from Helsingfors on *Hotel KÄMP* stationery *Måndagen den 13 Juli* 1931:

Dearest Folks,
Well I have just been to the *torg* market place and have had a most interesting time. Bergen's fish market was unique but this one almost has that beaten. I walked down the Esplanaden at about 10:30, through the avenue of lovely trees,

a lovely sun was shining. Soon I came to the fountains and there before me was the busiest place I have seen not except-ing New York, although this place did its business without yelling. Peasants and fishermen and small business people were there with all their wares. These consisted of everything from brooms made of switches, to the loveliest of flowers, vegetables, meat, eggs, and the ever-present fish, fish, fish. I stopped by an interesting fish stand, the fish sparkled green and silver in the sun, very lovely. I asked the old wrinkled woman wearing a *halsduk* what they were and lo & behold I was being fascinated by fish called *strömming*. Well I thought of Dad and all that he had been talking about *strömming* and here they were, sparkling, silvery green in the morning sun in Helsingfors. Well, I walked on and the faces of these people just interest me. I can't help but look-look-look at them. There is something about it all that does something to me. I don't know just what it is, possibly something strangely familiar, yet something that baffles me. Old, old women, just ever so old, faces wrinkled with age and tanned in sun and weather. Old! yet very agile and active. Their lot was to sell their pro-duce and it was a very serious business for them this day. Younger women, very young women hardly out of their teens but with all the earnestness of age, stood side by side their old veterans and selling *strömming, kött, ägg* or *gurkor*. Yes, younger women and very handsome, in fact beautiful. I could not help but wonder at the generations and generations of young women who have grown into old women at this market place. The inevitable cycle of life. I wondered some if there is a purpose in it at all, or is it but the changing of youth into age, selling and buying to keep body & soul (if such there be) together; to sell in order to buy, in order to live, and to live – what for? To grow old, to die? And the recurrence of this through limitless ages and time alone goes on.

One old face peered at me from under her *halsduk* – she gave me a faint smile. "*Främling*," I bet she mused to her-self. She looked more Swedish than *äkta* Finnish so I asked her the name of the small wild strawberries she had for sale, just to get into conversation with her. *"Smultron,"* she said. *"Smultron?"* Well! I've heard of that before but never dreamed they'd just be wild strawberries. After a bit of kindly remarks, she asked me if I wouldn't have a box. Indeed I did. So for 7 marks I bought my box of *smultron*. She wrapped it well in two papers so as not to leak out & stain my green suit. I said *"adjö"* and went my way wondering what I was to do with my box of *smultron*; sit on the quay and eat them one by one as I would watch the fisherman sell their fish from their boats?

I could have watched these people for hours, they simply fascinate me somehow. I'll just bet when Dad was a boy he used to lug *strömming* from boat to a stand and sell them, and my ancestors before that, and before that, and if America hadn't happened to have been; I'll bet I too would be selling fish and knitting (when business is slack) and talking half the time Swedish & half the time Finnish, depending on the customers. In the course of my conversation you'd hear *"Jo-o"* instead of the *Stockholmska "Ja-då."* *"Kitnxia palyo?"* I'd dicker with customers at the end of the market period so as to sell all my goods and for 1 kilo, small knobby new potatoes. I'd offer them to some *stads fru för neljä kymmentä markkaa*. If the *damen* would make a move to leave, I'd come down a bit and say *kaksi kymmentä markkaa*. Sure she'd buy & sure I'd sell and for her kindness I'll throw in an extra handful of spuds for good measure. *Jo-o* they always make it evident that they are giving *"go måtte"* and all in favor of the customer.

Stads fruarna city ladies would flutter around these stands, critically examine the produce, and her country sister would quietly and with decorum, bespeak its good qualities and the reasonableness of price. Many of these *fruarna* wore mourning veils. I also have noticed all through the Scandinavian countries how they wear cloths of mourning & black on their sleeves & hats. I'm glad we have ceased that custom in our country. The closing up of the market was none the less interesting. The tent-like city in 15 minutes had completely vanished and there in the city square were men & women with brooms (made of switches) sweeping, black headed seagulls fluttering so thick about the place, I was afraid they'd flutter into me.

Now as I think back over my experience in Helsingfors it seems like a page out of life, never changing life, a page unwritten, cannot be written. Runeberg's statue stands in the tree-lined Esplanade, he wrote of this and many things and around this statue & past this statue his people are continuing on in much the same way. Yes they wear more modern clothes etc., but down underneath it all there is something you feel has survived through the age, and will continue on stubbornly as it were.

Finland is different. Yes, it is different and fundamentally it bears the mark of Scandinavian tradition and culture. It is unmistakably Scandinavian but it bears the mark of other influences. Yes, a different race has mixed the bloodstream of the Scandinavian, a Russian influx of art in buildings and towers and a wistful earnestness, almost pathetic, peers out from pinched faces. This country stands on the borderline between the east and west. It has been the battleground of nations throughout the ages, heroes and the vanquished have paced and died on this soil, different types of traditions and cultures have struggled for existence here. Language now is having its battle. The Swedish-speaking element is now subordinate and the pure Finn is endeavoring to exert its character and personality. I sense a cruel scornful attitude toward that which is Swedish. I find I am better off if when meeting with just Swedish-Finnish persons whom I know can speak Swedish (otherwise), I can get along better if I just struggle along in English or German. Now isn't that pathetic? Here I come, as it were, to the land of my fathers, and they will not converse with me in the language of old. It is now the Finland of the Finns and they are trying their utmost to make it entirely

Finnish. They no doubt will succeed. There are just many more Finns. The Swedish Finn will just become submerged – yes, a people without a country – without a language – without identity, but a stubborn blond quality which no doubt will survive in spite of all these changes. I have read and talked with folks of late (educated folks) about the Swedish Finn in Finland. These Swedish Finns were old robbers and plunderers in the 9th, 10th, and 11th centuries who came from Sweden. Yes, they were robbers and plunderers – a finer name is Viking. Well the coast was the first place they settled, and we are of that outfit. They have more or less dominated the Finns in all this time both under Swedish and Russian rule, but now that Finland is a republic and has become a republic in which the Swedish Finn certainly has offered its strength, wisdom and blood – yet in the existence of this republic the Swedish element now seems to have come to the stage in its history where it is doomed to extinction. I wonder?

Leona

S.S.Ariadne, Baltic Sea,
Enroute to Germany from Helsingfors via Reval, Estland
(Tallinn, Estonia)

[Sunday] 2 Aug, 1931

Dearest Folks:
The sea is as still as the evening air in Finland's forests. *Helsingfors* is now far away and Finland is fast becoming a memory. A memory never to be forgotten. An experience which has been both painful and pleasant. It has been a lesson for me which schools and colleges could never give me. I have profited much by it in understanding of our own people and I hope that it will give me more patience with them in the future than I have had in the past. It has given me an understanding of myself and an explanation of some of my innate tenacious stubborn characteristics. I wish now that I had

allowed more time for Finland, but as it was, each moment was full and to be truthful, I'm glad it's over. There was much of it that was thoroughly obnoxious and down right disgusting to me, and I simply had to force myself to do, to eat and to sleep when all that was in me utterly rebelled. For the life of me I cannot understand why supposedly intelligent folks will submit themselves to such living conditions as are everywhere prevalent and common in the peasant areas of Finland. The townspeople are somewhat better but - this thing of education for ordinary, everyday living has a long way to go as yet, and I would say that we have gone a long way in the good ole U.S.A. Truly, in spite of all the hideousness, graft and greed of America and its heartless economic machinery that controls our destiny – yet it is America the beautiful for me and there is opportunity and a sense of freedom & liberty in customs, spirit and living that I have not sensed to such a degree in Europe. The most ordinary individual has a chance for anything in America if he wishes and wills it. And if his native endowment allows it, nothing seems impossible. But in Finland, one's life almost seems preordained at birth – the child steps right into the fetters of traditions and customs of the past and there he stands shackled for life and it hardly ever occurs to him to rebel or to change it. There is a resignation to life there that is as tragic as anything that I have ever seen or experienced. It's truly a living death to my notion. It is sadness and hopelessness and utter futility. And then to think that that part of Finland which I have seen is the most progressive part what must the rest be like? What must the northern part of Sweden be like? What must Lapland be like? It's unthinkable how this may seem like a terrible sordid picture which I have painted, but father and mother know that it is not a bit overdrawn and I wish that all of you might have been here. Now this is not peculiar only to Finland, the same conditions exist in Norway & Sweden in peasant areas, worse if anything in Norway, but it struck home more forcefully in Finland it was there my people, that my forefathers have lived and from which they have come with all that nature could give them and precious little of culture and that culture largely of Scandinavian origin somewhat influenced by Finnish contacts and Russian dominance, but not to a great degree. It has been interesting to observe how tenacious they hold to Swedish customs, traditions and habits after all these years since they colonized Finland. But now that Finland is a Republic the Finns are literally forcing the Swedish element to submit to that which is fundamentally Finnish. And the Finns as yet are largely a wild, untamed primitive folk who have for centuries lived in isolated areas in the upland forests, battling for life itself and its sustenance in the brooding gloom & darkness of those northern days and nights. They have had no time nor chance for those activities which we call cultural, for they have had to wrestle from an unrelentless nature a most poverty stricken existence, and that has taken all their time and energy and thought. And I can understand also that even though Finland has been under both Swedish & Russian dominance for hundreds of years, that the Finns have suffered under the bonds of the Swedish element in Finland. And now that Finland has become a republic, the Finns are now in control and the Swedish element is getting it right in the neck and between the eyes. The Finns have come into their own and the Swedish element is truly suffering and I feel sorry for them. They comprise but 10% or so of Finland's population & in voting upon any question the Finns naturally win. The Swedes are truly without a home. They must either submit to it all or else leave and most of them are too down right poor to pick up their traps and leave and so must stay and sulk in their huts and criticize all the Finns are trying to do. The whole situation is a tragic one but one which is of interest to watch in its further development. The whole country is full of what seems to me petty strife and hatred and really detrimental to Finland's welfare, but to those who are there these affairs are not small & petty but hugely important. My guess is that the Finns are out for to win and for once the Swedes are in for a licking, and another thing, the redness of Bolshevik Russia is not going to leave Finland untouched.

Eight years after Leona's visit in 1931, the Soviet Union attacked Finland in the Winter War 1939–40 and fighting resumed in the Continuation War 1941–44. Finland preserved its independence and sovereignty, but some territory was ceded to the Soviet Union.

Russia surely has left its mark with these folks. They simply hate anything that smacks of Russia. They hate Russia with all the intolerant vehemence that the human soul possesses. I am often thinking these days of Lithuania, Poland and a host of other similar countries that line the borders of Russia and the more western countries of Europe. They too, no doubt, have their feelings toward Russia & also toward Germany, as the Finns feel toward Russia & the Swedes. Honestly, Europe is a small place but a host of different peoples grouped in small knots, each wanting to exert its own personality over against the other and fears and hates born and nurtured through the centuries, they possess and cultivate. With all this I wonder not that wars exist & fights and feuds & poverty, strife & suffering, This! a civilized world? Christianity seems a farce, and I am wondering if in time, and that time not so far in the future, we'll lug (lunge) at each others throats again and modern science with all its vile weapons will just put an end to it all & this our age of modernism; only to start out again from the shattered ruins as of old in Rome & slowly & painfully again try to get our heads above the water. Life just does seem to have such a damnable time of it – no matter where you look or where you observe it. There's always such a struggle just to exist, no matter where you look. It wearies one just to think of it, and we humans with supposedly, brains in our heads, should be able to attain to something bigger & better. There's enough in all the world for all, but somehow a jealous something governs this human souls and with it we shut ourselves in from the possible. It's truly pathetic.

Leona

The principle of official bilingualism also covered signage directed at the populace, i.e. place names and traffic signs. Public signage identifies towns in both Swedish and Finnish language, and it is apparent in any given town which language is the majority as the information that appears on top of the sign is above the language of the minority. Sometimes Swedish, but more often than not, Finnish. By law, smaller communities may omit the minority language in signage, provided the minority language is less than ten per cent.

Leona lamented in a letter written to her mother the change in names from Swedish to Finnish that she noted as she traveled through Finland in 1931:

> You would never know any Swedish people ever lived in Finland. Everything is so Finnish that I declare I can't understand it. Kovjok is Kovjoki. Nykarleby is Uusikaarlepyy. Kronoby is Kruunupyy – gosh ma if you lived there now and I only had a Finnish map to go by, I'd never in all the world find you. I suppose Såklot is spelled funnier still and maybe my spelling of it is all off too – no doubt, but I can't even find it on the map, but I'll find Nykarleby and then there'll be some way out. Åbo is Turku. You'd think you were traveling in Turkey by the sound of it.

Old prejudices that arose centuries ago in Finland traveled with the immigrants to America, and as throughout American history, each new group of immigrants who were not of Anglo-Saxon origin experienced difficulties as they entered the American workplace. Finns were caricatured by the size of their heads and their "strange" language; they were even called Chinese in an attempt to have them deported under the Asian Act. In North America, during the years of major emigration from Finland in the late 19th century to early 20th century, Swedish-speaking immigrants from Finland called themselves *svensk* Swede or Swedish to distinguish themselves from the word *finne* referring to a Finnish language speaker. Expressions like *svenskfinne* were also used. In many cases, they would identify with the ethnic Swedes. Therein may lie the basis of our earlier confusion, thinking that our heritage was Swedish. And may also somewhat explain why Grandfather would chide Ida Maria with the comment that "somewhere in your bloodline a Finn is lurking," if her behavior should vary from normalcy. Any aberrant behavior was prejudicially attributed to *finne* in the bloodline.

Author Anders Myrhman, Finland Swede immigrant, wrote in his respected work *Finlandssvenskar i Amerika*: The Finland Swedes in America published by *Svenska Litteratursällskapet i Finland* 1972, that at first the immigrants were called Finns, then Swedish-speaking Finns and Swede-Finns, and finally Finland Swedes. He claimed that since the 1920's in Finland, the word *finlandssvensk* has been used to denote Swedish-speaking Finns, and *finländare* all people of Finland, while *finne* still continues to denote Finnish-speaking Finn. But there still remain some differences of opinion in Finland, America, and in Sweden also, as to what this particular cultural group should be called, considering the occasional lively discussions on the Finlander and Finngen Internet talk sites. Of note, Swedish-speaking Finn does not necessarily define cultural difference or identity, as many Finns whose first language is Finnish also speak Swedish.

Cousin Inger addressed the further question about centuries of migration between Sweden and Finland in both directions across land or Gulf of Bothnia:

> "The word Swede-Finn should not be used about us
> Swedish-speaking people in Finland. A Swede-Finn is a
> Finnish speaking person living in Sweden! And there are just
> as many Swede-Finns as there are Finn-Swedes! But we do
> not use the word Finn-Swede about us "Finlandssvenskar"
> we would probably call ourselves Finland Swedes in English.
> I don't think our identity is changing. We have the language
> in common with the Swedes and part of our culture too, but
> when I go to Sweden, I don't feel Swedish at all."

The Swedish spoken by *Finlandssvenska* is characterized by a local dialect that varies in intonation and most often noted as lacking melodic accent. Dialect or home language varies from region to region and among towns not too distant—Vörå dialect, Pedersöre dialect, Terjärv. Nedervetil dialect is a "hard" dialect with lots of consonants. Ida Maria spoke *krombisprååtzi* Kronoby dialect. In most areas, through inter-action of people from different areas and marriages across linguistic boundaries, dialects have incorporated loan words from other lan-guages and nearby dialects and differ somewhat from the spoken dia-lects 100 years ago.

My småkusin Inger explained their dialect in this manner:

> "It could be something like the difference between
> American English and Australian English or British English.
> Our variety of the Swedish language differs from Swedish in
> Sweden in much the same way as American or Australian
> English differs from British English."

Nature and society are in constant change. Even as each genera-tion experiences change in our cultural traditions as well as assimilat-ing new traditions outside of our own cultural values through "mixed" marriages and societal affiliations that fit our American amalgamated "melted-pot" lifestyle, that "stubborn blond quality" of our Finnish cul-tural heritage and historical identity remain as important today, as it was to the immigrants and the first generation born in America.

What does it matter if cultures fade away?

Author and anthropologist Wade Davis writes:

> "Distinct cultures represent unique visions of life itself,
> morally inspired and inherently right. Those different voices
> become part of the overall repertoire of humanity for coping
> with challenges confronting us in the future. If we drift toward
> a blandly amorphous, generic world, as cultures disappear and
> life becomes more uniform, we as a people and a species and
> Earth itself, will be deeply impoverished."

How will we succeed in preserving traditions and cultural heri-tage in the face of constant change? As an organized group, witness the determination and continuation of an international organization of Finland Swedes called Swedish-Finn Historical Society, based in Seattle, Washington, and supported by members across North America and world wide. Their mission: "To gather and preserve the emigration history of Swedish Finns across the world, to connect Swedish Finns to their roots in Finland and to celebrate our cultural heritage."

In Finland, the importance of the Swedish language culture and tradition today is recognized by the Finnish government and Parliament. Powerful endowments such as *Svenska Litteratursällskapet, Svenska Folkskolans Vänner, Svenska Kulturfonden* are cornerstones of present-day Finland Swedish culture and tradition. As an aside, great interest has been shown in the Markku T. Hyyppä and Juhani Mäki published study that shows that this group, although quite similar in societal respects to the Finnish language community, holds a higher amount of social capital measures associated with their well-being and health.

In North America, we have multiple opportunities within the American amalgamation to identify with Finnish groups through shared nationality and history, the Swedish group through shared culture, and for most descendents of Finland Swede emigrants, we relate to other Nordic peoples and other ethnic groups as well through marriage and friendship. Like a riverine estuary where saltwater tides flow in to mix with fresh water that sustain salmon smolt before they embark on their ocean-going journey, we are as an estuary nourishing a Nordic heritage of similar traditions and values.

I thought of my last visit with grandmother, both of us enraptured by the radio broadcast, "Mr. Keen, Tracer of Lost Persons." The theme song "Someday I'll Find You" played in my mind. Mr. Keen, the master detective, never failed. If only he could be engaged to find the girl that my grandmother once was and the answers to my questions. One hundred years had passed since my grandmother looked back upon her homeland as she, her husband John, daughter Leona Marie and son Johan Vincent boarded the ship to return to America after an eight-month visit, never to return to Finland again.

Foregoing engaging a master detective, my husband and I, one of my daughters, and five grandchildren set out on a quest to find Ida Maria, to learn about our roots, and to experience the culture and the sense of place that is Finland. Three generations together on a pilgrimage to our ancestral homeland, to the birthplaces of our ancestors, to find the girl my grandmother once was.

Chapter 4

Aged Tomes and Faded Photographs

Standing quietly amid the gnarled trunks of white-bark birch trees, listening to the whisper of a gentle breeze combing through silvery leaves, I looked out over a fertile landscape of tilled fields following the winding Kronoby River that flowed peacefully toward the vast sea beyond. This is the land where my grandmother was born in the region of Ostrobothnia in Western Finland. The rich soil bears as it had when my grandmother walked this farmland; the narrow stream flows on past a multitude of generations and into the future. The house where she lived is no longer there; only a grey weathered wood out-building remains.

At the end of the little wood bridge over the Kronoby River, I was drawn into my surroundings, and I sensed a remarkable spirit of place. A soft wind rippled the delicate serrated-edged birch leaves and rustled through unmowed grass, as if someone were passing through. I slid my hands around the peeling bark on the trunk of an enormous birch tree that my grandmother once climbed, played under, sat under; its now massive drooping branches created a dark green canopy over the tall grass. A narrow walkway constructed of two wood planks and a wood railing, dilapidated and darkened over time, extended from the grassy bank over tall reeds and out over the river where my grandmother once swam during the summers of her youth.

The bank of the river on the Lillbroända side was lined with the ethereal figures of ancestors. Ancient birch trees shaded the grassy bank as they have for generations, but it was only the imposing birches that I saw reflected in the placid water.

∽◌∾

Thus far, just getting to Lillbroända farm was by a circuitous route, gathering information, contacting newly found relatives in Finland, making travel arrangements from Seattle for my husband and me along with two granddaughters, and for daughter Lauren and three grandchildren from Switzerland. When I finally set foot in my grandparents' homeland, it was a coming-home experience in that magnificent setting, as I breathed deeply and savored the fresh green air of summer. We are here to explore our ancestral roots and the roots of our cultural traditions and to learn about the young girl whose presence I felt among the century-old birch trees.

Hans-Erik and Helena Andtbacka, who live in Kronoby, met us at our rented villa Fäboda. They had arranged an extensive program for us on our first day within the area where my grandparents were born, and we could not have been in better hands. They presented a book they had prepared for me: *Arlene's Ancestors to 1485.* They had gathered genealogical information about my grandmother Ida Maria and prepared an ancestor chart back to the 15th century. Hasse Andtbacka explained to me how he and I are related going back six generations. We began the day by visiting the farm at Lillbroända and then drove to *Gamla stans restaurang,* the old town restaurant in Karleby where we shared a beautiful midday meal topped off with dessert featuring cloudberries *Rubus chamaemorus*, a Finnish delicacy.

We were on our way to the impressive cruciform Kronoby Church where Ida Maria Andersdotter Lillbroända was confirmed and took her first communion. Andtbackas had arranged for us to see firsthand the centuries-old *Kyrkböcker* church books that hold information about our ancestors. Surrounded by an aura of anticipation and excitement, our single-file procession of three generations of Ida Maria's descendents quietly followed a narrow winding path through tall birch trees to the parish office beside Kronoby Church.

Andtbacka placed the nineteenth-century ledgers on a polished wooden table. The age-worn leather-bound books are simple ledgers but impressively large—some over two feet in length. He opened one book that recorded the people who had moved into Kronoby in 1881: *Inflyttade för år 1881 i Kronoby församling.* There we affirmed that Anders Andersson Björnvik, his wife Kajsa Greta, their children Hilda Sofia, Ida Maria and Wilhelmina arrived from Larsmo 19 March 1881. With them were Viktor Andersson Björnvik and Maria Kristoffersdotter Björnvik. Ida Maria had just turned five years old. Our family knew she had come to America from Kronoby, but there had been an erroneous assumption that she was born there. Now we have seen firsthand that the family moved from Björnvik to Kronoby in 1881.

Days later, we would meet genealogist Vidar Liljekvist, who verified through entries in the Larsmo church book that Ida Maria Andersdotter was born in Björnvik *Född* 9 February 1876, not in Kronoby. Her father: *Far:* Anders Andersson, *bonde på Björnvik* and mother: *Mor:* Kajsa Greta Simonsdotter, Hästö. Ida had been baptized by the Church Rector L.V. Schalin in Larsmo. Her baptismal sponsors *Faddrar:* Johan Mattson *(28.03.1843) bonde på "Mattas;" hustrun* Lisa Mattsdotter, Finne (02.09.1842); Anders Hansson Björnvik (07.12.1864) *bonde på "Nysto;" hustrun* Greta Sofia Mattsdotter (04.02.1855).

Hasse moved on to the aged tome that held the entries for the 1880s and slowly turned the brittle pages. With my first glance at a *kommunionbok*, the contents seemed unmanageable. There was no index and the farms were not in an alphabetical order. Certainly, we were fortunate to have a guide. Hasse explained that the contents are presented by village with pages designated for each farm. Usually in the same sequence as the pastor's annual round of visits to the farms to test the people about their knowledge and reading of Luther's Catechism. All the people who lived at a farm were recorded.

Hasse paused at page 463 marked Öfre Bråtö. My daughter, five grandchildren, and I edged closer together around the table and bent over the *kommunionbok* as we strained to see the faint nineteenth century script written by the pastor of Kronoby Church more than a hundred years ago. At the top, the name Nr. 15 Broända; a few lines below, I spotted the farm name Lillbroända, and a quiver of excitement raced through my body. My eyes scanned the names of people living at Lillbroända listed on the left side of the page, beginning with Anders Anderson, and I breathed, "There they are."

"There she is," Kristen shouted. She had spotted Ida Maria's name.

The head of household is listed first: Anders Andersson. Then, Kajsa Greta with *h* preceding her name indicating that she is Anders's wife, *hustru*. Following were their three daughters in order of birth: Hilda Sofia, Ida Maria, and Wilhelmina. Lower on the page were the names

49

of Anders' brother *Bror* Viktor Andersson and their mother *Mor* Maria Kristoffersdotter.

The *kommunionbok* is in a columnar ledger format. Each family recorded in the book covers two pages. Following the names listed on the left side of the page, the first two columns have information about birth, year and date: *Födelse: År och datum*, and place *Ort*. In the next column, where they came from *Kommen ifrån* and a column to identify if anyone had had smallpox. The next columns are under the heading *Läsning* reading and *Ut ur minnet* memorization. The church law of 1686 required the pastor of the Lutheran Church to instruct the parishioners through Martin Luther's Little Catechism and conduct a reading examination of all residents in each household, including adults, children, and servants.

My grandfather's cousin Helga Sunnell related her experience with *Läsförhör* before she emigrated to America in 1905:

> Läsförhör was conducted by the pastor. The examination was held at home or perhaps in the home of a prominent person in the community. Each was asked to read a portion of the Bible and catechism and to explain what it meant. At the end of the session, new portions were assigned for study to each child for the next meeting. Helga recalls her assignment: "It was to memorize both the Ten Commandments and the first chapter of Genesis. And I was only seven years old."

If the pastor approved of their accomplishment, he marked a tick in the square in each of the appropriate column in the *kommunionbok* signifying the person's proficiency in reading from the Bible, reciting from *ABC-Bok* and Luther's Little Catechism and *Hustafton A. Symb*, supplement to Luther's Little Catechism, reciting a Psalm from Psalms of David, and finally a column marked for proficiency in comprehension and understanding. The mark under each category could be an X if the confirmand had done very well, an incomplete X that appears as a Y or a slanted I would indicate they did not do so well.

My grandchildren leaned over the table, as we all strained to see the faint marks across the page that would signify she had passed her required learning. Everyone's eyes followed my finger across the line where Ida Maria Andersdotter name was written. Jessica called out, "Her marks were perfect," as we all nodded in collective satisfaction.

One of the inherent values of church book records to the researcher or genealogist, unlike normal records of births and deaths, is that family members are recorded together. The information recorded in the books concerns the church and religious life—baptism, confirmation, communion, marriage, burial; but there may also be additional information on the page relative to population registration: other people living on the same farm; when and where people moved. Remarks about growth abnormalities and physical disabilities are sometimes also found in the records. We were startled to find recorded that Ida Maria's father was *enögd* one-eyed; her mother *blind på vänstra ögat* blind in left eye; her sister stuttered *stammar*.

The pastor had entered in the Kronoby church book that Ida Maria completed *Skriftskolegången* in 1891, the requisite schooling that she must successfully pass before she could be confirmed in the church. Confirmation was an important rite of passage in the Lutheran church. From the time that Finland became Lutheran, every person was required to be confirmed in the church before they could partake in communion and before they could marry. There were variances among parishes, but generally confirmation occurred when a young adult was from fourteen to sixteen years of age. Since the 1600s, it was a Royal law that every person be taught to read and write before being confirmed. Upon confirmation, a young person was considered a full, responsible adult and was then allowed to marry, a law that remained in effect until the 20th century. As tradition dictated, the church confirmation was always held at *Midsommar*; fifteen-year-old Ida Maria's confirmation was held 24 June 1891, and she participated in her first communion. There were additional marks for communion on 21.8.1892 and again on 26.2.1893, but an indistinct tick for communion 2.1.1894.

Finnish church recordings are considered the best in the world. The earliest records from 1469 consist of births, marriages, deaths, as well as accounts. The Protestant reformation reached Sweden and Finland in the 1520s. (Its strength derived not because of the people or clergy, but it was instituted by royal decree.) With the Reformation, all ties with Rome were severed, and the Pope's power was replaced by that of the King of Sweden, King Gustavus Vasa at that time, who transferred the church's income and property to the crown. Lutheranism became the state religion in 1593, and record keeping was taken over by the Lutheran church. The state church then kept the records and the names of persons who were counted and taxed by the state. Everyone within a geographical area of farms and villages in the parish are found in the old books, making it possible to trace ancestry back for centuries. When the pages in a book were filled after a period of five or ten years, the pastor would begin a new book and a new page for each farm.

It may be easier to locate copies of church records at the national archives in Helsinki or regional archive at Vasa than in individual church offices where staff may be limited or unavailable, but we genuinely appreciated the assistance we received at Kronoby and Nykarleby churches. And for my progeny and me, there is nothing quite like the joy of touching the centuries-old ledgers and seeing the original script.

Not only does Finland have the best records; the country has the most genealogists per capita. In America, the simplest avenue to finding a Finland Swede ancestor would be to inquire of the Swedish Finn Historical Society in Seattle about a genealogist whose experience is in the area where your ancestors lived. *Småkusin* Inger Sandvik paved the way for us, but we found many friendly Finland Swedes eager to help. Besides Helena and Hasse Andtbacka, we had the good fortune to receive extraordinary assistance from friends and relatives Berit Backnäs, Alf Blomqvist, Patrik Hansell, Vidar Liljekvist, Rolf Törnqvist, Börje Vesto, Sven-Erik Wiik, Alf and Marianne Ödahl and others who responded to our queries.

The date of the requisite certificate permitting Ida Maria to leave Kronoby parish startled me—5.5.1893. I looked again at the indistinct tick for communion that appeared to be 2.1.1894. The discrepancy in the dates suggested several possibilities: Either she did not leave in 1893, as the certificate allowed her to do, or she had gone to America in 1893 and for some reason returned to Finland, or because the ink mark appeared to be only partially made, it might be a clerical error. Indeed, the 1894 communion date recorded in Kronoby church book was mysterious, considering the penciled date on the back of her photograph taken in Duluth – 1893. The pastor's final recording—*Betyg till Amerika* 5.5.1893. Ida Maria had gone to America.

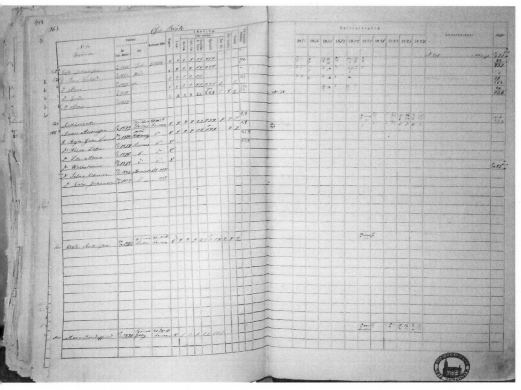

Lillbroända 1880 Kronoby church book

"Why did you wait so long to come to Finland?" a *småkusin* asked me at a "coffee party" after our family and an entourage of newly found relatives attended Sunday morning service at the beautiful cruciform Kronoby church where Ida Maria had been confirmed and took her first communion. Not wanting to usurp another family's preferred pew, we entered the church late and sat near the back where there were many empty pews. In earlier times, the top class was the clerical families, as there was no noble class in Kronoby. People sat in farm order, people from one farm always in the same pew. Also crofters, craftsmen, farm hands and maids living on the farm sat together. Centuries earlier, the women sat on the left side, men to the right.

The relatives sincerely expressed their regrets that they could not tell me more. "The people who have the answers to your questions are no longer here." And I felt remorse for not having made this quest when Ida Maria's sister Wilhelmina was still on this earth. Certainly, the decision to make this pilgrimage was reinforced.

The ancestors silently looked out at me from framed faded photographs hanging on wallpapered walls in the living rooms of our relatives' homes in Finland. I stared long and hard at their faces. I pondered their expressions and studied their individual and collective characteristics—their resemblance to the living. Notably, all of the homes we visited had ancestors' photos placed on a prominent wall. That they continue to honor their ancestors by keeping them in their presence impressed upon me not only how much I had lost, but also what I had gained—that the ancestors are with us for as long as we remember them.

Whether posed individually or in a group photograph, their faces appeared somber, if not intense. No one in the frames smiled, no doubt because of the length of time necessary to make the photographic exposure. But what we might consider in the twenty-first century as a somber pose was the norm for formal portraits in the nineteenth century. Modesty was considered a virtue. It was not only inappropriate to smile with the mouth open in a portrait; it was considered bad manners, sometimes even thought to be lewd. Today, the mindset is that a smile reveals personality and is a symbol of health and happiness, but that attitude came about in the 1920s. Along with the idea of saying "cheese" in America to create a facial expression most similar to a natural smile or saying "sex" and then everyone really smiles. The new custom of smiling for a portrait also occurred in step with the advance of dental work, which might suggest another reason for people not baring their teeth in earlier portraits.

What can we learn from these old photographs?

The intimate scene in the photo (ca. 1900) of my great-grandmother alludes to the eighteenth-century Dutch painter Vermeer in the simplicity and serenity of the interior setting, especially the light from an unopened window that illuminates one side of her deeply lined face. The photo was so exquisitely composed, that I wondered who was the photographer. Like Vermeer's inclusion of paintings-within-paintings, there is a photograph-within-photograph—a portrait of her mother—visible on the wall above her shoulder. She appears comfortably seated on a small chair, leaning against the side of a tall wooden cupboard in the farmhouse. Her feet are resting on a small *palla*; the century-old photograph reveals her handmade leather curled-toe shoes, *näbbskor*. The word *näbb* translates to beak in English. *Pjäcksona*, the shoes with the characteristic turned up toe are worn by the Sami people in northern Finland. The leather's durable nature and the practical nature of the curved toe design is a great advantage when walking in snow and a practical way to hold the ski on the foot. My eyes stroke the thick handwoven fabric of her full-fashioned floral-patterned dress. Her large hands, resting on her coarse striped handwoven apron, reveal a lifetime of hard work. Her eyes are closed.

My cousin opined, "No doubt she is dozing as at that time, a Finnish lady would never allow herself to be photographed in a pose with her legs crossed."

With relatives on hand to explain familial relationships, we poured over photos on the black pages of composed photo albums with black debossed covers. Some were albums of gathered family photos; others created by the deceased are their legacy and personality. As example, I was able to know Aunt Ida Elvira through her artfully composed book of photos and memorabilia, even though her life on earth was cut short by a tragic train crash. I never met my aunt; she was gone before I could put my arms around her and feel her warmth. Within her artistically designed album, I scan her body posture; I peruse her clothing and hairstyle; I muse upon the setting that was selected for recording that moment in time, while amused by her clever captions that she inscribed in silver ink on the black paper. Ida Elvira's photo album revealed her personality through her book design. She was vivacious, dramatic, and happy to be alive here and now; her arms thrust hither and thither in exuberant poses. Perhaps we interpret more meaning in the moment or in the scant few words under a photograph than was ever intended. We search for the depth of this blood relative; one who touches us, yet we never had the chance to physically touch.

A solemn, almost haunting, formal portrait hangs on the wall of my *småkusins* home in Kronoby. It is a family scene symmetrically composed around a one-meter-tall bronze cross bearing the name of Ida Maria's mother Kajsa Greta Lillbroända. The gravesite photograph pays homage to her passing 27 October 1910, but perhaps also commemorates the installation, nearly four years after her death, of the large black metal cross engraved with her name, date of birth, and death. The emotional content of the portrait takes precedence in the solemn faces and the stiff postures: On one side, Ida Maria's sister Wilhelmina sits on the fresh earthen mound holding young Sven beside her husband Johannes Sabel and Bertil. On the other side, the Sabel children: Eugenia sits on burial mound, Birger stands beside Ida's unmarried sister Hilda Sofia who sits next to father Anders on a wooden bench. Ida Maria had gone to America. Was the photograph taken graveside beside the cross also for Ida Maria's benefit, so that she could see that her mother was given a fitting tribute?

Following Sunday morning service at Kronoby church, three generations drove to Ida Maria's mother's gravesite, accompanied by many of our relations. I had earlier inquired of Andtbackas if it would be appropriate to bring flowers to the gravesite and then in the haste and hassle of getting eight people to church on time, the thought left my mind. As we exited our rented van at the roadside, I suddenly realized and expressed dismay that I had not brought flowers to place on her grave. My dismay turned to delight when I espied colorful wildflowers growing amidst the tall grass alongside the road—wildflowers not restricted from picking. We bent over to each gather flowers.

We entered the graveyard together. Any personal introspection at that moment blew away like dandelion seeds in the wind as ten-year-old Kristen immediately covered her cheeks with both hands and said, "This is scary!" while Cedric echoed, "And creepy." Marielle's Keane-like dark brown eyes widened; her lips pursed.

I looked into my grandchildren's young faces and said, "Let's talk about this a minute; this is a special moment." We walked amidst the silent markers of the ancestors and stopped at the tall metal cross over the grave of my great grandmother. We knelt together around her grave.

"This is a special moment that we are sharing to honor our ancestor Kajsa Greta Simonsdotter Hästö Lillbroända. Her daughter, my grandmother Ida Maria, went to America carrying with her the genes of the ancestors, the same genes that run within our blood memory. Kajsa Greta is my daughters' great great grandmother and your great great great grandmother."

I could tell by their quizzical expressions that they had never given thought that far back about their blood relations, as their hands raised upward to count generations on their fingers. Nor did I know my great grandmother's name until only months ago. She died before I was born. The family was a continent and an ocean apart, but that should not have excluded remembering her. No one talked about her; no one celebrated her life on Earth. I never knew. More troubling, I never asked.

Beneath the massive branches of a century-old birch tree drooping over Kajsa Greta's gravesite and bowing to the ground beside her grave like the arms of the Divine embracing all of us, we knelt and carefully arranged the delicate wildflower blossoms on her grave as our earthly gift.

Following our visit to the gravesite, we walked the grounds where Ida Maria's grandmother lived as a young girl. The stately house still stands surrounded by the omnipresent tall birch trees. The structure remains breathtakingly beautiful amidst the verdant summer landscape. We strolled the grounds with *småkusin* Alf Ödahl and his family through thick grass, deep green and damp, punctuated by spindly bright wildflowers. For my family and me, he expressed in perfect English his devotion to keeping up the Finland Swedish tradition, as we viewed his handcrafted model of Hästöby village 1945.

"For a time," Ödahl explained, "even in the mid-twentieth century, people were leaving this beautiful rural area and moving to the cities to be closer to their work, but now, there is a trend back to the country to live with Nature which Finlanders are extremely proud and protective of."

The Finnish love and adoration of Nature had not escaped me. Finland is the most heavily forested country in Europe. Only Finnish tree species are grown and the cutting rate remains below the growth rate, guaranteeing sustainability. Forestry is based on small-scale "family forestry," and you will commonly see forests of perhaps 20–40 acres on owners' parcels. Small "family forests" which have been left standing after clearing the land for cultivating punctuate the Ostrobothnian farmlands. I recalled that my grandfather had left a small forest of evergreen trees when he cleared his land in America. It was a good idea lost in America to maximizing development. In Finland, strips of wildness equal in length to the planted rows separate cultivated crops of rapsi, oats, and potatoes. On *småkusin* Bengt Enqvist's land, a small forest shelters the dense growth of wild blueberries. Bengt picked luscious berries for a sauce that smothered the pancakes that *småkusin* Astrid Sandvik cooked on an iron griddle suspended over an open fire on the sandy beach. The combination was an unsurpassed culinary experience, and as well, the setting by the sea, embraced by generations of Sundquists, left an indelible impression on my family of love and connections that we found in my grandparents' homeland.

Every Finn is guaranteed the right of access to the countryside through an entitlement called *Varmansrätten* Everyman's Rights—the right to move about freely in Finnish forests on somebody else's property—on foot, skis, bicycle, and horseback, provided you cause no damage. *Varmansrätten* dates far back in the Swedish realm. You can pick wild flowers that are not protected, berries and mushrooms. Importantly, you cannot misuse your right so that it causes damage to the landowner or to Nature.

The Finnish people are devoted to Nature, and they respond to that inner need. Much of the population makes pilgrimages to the lakes and forests in the summer. People camp and live in summer cottages, many without electricity, to enjoy Nature, to be restored, to replenish the soul and body, to enjoy the blessings of a natural wild environment. They honor their roots—in the forest, the water, the cabin, the sauna, and the silence.

I am emotionally overcome by the breathtaking beauty of the verdant summer landscape and the spirit of place. I softly breathe, "How could my grandmother leave this wonderful land?"

Certainly, the Ostrobothnian economy prompted many men and women to emigrate. After a period of strong development during 1764 to 1860 and prosperity through ship building and tar manufacturing, the economy slid into deep recession as the demand declined. But besides the economic reasons, Alf Ödahl proposed there may have been another factor in her decision to go to America: In the late 1800s, a young woman could only look forward to either working at another farm or getting married. The number of persons in each household was increasing in size in the late nineteenth century, and it was expected that by the time young women were confirmed, they would leave the family home.

To work elsewhere meant little pay, if any, and sometimes board and room were the only compensation.

Marriage, the other alternative, did not present the most ideal circumstances to a young girl whose dreams, imagination, and aspirations might carry her elsewhere. If she married, she would move into her husband's family home. The matriarch of the family was responsible for everything within the four walls, therefore, her husband's mother would be in charge of the household and the young bride, whose status was daughter-in-law, would work according to her mother-in-law's dictates—cooking, baking, weaving, sewing, washing. The tasks were endless and done by hand, and that did not exclude working outdoors too. Women took care of cattle, chickens, and in the summer, shocked hay, harvested wild berries and homegrown fruit and vegetables.

The role of the peasant girl upon marriage had changed little from earlier times as told in *The Kalevala*, the national folk epic of Finland comprised of ancient oral stories collected by Elias Lönnrot from among the peasantry in Eastern Finland and first published in 1835. From Rune 11, the son brings home a maiden:

> So the most delighted mother
> Spoke these words, herself them uttered:
> "Be thou praised, O God in heaven,
> Be thou thanks, O great Creator,
> Thou hast given me a daughter,
> One who smartly lights the fires,
> One who weaves the cloth so nimbly,
> One who spins with great adroitness;
> Sturdy one for doing laundry
> And to make the washing whiter."

I had found the girl called Ida Lillbroända, the Ida who lived by the little bridge, and the place called Lillbroända where she grew up in Finland. With Vidar Liljekvist, we walked the wind-swept grassy knoll in Björnvik where the house in which she was born once stood. We visited homes where our ancestors lived; we gave thanks as we knelt beside their final resting place on this earth. We connected with more than a hundred *småkusiner,* living cousins that we had not known existed—four generations of descendents of Ida Maria's sister Wilhelmina Andersdotter Lillbroända who remained in Finland and married Johannes Sabel. And four generations of John Sundquist's brother Henrik August Danielsson Sundquist who married Sofia Smeds. Henrik, after several journeys to America, returned to his homeland to carry on the Sundquist farm in Finland, that passed to his daughter Ingeborg Sundquist Enqvist and her son Bengt Enqvist.

In my own mind, I still had not resolved how my grandmother could leave this beautiful country and never again share the lives of her sisters? Those answers will come. In the moment, I celebrated the beauty of place and people as one being. The spirit of place that a cultural landscape exudes after centuries and generations of people being on the land and of the land in one relatively small geographical area still makes its presence felt. But a strange sensation of time overcame me, as I felt I was there in her place. I withdrew myself, as if to stand at the center of circular time—looking back, looking forward. Ida Maria left Finland and her family over a hundred years ago and had gone to America before her nieces and nephews were born, and there I was in her homeland amidst the generations following Ida Maria, mingling with people with familial characteristics, similarities, and like mannerisms—beautiful people with intense blue eyes, many who looked like us, laughed like us, whose body movements were hauntingly similar to our own. My family felt comfortable in their embrace, as if we had always known each other, as the blood of a common mother flowed in our veins. We came together; we sang together, and true to our cultural tradition, we drank gallons of coffee together. We marveled at coincidences: My daughter Lauren Lindskog Blanc directs a choir in Lully, Switzerland called "Take Off." Our *småkusin* Camilla Cederholm in Finland conducts a choir coincidentally named "Take Off." Lauren sings in a choir; Camilla sings in a choir.

Leona recognized a blood connection through "body language" that occurred at a school assembly in the late 1920s where a string quartet from Whitman College performed. She shared that serendipitous event:

It was not only that the leader's name in part was Esther Sundquist Bowers (Esther Sundquist is my sister's name) but also that there was something hauntingly familiar in her movements and general behavior. I couldn't resist meeting her after the program. I introduced myself and remarked about the fact that we both had the name Sundquist.

She asked, "Did your father come from Finland?"

"Yes," I answered.

"Where from?" she hastily asked. "Nykarleby?"

I answered, "Yes; is your father's name Jacob?"

She said, "Yes."

Well, of all things! I had heard Father recall the memories of an Uncle Jacob, who was considered a ne'er-do-well because he would rather "fiddle" on a violin than work. He had eventually taken a job as a carpenter on a boat destined to sail for St. Petersburg, Russia. It turns out that I was talking to his daughter, who was born in St. Petersburg.

Did I feel resolution or was there more gained in addition to gathering the comprehensive story of Ida Maria's young life? Yes, I found my roots, I connected with relations that I had previously not known, and I learned about my ancestral homeland. But there was more that deeply moves me: I fell in love. I fell in love with the contemporary country that is Finland, its Natural beauty and substance, and its people who deeply care about their country, elevating its status in the world to the highest in the arts, education, and environmental conservation.

Reading and research opens horizons not seen before, but only by being in a place can one assimilate the spirit of place that is Finland. I searched for words that would do justice to the magic of our summer nights in Finland when earth slept, and it seemed that someone forgot to turn out the lights. An experience that will remain with me forever, as I contemplate that haunting, lingering luminous color and sound of the northern night when the sun doesn't set.

Alexandre Dumas (1802–1870) lamented after his visit to Finland:

"I have searched everywhere for that soft twilight which was engraved on my mind forever in the dusk of a Finnish summer night, but I have never experienced it again."

I found in the poetic words of the Finnish author Zachris Topelius, the thoughts and feelings that explicitly explain my encounter with the awesome silence and the radiance of the night, that dim, silvery light that spread through the still forest behind our villa, through the birch trees and across the shore:

THE GLORY OF A SUMMER NIGHT
from "Our Land" by Zachris Topelius (1818–1898)

Painters have sought to depict all the loveliest effects of light in the sky. They have portrayed the sun and moon in all their different positions in the sky but no one has yet succeeded in capturing on canvass the miraculous brightness of the northern summer night.

Light from the sun and the moon spreads from one direction over all the objects within its circle of influence, whilst others remain in shadow. But on a clear summer night in the far north, the whole sky glows and the air itself seems to shimmer in soft, gentle light. When the northern sky is cloudy no shadow can be seen because the light comes from every direction and seems to radiate from objects themselves? When the sun goes down to rest briefly, the whole of nature settles into a strange dreamy mood. The bringer of the day is gone, birds have fallen silent, people and animals seek rest and plants wait for night that does not come. Instead, a dim, silvery light spreads over forests, waters and shores. It is not the light of the sun, the moon or the stars, nor is it dusk. It is the night's own radiance, serene yet festive, like eternal joy amid the transience of spring.

I search for something in life that I could compare to this, but I can find no picture to equal this luminous night except perhaps the glow of evening reflected in the windows of a deserted house wherein have lived cherished friends, or the brightness of dear eyes looking at one through the tears of inexpressible love.

In such a picture of night there is nothing that would shock. The eyes are not dazzled, the heart beats calmly; everything appears to be unchanged, yet all is different. The whole of nature glows, everything is soft, clear, contemplative. The grass is like the finest velvet, the leaves translucent. Commonplace objects: a fence, a barn, a horse in the meadow, look strange and wondrous. When I walk in the forest the rugged pine trees appear to be wrapped in cotton wool. When I row on the lake, I feel as if the shore has never looked so enchanted. All around is silence, interrupted only by the melodious song of the blackbird, and the loneliness that always accompanies the night. All of this pours into the soul of the beholder who experiences the invisible bond that links nature to all living creatures. One feels as if the glory of the night might enter the beholder's eye.

The birds know time. They sleep as little as possible. For an hour or two they keep their heads under their wings then again start to sing. Country people, too, know time. In winter they often sleep ten or twelve hours a night, but in summer only three or four. Only amongst the gentry are there those who upturn the order of nature. On long winter nights they may stay awake with lamp or candle, but on light summer nights they sleep behind closed curtains. It is a pity to lose what is most beautiful in nature.

—Translated by Joe Brady. Copyright 1999 Virtual Finland.

ASE

Ida's parents Kajsa Greta and Anders Andersson Lillbroända

Ida's sisters Hilda Sophia and Wilhelmina

Kajsa Greta Simonsdotter Hästö gravesite: Ida' sister Hilda Sofia, father
Anders; sister Wilhelmina, husband Johannes Sabel and children (l. to r.)
Birger, Eugenia, Sven, Bertel.

Chapter 5

Amerika Feber 1893

I da Maria Lillbroända, the young girl who lived at the end of the little bridge over the Kronoby River, had left her homeland. She embarked on a journey that would take her halfway around the globe—from the West Coast of Finland on the Gulf of Bothnia and across the Atlantic Ocean to a continent known to the 19th century emigrants as the New World. *Amerika!* The touted land of opportunity and riches. Indeed, this would be an extraordinary journey for a seventeen-year-old farm girl in the 1890s.

Ida Maria emigrated to America in 1893 at a time when the greatest numbers were leaving Ostrobothnia. The cause of this mass emigration was due in part to the population increase at an unprecedented rate as industrialization advanced during the 19th century. Emigration to America had begun in the 1600s when the first Finns emigrated to America and established one of the first colonies, New Sweden in Delaware. But it was not until the 1890s that there was a surge in emigration. The subject was on everyone's lips. Wherever people gathered together, the ongoing topic of conversation was about those who had gone to America. *Amerika feber,* as it was called in the mid-1800s, referred to that intense desire to emigrate to America prompted by economic and social conditions within the homeland and nourished by letters from earlier emigrants to America. Neighbors returned with stories about America; others sent letters that were passed around the village. Hasse Andtbacka recalls conversations with the elder Huggare who affirmed that letters from America back to friends and relatives in Kronoby brought not only reflections on the joys and sorrows of settling in a new land but news about the New World, the wealth of opportunities for employment, and ultimately the chance to own land, which was every countryman's dream. With an entire continent as opportunity and a new country that proclaimed Manifest Destiny as its guide, Finland was not the only country to pay attention to opportunity. Author Wallace Stegner wrote, "The initial act of emigration from Europe, an act of extreme, deliberate disaffiliation, was the beginning of a national habit."

The reasons were many for men who departed Finland in record numbers, particularly from the Ostrobothnian region along the West Coast of Finland. The coastal area of Ostrobothnia had experienced strong development 1764–1860 as ship building and tar manufacturing brought prosperity and employment. Following the flourishing economy, however, began the equally rapid decline into economic recession as demand for tar and wooden ships declined. There had been burgeoning population growth during 1800–1850 followed by years of crop failures and the famine of 1867–68. The economy was not industrialized until the late nineteenth century and could not support the growing population. People became poorer.

For some, the search for adventure may have been the driving force, but for the male breadwinner, opportunities were lacking in Finland: Farms had been divided over the centuries and could no longer support the number of people with the population expanding as it was; the oppressive tenancy system kept the landless laboring class at the mercy of large landowners. Large families were the norm, and it was common that a farmer couple transferred their farm to a son and his wife, usually the eldest son, or perhaps to daughter and her husband. The other siblings who were not so privileged; many left for America. And not the least, there was the lure of the New World that beckoned Finlanders to participate in its many opportunities and great riches. America needed workers, and there were colorful appeals to encourage immigration to the New World. Steamship agents traveled about and recruited emigrants through newspaper advertisements; lavish posters beamed their message to passersby. Recruiting was finally prohibited by the United States in the 1880s, but Canada continued into the 20th century to encourage immigration.

"Who is this new man, this American?" wrote Alexis de Toqueville, (1805–1859) French political thinker and historian in his books *Democracy in America* (1835) an early work of sociology and political science.

"He was Adam in the Garden, man beginning again, leaving all the history and heartbreak of the Old World behind.
The idea that what made America unique was the opportunity for man to live in a state of nature, a society of farmers whose perception of Truth is unfettered by ancient social and political conventions lies at the base of Jeffersonian democratic theory."

Why would a young girl leave her familiar surroundings, her parents and siblings, and break with her homeland? We can only surmise that the economics of the period also played a part in Ida Maria's decision to go to America. If it were a response to the times, those who emigrated were distinctive, as only a small minority of single women became emigrants in the 19th century. She was the first female in generations of her family to leave Finland. At that time, future choices were limited for Ida Maria and other adventurous young women in Finland: She could marry, move in with her husband's parents and be subservient to her mother-in-law's demands. As an unmarried young woman, she might face a similar future, if it were necessary for her to leave her father's home and take a servant position at another farm.

Nordic women did not shun hard work, but the news of opportunity and education in the New World, possibly riches, did not escape a young girl's notice. There were reports of young teenage girls from Ostrobothnia who had found careers as maids in wealthy East Coast homes in the United States. Ida Maria weighed her options—if she married into the wrong family, she might possibly have to endure years of scorn by her mother-in-law; if she emigrated, her destiny would be of her own making.

For Ida Maria and others, emigration—leaving one's homeland—took immense courage. Simplified, it was hopelessness on the one hand, hope on the other. Ida moved forward with her plan to go to America. First, she submitted the required *Ämbetsbetyg*, the official certificate that would allow a resident to leave a parish in Finland. The paper was then recorded by the pastor under the Lillbroända farm name in the Kronoby church book: Ida Maria *betyg til Amerika* 5. 5.1893.

Ida Maria Andersdotter Lillbroända crossed over the actual little bridge that was her namesake, perhaps for the last time. Or was the bridge itself the metaphysical, genetic, spiritual, metaphoric bridge to a new world, Ida herself being the avenue or bridge, from the Old World to the New World, carrying across her beliefs and descendents.

∞∞

Leona's manuscript revealed that at the age of 16 or 17, with a girl friend, Ida Maria decided to find her fortune in *Amerika*.

> They landed in Quebec, Canada, and were promptly quarantined for weeks, as an infectious disease had spread among the passengers. Mother was very miserable there, unhappy and homesick. Once, in recalling the experience, she said that if she had had the money she would have taken the next boat back home.

There were no Canadian arrival records online, and I was uncertain how I should begin my journey to find Ida. Passenger Arrival Records at New York's Ellis Island began in 1892 and are accessible online, so even though my aunt had written that Ida Maria landed in Quebec, I searched Ellis Island Passenger Arrival Records website on the off chance she may have landed in New York.

I searched passenger records for Ida Maria's patronymic Andersdotter and her place name Lillbroända with no results. *Småkusin* Inger Nyman suggested that she might have used Vikstrom, as it would have been an easier name for immigration officials in America to pronounce. Her father's brother went by the name Vikstrom, and her father was sometimes referred by the family as Anders Wikstrom. I searched Vikström/Wikstrom and other similar spellings such as Wickstrom/ Vykstrom, as it is not uncommon that immigration officers had difficulty with spelling foreign names on the passenger entry cards, and V and W are one and the same in Swedish.

I found a passenger named Ida Wikstrom. I relate this story not only to show how easy it is to go off on a tangent with the right name, wrong person, but also that historic records are not always correct. Ellis Island records listed Ida Wikstrom from Norway; the year of her voyage 1892. I noted the discrepancy between the *betyg till Amerika* 1893 recorded in the Kronoby church book and the year of the voyage, but it behooves a researcher to check further, as errors are replete within Ellis Island records, mainly in deciphering illegible handwriting. On their website, I brought up the copy of the original handwritten passenger manifest. The names adjacent to hers on the passenger manifest were familiar Finland Swedish names—Östergård, Kronholm, Smeds. I went to the Finnish Institute of Migration website, and there I found the same group had departed from Finland! The Ellis Island records said origin: Norway; however, this group was originally from Finland. I was certain that I had found Ida Maria Wikstrom's passage, but I didn't stop there; I needed to verify.

I posted queries on internet sites Finngen and Finlander and in *The Quarterly* of the Swedish Finn Historical Society in an attempt to find a descendent of one of her travel companions who might shed some light on their passage. Months later, no response to my queries. Fortunately, I had connected with Hasse and Helena Andtbacka in Kronoby, Finland. They drove to the Vasa archives and located a record of the passport for this Ida Wikstrom. Wrong birthdate; wrong place of birth. Yes, there was an error on Ellis Island Records in posting the country; this person was from Finland, not from Norway, but she was not our Ida Maria Lillbroända Wikstrom. Disappointing news, to be sure. Months had passed while I attempted to verify the wrong Ida.

Thousands of emigrants arrived by ocean-going steamships at North American ports in the 1890s, so it is necessary to have some clues in order to narrow down the search - an exact year is almost a must; a ship name is helpful. To find information about Finnish emigrants, the first stop should be the Emigrant Register of the Institute of Migration in Finland. Finland is noted for the best genealogical records in the world. Their web site data is mostly related to the migration event itself with relative articles, statistics concerning Finnish emigration.

The Emigrant Register was established in 1989 as a service for genealogists and the descendants of Finnish emigrants. The foundation of the Register was a part of the Delaware 350th Anniversary to commemorate the beginning of Finnish Emigration to North America. The searchable database contains 318,000 detailed passenger records of people leaving Finland with the Finnish Steamship Company (year 1892 up to 1910) and 197,000 passport records from the year 1890 to 1950. Passenger information is available from 1892 forward when the law required that all passengers had to be listed on the ship's manifest, although there are some years missing and limited entries for departures prior to early 1900s. Besides names and age or age group, i.e. adult, passenger information would include number and page of the passenger manifest, date of departure and name of the ship leaving Finland, the Ocean Liner Company, port of call in England and port of arrival, and sometimes persons traveling together. The passport record information includes birth date and domicile, date of issue, period of validity, and may include occupation, religion, and country of destination. The records are preserved at the Manuscript Department of Åbo Akademi University Library, Åbo, Finland. The index to the passenger lists is entered on computer by the Institute of Migration in Åbo, Finland.

Considering the prospect of finding significant information, I was dismayed when I searched for Ida Maria Andersdotter Lillbroända Wikstrom using each of the names, and she was not to be found in the Institute of Migration emigrant records. The only information I had to go on was her certificate *betyg till Amerika* 5.5.1893 recorded in the Kronoby Church book and my aunt's manuscript that said she landed in Quebec. So the next step would be to calculate the earliest date she might have arrived in Quebec, assuming she left Finland after receiving her certificate, and look for her on Canadian passenger arrival lists. In most cases, emigrants departed Finland soon after receiving the certificate.

Emigrants did not depart directly from their homeland to America. There were several routes by which the emigrants reached America, but most often, Finlanders would first take a smaller steamer, referred to as a "feeder ship" to a British port, then by train to larger emigration ports such as Liverpool, Glasgow or London, to embark on a transatlantic steamship. Most feeder ships carried passengers from Hangö on the south coast of Finland to Copenhagen, Denmark and to Hull in England, but also to Stockholm, Sweden and Lubeck, Germany. The emigrants who traveled by this "indirect" route were referred to as transmigrants. There was also transmigration via Hamburg, where Finland emigrants boarded German transatlantic lines. Some emigrants, such as my grandfather Johan Leonard Danielsson Sundqvist, crossed the Gulf of Bothnia by boat to Sweden and departed from Gothenburg to Liverpool where they boarded an ocean-going vessel.

Finland steamship company *Finska Ångfartygs Aktiebolaget/FÅA* began a regular route autumn 1891 between Hangö and Hull, England, so it was likely in 1893 that Ida Maria traveled by train from Kronoby to Hangö, then boarded a "feeder ship" to Hull. From Hull, it would be about a four-hour train ride to Liverpool to board an ocean-going vessel and then at least another two weeks at sea before her arrival in Quebec. The ticket arrangement made in Finland connected passengers with certain ocean-going passenger lines such as Allan Line, Dominion Line, and Cunard. If the passenger were listed on the Finnish Migration Institute records, one of the items posted would be the line traveled to America. Morton Allan Ship Directory lists European ocean-going lines, the names of ships connected with each line, and passenger steamship arrivals.

It was not unusual that Ida Maria entered North America via Quebec. Quebec was a common port of entry for many European emigrants who disembarked in Canada on their way to the United States. By 1865, there were excellent rail connections on Canadian Pacific Railroad or river steamers down the St. Lawrence Waterway to Midwest destinations such as Duluth, Minnesota.

The word was out that Port of New York was becoming increasingly restrictive. America had welcomed immigrants, even encouraged and actively recruited immigration through advertisements in the northern European countries, but by 1890 attitudes in America were changing and restrictions were being applied to screen passengers arriving in New York. If one person in a family were ill, they might all be sent back. Immigration officials were looking for any sign of disability that might put the immigrants on welfare rolls. Canadian entry ports meant less personal inspection and harassment than an emigrant might encounter at New York's Ellis Island or earlier at Castle Garden.

Between 1815–1860, five million immigrants had settled permanently in the United States, mainly English, Irish, Germanic, Scandinavian; the second wave of ten million immigrants 1865–1890 again were mainly from northwestern Europe. But from 1890 to 1914, a ship from Liverpool or Bremen, Germany might include Austro-Hungarian, Turkish, Lithuanian, Russian, Jewish, Greek, Italian, Romanian. The Americans who thought of themselves as "natives," not including Native American Indians, felt threatened by the southeastern Europeans who they felt were inferior.

There were several "immigration acts" that arose during this latter period. The 1891 Immigration Act was a revised version of the 1882 act that declared certain classes of individuals were unfit to become American citizens including idiots, insane persons, and paupers. Any person who could become a public charge on society was not allowed to enter. The immigrants who came to the United States carrying a contagious disease were also not permitted entry. Anyone who had been convicted of a felony, misdemeanor, or any other crime such as any activity deemed contrary to the beliefs and standards of society such as polygamy were not granted citizenship. Any person whose ticket was paid for by another was not allowed to enter into the country as well. The United States wanted only those who could care for themselves without the assistance of others.

Upon arrival to the United States each individual was inspected by the Commanding Officer or agents. The immigrants were required to supply their name, nationality, last residence, and where they were planning to go in the States. They were not allowed entry to the land until they supplied the necessary information. Once on land they had to submit themselves to a medical examination. If any diseases were found they were immediately sent to quarantine or sent back to their country of origin. If an immigrant entered into the United States illegally they were sent back to their home country on the ship in which they arrived. If an immigrant came illegally it was the responsibility of the shipping company to take them back at their own expense as well as pay a fine of $300 per offense.

Ship passenger records are kept in the National Archives of the United States and Canada, and they are available on microfilm reels. The roll of microfilm can be ordered through interlibrary loan at the public library if there is a microfiche available with which to view the film or through Church of Latter Day Saints Family History Center.

Ida Maria purportedly landed in Quebec; therefore, her arrival would be recorded on Canadian records. The port of Quebec was the first Canadian port to archive passenger lists in 1865. The National Archives of Canada holds immigration records from 1865 to 1935. Few lists created prior to 1865 survive, as shipping companies were not required by the government to keep their passenger manifests. The lists are not indexed.

I posted a query on Finngen to enlist help in the process of finding Ida and soon received an email response from Finnish researcher Staffan Storteir:

> "I'd suggest a query to TheShipsList. Their foremost expert on Canadian arrivals and owner of the list is Sue Swiggum, who will be back in a few weeks. There are no online records as to Quebec 1893, but perhaps she can do a lookup on the microfilms."

With this new information, I posted a query on TheShipsList and listed vital information about Ida Maria Lillbroända aka Ida Wikstrom and date of her certificate to leave Finland—5.5.1893. By chance I added: My aunt wrote, "They (Ida and a friend) landed in Quebec, Canada and they were promptly quarantined for weeks, as an infectious disease had spread among the passengers."

Harry Dodsworth, a subscriber to TheShipsList.com responded to my posted query:

> "Allowing the usual two to three weeks, I expect an arrival in Canada near the end of May. As the *Montreal Gazette* was printing useful arrival notices in 1893, I read them for May. There was one note in mid-May saying that quarantine at Grosse Island had been very quiet. But on May 31: The Dominion Line SS Oregon was detained at Grosse Island – diphtheria among the steerage passengers – all landed. Measles and diphtheria were noted. It would look as if the Oregon might fit with Arlene's aunt's story.
>
> Emigrants from Ostrobothnia (probably) never left Finland on the same date the certificates or passports were issued, at least not if they departed from Hangö."

Staffan Storteir advised, "In my experience one should add at least one week to assumptions of the first possible date of departure from Finland. But the Dominion Line SS Oregon on May 31 is possible."

Sue Swiggum responded with information:

> Reel #C-4539; Ship Name OREGON; Departure Liverpool, England 1893-05-19; Arrival Quebec, Que. 1893-05-31; DOM (Dominion Line) British and North Atlantic Steam Navigation Co. Ltd., Liverpool, U.K.; List Number 24.
>
> "As Harry suggested, this looks like it might be the ship. "Weeks" in quarantine sounds a little long…maybe it just felt like weeks. :-} I would have expected a Liverpool departure more in the range of May 10–15 so if she isn't found on Oregon, check List Number(s) 17, 18, 20 and 22. The List Numbers are clearly written on the manifest (grease pencil?) Even though there is usually limited information about US destined passengers, the list may include at least her destination State, and if you are lucky, the town."

Swiggum continued with elaborate instructions for this grateful neophyte:

> "The passenger manifest is on Microfilm at the National Archives of Canada (NAC) in Ottawa. The Ships are placed on the reel, in order of arrival. You can borrow this reel on an Inter Library Loan (ILL). You can find the details for this procedure at the NAC Genealogy Research. You are also able to ILL from Ottawa, to libraries in the US, and outside North America. These microfilms contain arrivals from ALL ports; they are not indexed. The LDS also have copies of Quebec films 1865–1899 if that is more convenient than borrowing via ILL from Ottawa. For a copy of this microfilm, the LDS number 0889463 ~ 1893 ~ port of Quebec. Good luck!" Sue

Staffan Storteir echoed her response:
"I'd start from List Number 24 for Ida."

Three keen researchers were certain that, because of dates and information that she had been quarantined, Ida would be found on the SS Oregon, and so was I.

I ordered film # 889463 of passenger manifests 1893 port of Quebec and impatiently anticipated its arrival. At the Church of Latter Day Saints Family History Center, I briskly wound the reel to passenger list number 24. The first manifest I perused were passengers on the Dominion Line's vessel SS OREGON, departing from Liverpool, England 1893-05-19, arrival Quebec 1893-05-31. To my astonishment and dismay, the end of the list appeared, and I had not found Ida.

I continued on, checking the ships that departed prior to mid-May and then later ships. After an hour or two, I began to laugh. This is a two-handed operation: With one hand raised to adjust the focus knob overhead, and one hand on the lever at table level to scroll the film forward or backward, I felt like I was playing the old trick of rubbing one's head and stomach at the same time, with hands going in opposite directions.

Thousands of names handwritten in 19th century script danced on the white surface under the light of the microfiche. Often each page's entries were a different handwriting. Some of the entries were faded; some lists appeared distorted. There was also the matter of spelling. Passenger lists for steam ships were mostly created by British pursers. Their knowledge of foreign naming practices or pronunciations was obviously lacking. The Englishmen on the ship leaving Liverpool, hearing strange foreign names, wrote down what they heard; misspellings were rampant. Each time I came across a group of recognizable Nordic names, my eyes concentrated on seeing the names Ida or Andersdotter or Lillbroända or Wikstrom/Vickstrom or similar spellings. As I learned of Ida Maria's relatives who had emigrated to America, I would also look for their names. Finding any one of the chains of migration from her Kronoby parish might lead to finding Ida.

Some passenger lists had scant information; but if the country of origin was identified on the manifest, I could quickly skim over names from other countries and concentrate on Scandinavian names. On each page, I would first scan the notations on the right side of the manifest. If the captain had noted the country of origin, I would check emigrant names on the list where the country of origin was marked Finland/Finnish, Sweden/Swedish, or Scand/Scandinavian. Perhaps the Finnish emigrant had remarked, "I am a Swede from Vasa (Finland)." If the purser heard the word Swede or did not recognize the dialect of the Swedish-speaking

Finns, he might have classified Finland Swedes as Swedish, or perhaps he might have listed all Nordic emigrants under "Scandinavians." The Finland Swede emigrant had a Finnish passport in most cases, but I also scanned names when Russia was noted as country of origin. Until 1917, Finland was an autonomous Grand Duchy under Russia's rule, so there was the off chance the emigrant might be listed under Russia.

I perused twenty-four passenger lists and thousands of names on the microfilm reel of Canadian passenger arrivals 1893 Quebec from Liverpool. For days and for hours at a time, I sat in a quiet, darkened room at the Family History Center, bent over the microfiche table, as my eyes strained to discern the faint writing. Occasionally, I would hear a muffled gleeful outburst in the room, "There she is!" when someone came upon the person they were looking for. That is the moment I yearned for, but Ida Maria Andersdotter Lillbroända Wikstrom was not to be found.

Weeks went by, and I had gone through thousands of names with no result. I explained my plight to Sue Swiggum: I had carefully looked for Ida, and more so for the last name Wikstrom, the name written in pencil on the back of a photo of Ida Maria had taken in Duluth, Minnesota. Now I must return to those lists again because I had received information from the National Archives of Finland in response to my query.

Ida Suolahti, Research Assistant wrote:

> "In the lists of Rural Police District of Kokkola
> (Gamlakarleby) from year 1893 (file 9), there is a note that on
> 6 May 1893, farmer's daughter Ida Maria Lillbroända, b 1876,
> home place Kronoby, was issued a five-year passport."

The date was concurrent with her certificate to America, but this suggested that I should be looking for Ida Maria Lillbroända, not Wikstrom.

Sue Swiggum succinctly responded, "This is number 24." She repeated the information she had previously sent for the SS Oregon and wrote: "Ida Maria Lillbroända will be there I'm sure, maybe hiding in "plain sight."

If Ida Maria was hiding, she was doing a good job of it. Again, I perused the list to no avail.

I dropped my search for Ida Maria for the time being and as a diversion, I turned my attention to finding my grandfather John Sundqvist's passage. While he came from another parish in Finland, and they did not meet until they were in America, I thought perhaps learning his passage might give me further insight into how the emigrants from Ostrobothnia found their way to America.

Before we made our family pilgrimage to Finland, my *småkusin* Bengt Enqvist went to Nykarleby church to look for John Sundqvist in the church records. The Sundquist brothers Johan and Henrik, Bengt's grandfather, were born at the farm named Gertrud Olin nr 19. Henrik's daughter Ingeborg Sundqvist and her son Bengt Enqvist continue the farm tradition in Finland. Bengt found Johan Sundqvist's *betyg til Amerika* recorded in the church book 11 October 1890.

I first checked the Finnish Migration Institute website for his passenger record leaving Finland or his passport. I found neither. Since 1862, all Finns needed a passport to travel abroad, but all emigrants are not found in passport lists. It was easy to cross the border to a neighboring country without a passport, and it was no problem to continue the journey without official documents. Quite often, the way to America from Ostrobothnia was the route into Sweden from Munsala to Umeå, commonly known as the Munsala *passet* passport.

A query to the National Archives brought the following response from Ida Suolahti, Research Assistant:

> "There was no mention of John Sundquist in the lists
> sent by Parish Records Offices, but in the list of people who
> left from the Province of Vasa to America in 1890 (file 3),
> there is a note that farmer's son Johan Leonard Danielsson
> Sundqvist, b. 1870, home place Nykarleby, was issued a one-
> year passport."

There were several migration routes for emigrants leaving Ostrobothnia. As the family story goes, Grandfather chose a different path. He and his uncle Anders Olin rowed a boat across the Gulf of Bothnia from Finland to Sweden and from there, they went on to Liverpool.

With the help of Staffan Storteir in Finland, I learned that my grandfather Johan Leonard Danielsson Sundqvist was listed departing from Gothenburg to Liverpool.

The Church of Latter Day Saints Family History Center boasts the most complete genealogical records at their Family History Library in Salt Lake City, Utah. Teams of Mormon members have been traveling the world since the 1930s microfilming images of records. I ordered film #889461 Canadian Passenger Arrival List 1890 through the local Family History Center at a nominal fee for several weeks use and engaged the microfilm reel to embark on another scroll through passenger lists for my grandfather John Sundquist's arrival in North America, beginning with ships departing from Liverpool in the weeks following the date of his *betyg till Amerika*.

I scanned names of passengers on four ships from Liverpool that arrived in Quebec in October, just as I had scanned thousands before while searching for my grandmother's passage. The names and information were written in 19ᵗʰ century script; the handwriting on each page was by a different person; some pages were torn and faded, and my eyes strained to see the names. Then, I came across an Allan Line vessel, a good bet for finding Finlanders.

Heavy handwriting in grease pencil at the top: No. 88 SS Corean. I quickly scanned the first page of the passenger manifest:

Port of Embarkation Liverpool. Bound for Quebec &
Montreal. The Master, Chas. Menzies, certified on 30 October
1890 "that the Provisions actually laden on board this Ship are
sufficient, according to the requirements of the Passengers'
Act, for a voyage of 37 days," although the ship would arrive
at its destination Quebec 15 November 1890. Total 185
Passengers: 1 Cabin; 184 Steerage.

I scrolled to the next page. There, on the fourth line, a name jumps out at me—Johan Sundqvist. I had opined that the excitement and joy that I would feel finding my grandparent would elicit a shout, but what came out of my mouth was barely an audible whisper: "Omagosh, there he is," I breathed, as Johan Sundqvist's name came into focus.

My eyes darted across the page to the column that lists Profession, Occupation, or Calling of Passengers: Sundqvist was entered as Lab (Laborer); Destination Ely, Minnesota. The next four columns are divided: English, Scotch, Irish, and Foreigners. All passengers not of "British birth" were designated "Foreign" until mid-1890s. The Foreigners on this manifest included Scandinavians, Germans, Russian Poles and Russian Jews. Under the Foreigners column, Sundqvist's age—20 years old. Yes, he is the right one. I quickly glanced back across the page to the passenger names column to see who was traveling with him. Above his name and number # 3335 was Sundqvist's uncle Anders Olin, age 43; following his name is Karl Karlson, age 18, not known; all laborers destined for Ely, Minnesota. A further glance over the passenger names revealed wide grease pencil lines that struck out two families of four. "Rejected by B/Y Doctor" was written beside the names. They would be sent back to their homeland. A sobering thought when one considers the long journey they had just undergone.

Johan Sundqvist wasted no time leaving Finland after receiving his *betyg till Amerika* certificate 11 October 1890. The ocean-going vessel SS Corean was the second to last ship leaving Liverpool for Quebec October 1890 before ice would cut off passage, as the St. Lawrence waterway would be closed to shipping during the winter months. His destination—Ely, Minnesota. Many Finland-Swede emigrants headed for Ely where they would find employment opportunities in the iron mines. And there was much about the northern territory that was geographically familiar: Glistening white snow covered the ground for months on end. Then the lingering light of long summer days that made up for the long dark nights of winter. Minnesota, the land of a 1000 lakes and thick forests, reminded the emigrants of their homeland.

The little bridge at Lillbroända (ca. 1930)

Chapter 6

Finding Ida

Where was Ida Maria? I pondered my dilemma and returned to family manuscripts and documents to search for clues I might have overlooked. I reordered 1893 passenger lists from the Canadian National Archives and perused the ships' manifests again, thinking that perhaps I had missed a ship if I had scrolled backward with the microfilm instead of forward or vise versa. I had made a list and placed a check by the name of each ship; now I was checking the same names again—still no Ida. I continued into 1894. There were thousands more names. I scanned arriving ships looking for a handwritten notation on the top right hand side of the first page of each manifest that would indicate passengers were dropped off at Grosse Île.

I decided to back off for a while with the thought that perhaps Ida Maria would find me. Then, the breakthrough came: An unexpected email from Staffan Storteir, Finnish researcher, who grew up at Nylassfolk farm in Sideby, Finland:

> From time to time I have tried new searches re your grandmother Ida Maria Andersdotter Lillbroända. Now I tried Andersson as optional last name and found among others the name Ida Andersson. I was on the verge to leave it, because it was in 1896, but decided to study copassengers. What makes this particular interesting is that there is a passenger Anders Lillbrända, which might be misspelled Lillbroända. Furthermore several of the passengers have Ostrobothnian sounding names (Olin, Rönkrans (Rönnkrans?), Skuthälls (Skuthälla?), Sundell, Warg, Lybeck ...). Below I have pasted the record for Ida Andersson and all copassengers on 15.05.1896 aboard the Urania from Hangö. (All five were bound for Quebec.) What do you think? Is there any

possibility that Kronoby church book *betyg till Amerika*
05-05-1893 could have been 05-05-1896?

His message had the ring of possibility. So in consideration of the
date possibly being 1896, I immediately ordered the Canadian passenger arrival list to Quebec #889465 and scanned May and June 1896 arrivals for the aforementioned names. I found none of the names arriving
Quebec 1896. I checked Ellis Island records; again, not one was listed
there in 1896.

Where are they?

Staffan Storteir emailed again; over a year had passed since he had
responded to my initial query.

> "I've made many attempts to find your grandmother in
> passenger records during the last years and she has every time
> eluded the searches. It is evident the year was 1893. I do not
> doubt that you have carefully checked the Canadian rolls, par-
> ticularly the arrival on 31. 5. 1893, which I still bet is hot."

He was still on the trail of Ida Andersson. I was slightly amused that
in my mind, he took on the role of the Finnish equivalent of my grandmother's and my favorite radio character: Mr. Keene, Tracer of Lost
Persons! His dogged perseverance would not allow him to give up on
finding Ida. He responded that he has learned to esteem his (Finnish)
incredible stubbornness as one of the main factors for eventual success
in his own research.

After long searches, Storteir was inclined to think that Ida
Andersson was Ida Maria Andersdotter Lillbroända, my grandmother.
"It must however be confirmed in some way," he wrote.

Uncannily, Storteir's astute observations and keen eye noted that
the ages noted for the 1896 departure were off by three years! He had
discerned that this group of twenty Ostrobothnians recorded in Finnish
migration records as leaving in 1896 might actually have departed
Finland in 1893. Now he supported his supposition with information
that Anders Lillbroända left Finland for the USA in 1893; Ida Skuthälla,
born 1876, emigrated to USA in 1893. Their recorded ages and their
birth dates on passenger records would indicate an 1893 departure!

Storteir's keen research eye noted something else:

> "Also there is another reason that the list of 15.05.1896
> makes me suspect that the year might be wrong. Why should
> the Urania sail with only a small (20 people) contingent of
> emigrants mainly from Ostrobothnia? At least 8 out of only 20
> passengers on this date have obvious Ostrobothnian Swede-
> Finn surnames like Warg, Sundell, Skuthälla, Ronnkrans,
> Lybeck, Lillbroända."

In 19th century Finland, names could be associated with places. As
Storteir noted, "Lindbeck (Lindbäck, Linbeck, Linbäck), also Lybäck
(Lybeck) and Rönnkrans are Kronoby names. He followed with another
startling email after searching May 16th as date of departure, rather than
May 15:

> "Well, one good reason is that Urania apparently did
> not sail on May 15 because searching the passenger lists with
> 16.05.1896 as input reveal about 150 passengers on this date
> on the same ship Urania. I still keep it as a strong option that
> the twenty mainly Ostrobothnian passengers might belong to
> 15.05.1893, three years earlier."

The Ostrobothnian names added titillating and important clues to
the unfolding drama. For one, Anders Lillbranda was no doubt from
the same place Lillbroända as my grandmother, but I was riveted by
another name in the group—Amanda Lybeck—a name that I had seen
before. *Småkusin* Patrik Hansell in Finland had earlier asked for help
in locating his ancestors in America and had sent me a list of names.
On the list was Hansell's ancestor *Bonde* Johannes Ödal from Hästö,
a cousin to my grandmother Ida Maria. Johannes Ödal emigrated to
America and to Duluth. I recalled from my aunt's manuscript that Ida
went to an uncle in Duluth. Was that uncle perhaps Johannes Ödal? But
most importantly, Patrik's information revealed that Ödal had married
Amanda Lybäck.

Could Amanda possibly be the "girl friend" who my aunt indicated in her manuscript had traveled with Ida Maria to Quebec? Indeed, when I first saw her name on Patrik Hansell's list and that she had married Ida Maria's Duluth cousin, a strange feeling went through me at the time that she could be Ida's travel companion.

I emailed genealogist Hasse Andtbacka in Kronoby, Finland to inquire about Amanda Lybäck and to verify the 1893 date proposed by Staffan Storteir's keen observations. Andtbacka immediately responded with startling information:

> *Pigan Maria Amanda Karlsdr Lybäck, b. 11.10.1872. Betyg till Amerika 5.5.1893!!!* The same day as Ida Maria. She also took a certificate that she was free to get married.

The information Andtbacka retrieved from the church records verified the date 1893. Amanda Lybäck, born 1872, would have been 21 in 1893, rather than 21 in 1896 as reported on the Finnish Migration Records. The certificate indicated that she had been confirmed in the Lutheran church and had her first communion, both of which were compulsory before she could marry. That a young girl felt obliged to carry proof with her to the New World to affirm she had fulfilled her religious obligations speaks to the power of the authoritarian, patriarchal Lutheran state church.

Andtbacka further noted:

> "The girls lived less than a mile from each other, and Ida Maria's Uncle Viktor Vikström lived next door to Karl Lybäck's family. It is obvious that the girls intended to go together to America."

I was convinced that Storteir's observation about my grandmother traveling under the name Ida Andersson was correct. Their *betyg till Amerika* certificates were issued on the same date. Amanda Lybäck and Ida Andersson left Finland together on the "feeder ship" Urania (1136 gross ton FÅA ship) from Hangö to Hull. Their passenger ticket numbers found on Finnish Migration Passenger Records follow one another and were prepaid, that is, money was sent by a relative or friend in America: Amanda's ticket, Ppd. #68786; Ida's ticket, Ppd. #68787.

Hasse Andtbacka also recognized Ida Maria Skuthälla's name on the passenger list. Andtbacka noted that she was also from Kronoby, born the same month and year as my grandmother. Skuthälla received her *betyg for Amerika* 8 May 1893, three days later than Amanda Lybäck and Ida Andersson. Staffan Storteir had noted Ida Skuthälla's birthdate 1876 in the passport record; yet she was recorded as 17 years of age in the 1896 passenger list. The departure date 1893 fit her year of birth. "I seriously assume that the year (1896 departure) is wrong in the database," Staffan concluded.

I reordered the 1893 Canadian Passenger Arrival List Port of Quebec through the local Family History Center. By chance, while awaiting the microfilm's arrival, a query on TheShipsList website regarding Canadian Records prompted me to return to the Canadian Library and Archives website and the Canadian Genealogy Centre. There I discovered a database of Hospital Registers at Grosse Île Quarantine Station (often spelled "Grosse Isle" in English) for the Port of Quebec from 1832 to 1937.

The words from my aunt's manuscript flashed across my mind: "They landed in Quebec, Canada, and were promptly quarantined for weeks, as an infectious disease had spread among the passengers."

I entered only first name Ida in the Grosse Île online database search, and there I found Ida Anderson's name. She had been admitted to the hospital. The information on the Hospital Register revealed that she had been a passenger on the SS OREGON and was dropped off at Grosse Île on 12 June 1893. I entered the same date to search for other passengers who may also have been dropped off, and even more exciting, two other familiar names were listed on the Hospital Register. Amanda Lindbeck (or should it have been Lybeck?) Hilma Lindbeck, and Ida Anderson, passengers on the SS Oregon are all listed on the Hospital Register at Grosse Île. The girls had been admitted June 12, 1893 and released June 20.

Grosse Île database reveals in total 126 passengers from the SS Oregon in the Hospital Register. Forty-six passengers had been admitted to the hospital May 30-31; the remainder were admitted between June 1 and June 12. It appears the infectious disease was confined to steerage passengers, as it is noted on the manifest, "Cabin to Montreal in vessel." Six children from the SS Oregon died and were buried at Grosse Île.

The Montreal Gazette, May 31, 1893 reported: "The Dominion Line SS Oregon was detained at Grosse Île - diphtheria among steerage passengers – all landed."

I excitedly emailed Staffan Storteir that I had found the girls on the Hospital Register at Grosse Île Quarantine Station.

Storteir responded, "I suggest you have found your grandmother."

Steamship *Urania* with 509 passengers on board spring 1893
Photograph by Captain J.A. Rosqvist, FÅA courtesy Institute of Migration

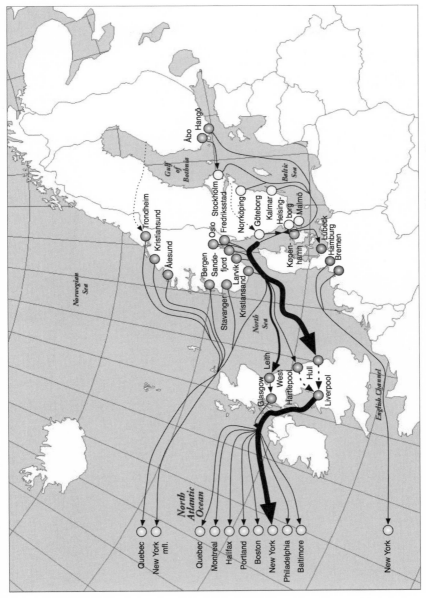

Emigrant migration map compiled and drawn by Hasse Nygård from *Emigrantfolska! Steg för steg.*

Steamship *Oregon* Liverpool to Quebec
University of Washington Libraries, Special collections, UW29112z

Chapter 7

Quebec, Quarantine and Quirky Passenger List

One sentence in my aunt's manuscript embodied all that our family knew about Ida Maria's emigration and her arrival in North America:

> They landed in Quebec, Canada, and were promptly quarantined for weeks, as an infectious disease had spread among the passengers.

But within that one sentence were the two important clues—Quebec and quarantine—that ultimately led us to the name I. Andersson.

Ida Maria had told her family that she had been quarantined for weeks, but her comments were few and brief. The SS Oregon officially arrived Quebec May 31, but according to the Grosse Île Hospital Register, some passengers were admitted May 30 and 31. Ida, Amanda, and Hilma were apparently quarantined for twelve days before they were admitted to the hospital June 12; then they spent nine days at the hospital. Yes, it appears my grandmother remembered very well that they were quarantined for "weeks."

Ida Maria's daughters recalled:

> Mother was very miserable there, unhappy and homesick. Once, in recalling the experience, she said that if she had had the money she would have taken the next boat back home.

When an outbreak of an infectious disease occurred aboard ship, the quarantine station at Grosse Île was required anchorage for all vessels from 1832 to 1937 to help control the spread of diseases. At an earlier time, ships arriving from foreign ports were detained in quarantine for forty days, hence the name "quarantine." The island, approximately two kilometers in length and 800 meters in width, lies in the middle of the St. Lawrence River, 46 kilometers downstream from Quebec City. Grosse-Île is now a Canadian National Historic Site.

Emigrants were filled with anxieties about the stop at Grosse Île, although most passengers passed medical inspection with good health. A Medical Officer would board and if there had been no sickness on board, the ship would be released to land passengers and cargo. If there had been an infectious disease aboard, the ship could be detained and disinfected.

Being dropped off at Grosse Île was not a pleasant experience even for those who were not ill. If they had been exposed to an infectious disease, it meant that the emigrant must present their clothing and possessions for sanitizing. Items were placed in metal baskets and run through boiling steam-filled chambers, while emigrants endured disinfecting showers. Passengers under observation stayed on the island; the sick were admitted and cared for in the hospital. From baptisms to burials, life and death mingled at Grosse Île.

As I removed the microfilm entitled 1893 Canadian Passenger Arrival List from its square white box for the fourth time, I thought of Sue Swiggum's remark over a year ago: "Ida Maria will be there maybe hiding in plain sight." This time I felt confident. I would find Ida. I cranked the microfilm forward on the microfiche to cover sheet No. 24. Ships are numbered according to the sequence of arrivals; the SS Oregon was the 24th ship to enter Quebec in 1893. Printed at the top of the form was "DOMINION LINE." According to her emigration record at the Finnish Institute of Migration, Ida had been ticketed on the Dominion Line, although the ship's name was not noted. The date of departure of the SS Oregon 19 May 1893 would be time-consistent with her certificate 5.5.1893 and the date of her passport, allowing for travel time from Kronoby to Liverpool.

On the Schedule B Form of Passenger List, SS Oregon was written under Ship's Name and under Master's Name, Joseph Gibson 2373, who presumably certified by listing himself "that the Provisions actually laden on board this Ship are sufficient, according to the requirements of the Passenger Act for a voyage" although he did not render his signature after the declaration.

The SS Oregon sailed from Liverpool 19 May and arrived 31 May with 43 adults and two infants in Cabin, 663 Steerage, 708 Total. June report: Passengers left at Grosse Isle. On the Summary of Steerage and Cabin Passengers: Master Joseph Gibson had written 561 adults, 114 children between one and twelve years, and 33 infants. The grand total: 708 Souls. Of 561 adults, 365 were single men and 14 single women. Forty-five persons were traveling Cabin; the remainder of the 708 was Steerage. Consider the cacophony of languages and dialects: Swedes, Finns, Russians, Russian Jews, Germans, German Jews, Italians, French, and Austrians. Imagine, too, the foods transported by the emigrants and the aromas that permeated steerage from pickled herring to garlic, cheeses, and bratwurst.

The SS Oregon was launched in 1882, 3,672 gross ton ship, length 360.7 ft. x beam 40.3 ft. with a speed of 12 knots. All the ships in the Dominion Line, except Vancouver, carried livestock; however, there is no mention of cattlemen on this manifest. A dozen or more cattlemen might be aboard on the trip to North America to accompany a load of live cattle on the ship's returning voyage to England. Earlier, cattle were shipped westward for breeding stock more than for meat or dairy. Canada quickly became a cattle-exporting nation, so then the cattle were going in the other direction. While not true, the thought crossed my mind, being a Westerner, that "steerage" was the name given the compartment within a ship conveying cattle, and that in turn became the lowest and cheapest class of passenger accommodations the ship offered. Many family oral histories have ancestors arriving on Cattle Boats relating their travel to hardship, but while steerage class was uncomfortable, many passenger ships also carried cattle.

This time, I was not perusing the manifest for names Ida Maria Andersdotter Lillbroända or Wikstrom as I had done three times before, but for a group of Ostrobothnian passenger names, including Ida Andersson, that Staffan Storteir proposed would be on this vessel because of the consistent three-year discrepancy in ages vs. birth dates that he had found recorded in the Finnish Migration Institute records, that indicated to him they had sailed in 1893, not May 1896. We had already ruled out the later departure when they were not to be found on 1896 passenger lists.

Staffan Storteir was quite certain that the Ida Andersson in this group was my grandmother, and I mused that quite possibly she might have used the name Andersson rather than Andersdotter when she was ticketed for America, as the name Anderson was commonly used in America, not Andersdotter.

Written on the upper right corner of the first page of the manifest: "4 foreign children died at sea, and 1 English child, ditto. From 6 to 3 years of age." On pages one and two: 50 Austrian musicians bound for Chicago. It is interesting to note that on most manifests of passengers departing from England, British passenger names are identified as Miss, Mr. or Mrs., and as a rule, the names are written quite legibly. Not so, with the "foreigners" traveling in steerage.

Page by page, I slowly scrolled and scanned passenger names. Page three revealed 20 British "Home Children," child migrants on their way to Belleville, Ontario to Rev. Wallace. Emigration had become a solution to the vast number of homeless, desperate children in Great Britain at a time of overpopulation, poor living conditions, and lack of employment. Children's homes were filled beyond capacity. In 1869, the first group of children was taken to Canada. Between 1869 and the early 1930s, over 100,000 children were sent to Canada from Great Britain during the child emigration movement.

Finally, on the next to last page—Page 11 of 12 pages of steerage passengers— the names of the five Ostrobothnians appeared together:

I. Anderson; A Rankrans; H. Lindbeck; A. Lyback; and A.W. Olin. "Foreigners" and it was noted that they were all bound for Ely, Minnesota via C.P.R. (Canadian Pacific Railroad).

The initials and surnames on the ship manifest at the arrival port in North America, albeit with some misspellings, coincided with the names of the group on the Finnish Migration Records: Ida Andersson, Anna Rönkrans, Hilma Lindbeck, Amanda Lybeck, and Anders Olin.

On this manifest, unlike some of the others, there was scant information: name, age, and destination and irregular postings. The column marked Married Male is checked for each passenger; Single Female column lists their ages. The SS Oregon's purser lumped them all together as Laborers, when usually, single women traveling in Steerage were listed Domestic, as a young girl's likely position in America would be as a maid. Men were marked Laborer as mining, logging, and sawmill workers were most commonly the jobs awaiting them.

Staffan Storteir had also sent the names of the entire group of twenty who purportedly had left Finland in 1896. I scanned the list again, and on page eight, I found the remainder of the names traveling together. Immigrant names are often misspelled on the records, and the SS Oregon's passenger list is rife with errors. From the spellings of names, it is apparent that the person recording names at the Port of Embarkation—Liverpool, U.K., was not looking at passport identification, he wrote what he heard pronounced by the foreigners or copied from the ship's manifest. Therefore, we see a list of misspellings, as is so often the case with passenger lists, but fortunately, each of the two groups traveled together and were listed together, so I could discern who was who.

In addition to the group of five previously mentioned, the other names, as best as I could determine as written on the passenger manifest, corresponded with the names of the group listed on the Finnish Migration records. From this list, one can observe how names often are misspelled in the records:

A.Bostrom, to Duluth MN appears as A. Bostrum; Erik
Carlsson, to Escanaba MI appears as E. Carlson; Johan
Carlsson, Escanaba, MI appears as J. E. Carlson and also a
R. E. Carlson to Escanaba, MI. I. A. Frodo could be Ida Frojd
to Ludington MI; M. Herik could be Maria Heikkila to Duluth
MN; Edla Honka, Duluth MN appears as E. L. Honga; H. M.
Kauffe to Duluth could be Hilma Kauko.

Johan Kotka, Neagaunee MI appears as J. W. Kotka; Anders
Lillbranda, Ludington, MI appears as A. M. Littranda; another
passenger to Ludington appears as S. Kvi (Maria Kivijarvi ?)
Johan Linback, Ely, MN appears as J. Linbuck; Alexandia
Sundell, Duluth MN appears as A. Lundell.

Ida Maria Andersdotter Lillbroända was aboard the SS Oregon, but it appears that along the emigration route, Ida Maria had changed her name to Anderson, which would be a more commonly used name in North America than Andersdotter. After over a two-year quest and with the help of Staffan Storteir, an astute Finnish researcher, I found my grandmother on passenger manifest No. 24 arriving Quebec 1893 aboard the SS Oregon, the ship that was first suggested to me over two years ago, the passenger list that I perused four times. And just as Sue Swiggum of Ship's List had earlier said: She was hiding there in plain sight. Indeed it had been a lengthy, indirect, often frustrating route to finding Ida Maria's passage to North America. The discovery was circuitous, yet exciting, which also makes a good story. For me, the culmination of the experience was as if I had received my grandmother's blessing toward publication of her story.

In my mind's eye, however, I reflected on two young girls huddled together in steerage within the dark confines of the ship. After two weeks at sea, their arrival in North America was not so glorious as they had dreamed, when they were dropped off at the Grosse Île quarantine station.

Ida Maria shook out the square woolen scarf she had woven, folded it carefully into a triangular half that she flung over her dark hair and tied in a square knot under her chin. One final tug brought the scarf forward over her forehead. She tucked her knitted wool mittens into the sleeves of her wool coat and pulled the heavy cloth around her legs.

I reflected back to my last visit with grandmother: On Wednesdays, we were enraptured by the radio broadcast, "Mr. Keen, Tracer of Lost Persons," radio's longest-running detective melodrama with Mr. Keen, a sage old tracer of missing persons, and his sidekick Mike Clancy. Mr. Keen, the master detective, never failed. When I wrote those words at the beginning of my story, I had mused: if only he could be engaged to find the girl that my grandmother once was and the answers to my questions." The theme song "Someday I'll Find You" played in my mind, as my eyes misted. Once again, grandmother and I together had solved a mystery, this time with the help of Staffan Storteir in Finland. I sent my thanks and appreciation to Storteir, the modern-day Mr. Keen, master detective and tracer of lost persons! He deserves kudos for his excellent deduction of dates and ages, and most of all, his sticking with the task of finding my grandmother, Ida Maria Andersdotter Lillbroända (Wikstrom in America) aka Ida Andersson/I. Anderson. The correct ship was there from the start, but not until Storteir located the group traveling together from Finland in 1893, not 1896, do we make the connection with the passenger I. Andersson, who is my grandmother, who will debark at Grosse Île Hospital under the name Ida Anderson.

Of note, Staffan Storteir made an important discovery of several people misplaced in the historical record. How many other descendents of this group may have tried to locate their ancestors without success? Not only because the incorrect date was posted on the emigrant list from Finland, but also because of misspelled names on the ship's manifest.

I pondered the sequence of events, people, and information that appeared over the two-year period to find Ida's arrival in North America, beginning with the synchronicities of finding Sue Swiggum's ShipsList and Staffan Storteir. By chance—were the discoveries all by chance? Certainly the highest credit is due Staffan Storteir, the Finnish researcher, who would not let this drop. He wrote, "I have learned to esteem my (Finnish) incredible stubbornness as one of the main factors for eventual success in my own research."

Storteir's decision to search for Andersson as optional name led him to Ida Andersson. He found the name Anders Lillbranda to be of interest, because of place association with Ida from Lillbroända. His keen observation of ages of the passengers from Ostrobothnia, inconsistent with their birthdates, led him to confirm that the three-year discrepancy meant they did not leave Finland in 1896; rather it would have been 1893. In true researcher's mode, Storteir was compelled to find the interlocking piece to the puzzle.

For me, the name Amanda Lybäck was key among the five passengers leaving Finland together aboard the SS Urania who reported Quebec as their destination. Hasse Andtbacka said the girls lived less than a mile apart, and he confirmed from Kronoby church records that Amanda Lybäck got her *betyg till Amerika* on the same date as Ida. Amanda lived next door to Viktor Vikstrom, Ida's uncle. My aunt wrote in her manuscript that Ida traveled with a girl friend, but the name I. Anderson on the passenger list did not make an impression until I learned who she was traveling with; only then, the name I. Anderson fit with my grandmother, as her ticketing number was consecutive with Amanda Lybäck, her close neighbor in Finland.

And finally, by chance, I came across the database at Grosse Île Quarantine Station. Just as my grandmother had related, I found the girls there—on the Hospital Register.

All the pieces of the puzzle fell into place like the rhythmic force that topples a row of dominoes. It had been a long journey of my own between writing and being immersed in long periods of research. I felt enormous satisfaction.

Who or what directs our actions that ultimately leads to results? I found Ida with the persistent help of Staffan Storteir or conversely, did Ida find us? I never gave up on finding Ida, but I did resign to back off for a time with the thought in mind—perhaps Ida would find me. Everything happens in its own time. Ida had finally appeared, and her appearance seemed to me that she approved my telling her story in the 21st century. I honor that magic presence, that intelligence that directs us unerringly to persons, places, and conditions at the time they are needed.

I pause to reflect on how courageous and adventuresome my grand-mother was. She traveled to North America from halfway around the world in an era when there were no cars, no airplanes, and the steam-ship was just coming into its own. Today, it is less than a day's travel by commercial airline from the West Coast of North America to the West Coast of Finland where my grandparents lived in the late 1800s. To con-trast that period slightly over 100 years ago with the second and third generation born in America, one of my daughters has chosen to live in Switzerland. Our connection at first was a telephone call; today I see her smiling face and the faces of my grandchildren on Skype!

Ida Maria was a renaissance woman, resilient, strong, and asser-tive—with a goal in mind and "a mind of her own," as she was described in her daughter Esther's University of Washington thesis. I ponder her determination to emigrate, as well as my grandfather's. Did either of them contemplate the consequences of that decision that effects gener-ations hence and also affects those left behind, those who chose not to leave their country? Or was there an immediacy to rise above economic conditions that precluded the luxury of contemplation?

Was there, or is there, any lingering resentment by people in their homeland toward people who left their country to find a new life in another place? Certainly, not among today's young people in America and in Finland who see the world as a global community. Certainly not among many of Finland's people who experienced emigration from the West Coast of Finland to Sweden in the 1950s and 1960s. Certainly not Ida Maria's mother-in-law Greta who knew the poverty of her own existence and was supportive of her daughter-in-law's decision to return to America after her visit in 1901.

Many came to America; some returned. John Sundquist's brother Henrik traveled to America three times to work in the logging camps in the Pacific Northwest. On his last trip, he returned home to see only a photograph of his newborn daughter wrapped in her baptismal blanket. The baby girl had died shortly after birth. Henrik remained in Finland, and with the money he had earned in America, he purchased Gertruds-Olin nr 19, the farm where he was born, and there, he lived out his life with his wife Sophia, children, and many grandchildren.

Were there others who longed to return "home" but could not afford to, or could not do so for myriad reasons? Thoughts race through my head. I have a strong sense of place and perhaps a characteristic of my Nordic heritage that I sometimes brood about matters. Were they captured by circumstances? Do those who remain at home think about the road not taken? In any case, is there regret somewhere inside? Somewhere inside, the emigrants must have felt pangs of regret, of missing, of yearning, longing for home— *hemlängtan.*

The connection to homeland carries on in our blood memory; otherwise, why would we second- and third-generation American-born descendents have tears in our eyes when we hear played on the accordion the plaintive strains of the song *Hälsa dem där hemma*? Greet the folks at home. Listeners hardly dare breathe, as soul thoughts consume the body.

Certainly migration is important to the history of the people of Finland— emigration and immigration. And in the United States, everyone except the First Peoples of North America came from another continent. America is a country of nomads, where today people still continue to move West.

I ponder also if there is something within our genes that causes restlessness? Do we humans have a migratory impulse? Bruce Chatwin, British novelist and author of *The Power of Travel* wrote:

> "From the very beginning of our creation, we are continuously moving, traveling . . . I like to think that our brains have an information system giving us our orders for the road, and that here lie the mainsprings of our restlessness."

Were the young emigrants the restless ones? Was it a journey that had been programmed in their DNA? Is it plausible to think that we might carry some of the characteristics of migratory animals? I contemplate others' migrations in the spring of the year. Whales migrate northward. Monarch butterflies *Danaus plexippus (Linnaeus)* descend from thousands of feet to rest and feed, as these wanderers make their way from the mountains of Michoacán, Mexico, to their summer place in the northern territories. The Monarch is the only butterfly that annually migrates north and south as birds do. When I lived in the arid southwestern part of the United States, away from my birthplace in the Pacific Northwest, there were times of the year when I sensed a strong, almost magnetic pull to go northward. There was a yearning, a mysterious disturbance that permeated my physical being. A wedge of geese that passed by overhead tugged at my mind and heart with a strange intensity. I called to them. "I will see you up north in Washington."

Is it the animal and bird migrations or is it the season that stirs this restlessness encoded in our brains and cells? Is migration an ancestral or blood memory? Sometimes, when experiencing a place for the first time, I am brought to tears when the sensation comes over me that I have been at that place before. What does that mean? And why should we think that migration is unique to animal and bird species? We are part of this great universal kingdom. But migratory species don't just go one way; they return, unless captured or killed. Does "captured by circumstances" fall into that same category?

Ida Maria may have not read about Samuel Langhorne Clemens aka Mark Twain (1835–1910), but it is not unreasonable to suppose there were others reiterating the same message at the end of the 19th century, including my grandmother, as his words continue to echo into the 21st century:

"Twenty years from now, you will be more disappointed
by the things you didn't do, than by the ones you did. So
throw off the bowlines. Sail away from the safe harbor. Catch
the trade winds in your sails. Explore, Dream."

My family and I had found the girl my grandmother once was—in the old church books, in old photos, in the trees along the banks of the Kronoby River at her homeplace Lillbroända, at her church *Kronobykyrka*, and finally, on the ship to America. Bit by bit, piece by piece, with the help of friends and family, we had fit together the pieces of the puzzle.

Her life in Finland as a young girl was finalized when the pastor wrote the few words in the church book that she had been permitted to leave Finland: *Betyg till Amerika 5. 5. 1893.*

Ida Maria's life in America was just beginning.

Amanda Lybäck and Ida Maria Andersdotter Lillbroända, Ely, Minnesota

Chapter 8

A Cultural Landscape — Telluride 1895

The black huffing, puffing, steaming engine Number 278 chugged noisily into Telluride that bleak winter day in 1895. From a distance, the train's whistle signaled its arrival and shattered the calm of the Colorado Rockies as the echo rebounded up and down the rugged canyon. The train not only carried passengers, but each week brought news and letters from afar to the European immigrants who made up the majority of the populace in this mining town. Greeting an arriving train and passengers was one event that brought the townspeople together; otherwise, each ethnic group tended to stay within the boundaries of its own tightly knit neighborhood. In 1888, a telegraph line connected Telluride with Montrose and Ouray and points beyond, but it was the narrow-gauge railway line that was their connection to the outside world on the other side of the lofty San Juan Mountain range that nearly encircled the small mining town in southwestern Colorado.

Telluride's inception in 1878 was a direct result of silver discoveries in the area, but with the arrival of the Rio Grande Southern Railroad into Telluride in 1890 and its connection to the larger Denver & Rio Grande Railroad system, the town experienced its greatest building boom. Otto Mears built the short lines of narrow-gauge railroads that served the mines, and the Rio Grande Southern line had a profound effect on mining and expanding population in the rugged San Juan Mountains region. The name "narrow gauge" came from the short three-feet distance between the light rails upon which these little trains rolled. The entire system was designed to facilitate the building of a railroad through the rugged high country of the Rockies. Light rails could be bent sharply to make the necessary curves and the little trains could take these sharp curves without derailing.

It must have seemed to Ida Maria like an endless white journey across the snow-covered flatland prairie states, and then, the train's onerous climb into the Rocky Mountains, twisting, turning, rising higher and higher into whiteness that melded into a grey sky. The cowcatcher projecting from the front of the teakettle locomotive pushed through snow on the railroad track and screamed when metal abraded metal on the rails. The grades were so abrupt and the railroad track so worn and uneven, that the cowcatcher was disfigured.

The last leg of Ida Maria's journey was almost the last straw: The Rio Grande Southern Railroad ran between Ridgeway and Durango and linked to Telluride. The train engineer negotiated amazingly sharp curves and slowed through totally darkened tunnels. The train crept over spectacular high wood trestles as apprehensively as the passengers who stared out the windows into deep chasms below. The Telluride branch of the narrow-gauge railway left the main line at Vance Junction, turned 180 degrees at the Ilium Loop, and made a long, deliberate climb up Keystone Hill before it regained speed toward Telluride on the floor of the San Miguel River Valley.

A cacophony of languages arose from the excited crowd of Finns, Finland Swedes, and Swedes from the Nordic hinterlands; northern Italians, Welshmen and Cornishmen as the expectant townspeople crowded the rough wood-plank platform at the Rio Grande Southern Railway Depot on San Juan Avenue. Ida Maria was one of the newcomers who disembarked during the winter of 1895, bruised and shaken from the last leg of her extraordinary journey into the heart of the Rockies to Telluride in southwestern Colorado. She ran her hands downward over her long black wool skirt to smooth out the wrinkles and adjusted her flat-brimmed hat. Had the train's conductor really announced, "To hell you ride!" when the train pulled into the Telluride depot?

Waiting on the railway station platform to greet Ida Maria were her unmarried uncle Matts Leander Simonsson Hästö, who emigrated from Hästöby in 1892, and John Sundquist, Finland Swede emigrant from Soklot, Nykarleby, whom she purportedly had met in Ely, Minnesota. Both men were miners who drifted west to Telluride when the Crash of 1893 staggered the American economy. On 5 May 1893, the New York stock market tumbled, setting off the Panic of 1893 that swept across the United States. They and other miners followed a chain of migration west to where some of their fellow countrymen were already established and workers were needed for lode mining. There was gold and silver to be mined in those hills.

The threesome emerged from the wood-frame railway depot building with Ida Maria's belongings in hand, stopping as she scanned her new surroundings. Ida Maria's journey had taken her from the "flat-as-a pancake" Ostrobothnian region of Western Finland beside the Gulf of Bothnia to Quebec, to Minnesota, "land of a thousand lakes," and to Telluride, to the highest mountains she had ever seen.

The grey clouds lifted and revealed the east end of the canyon laced with cables of aerial trams that lowered ore from the mines to mills in the valley below. Ida Maria raised her eyes to peaks and crags that rose upward from Telluride's elevation of 8,756 feet to pierce the sky at 14,000 feet. There she stood: feet apart, head tilted back, flanked on three sides by mountains. Sullen clouds overhead laden with moisture waited to descend on the town. Nature had never seemed so overpowering.

John pointed out Ajax Mountain that rose almost vertically from the valley floor, and east of Ajax, Ingram Peak, framed by two spectacular waterfalls—425-feet-high Bridal Veil Falls and Ingram Falls. Ida Maria was keenly aware that she was standing in a box canyon surrounded by the rugged San Juan Mountains, a dead-end chasm in the mountains of Colorado. Only one road and a railroad track led to the western end of the canyon that opened into the San Miguel River Valley beyond. It was a choice she had made that had brought her to a place far from her native homeland in distance and geography. Did this overwhelming feeling that rippled through her body portend a personal abyss as well?

Ida Maria, John, and Matts Leander walked away from the train depot and began their trek through the snow to their house on Pacific Avenue. Ida Maria was startled to see such bustling activity—and the lights! The entire town of Telluride had become electrically lighted only the year before, following the success of the world's first commercial alternating current (AC) electrical system to power mine operations.

They passed warehouses, livery stables, blacksmith shops, and then the modest homes of foreign-born laborers. Ida Maria quickly detected the not-unfamiliar speech of her countrymen, though not her own language, as they passed through the Finnish settlement called Finn Town.

Two distinct languages and cultural differences separated the people who emigrated from the same country. The Finnish language originated from Ugro-Hungarian roots; the Ostrobothnian Finland Swedes spoke a dialect of the Swedish language.

The two groups from the same country generally didn't mix socially. The Finland Swedes lived in homes and boarding houses mainly on Oak Street, Town's End Street, and West Pacific Avenue. Together, the Nordic emigrants were Telluride's largest ethnic groups: 250 Finland Swedes, nearly all of them from the Ostrobothnian region, the majority from the area between Kronoby and Vörå, and approximately 200 Finnish Finns.

The town's cultural landscape was typical of other nineteenth-century American mining "boom towns." Platted on irregular sloping hillsides, Telluride's main street, Colorado Avenue, was the town's commercial center dividing the town into higher and lower elevations and historically, separating the social classes. On the slopes rising north of Colorado Avenue were the school, hospital, and fine Victorian-style and brick residences of Telluride's upper-middle-class citizens. Telluride's working class lived south of Colorado Avenue, near the town limits bounded by the San Miguel River and the railroad tracks. Their small, wood-frame weatherboard homes had few details; the gabled architecture echoed the peaks of the mountains.

At the east end of Pacific Avenue was the bordello "red light" district. "Soiled doves," as the prostitutes were called, worked out of bordello "cribs." These tightly packed two-room structures lined the street along with gambling houses, saloons, and dance halls. Miners would return to town after working a length of time in one of the high tunnel mines and could easily drop their hard-earned money if they sought prostitutes, gaming tables or moonshine.

Before the trio settled into their destination—the house at West Pacific Avenue, they strolled to Telluride's main thoroughfare to show Ida Maria the impressive brick structure of the San Miguel County Court House at the corner of Colorado Avenue and Oak Street and the New Sheridan Hotel flanked by storefront facades with large windows displaying mostly mining supplies. The exceptionally wide avenue covered with snow and muddy tracks was wide enough to turn around a mule train, indeed a contrast to the narrow cobble-lined village streets in their homeland.

Ida Maria and John were married on a Saturday. There are scant details leading up to their marriage. Purportedly the young couple had met in church in Ely, Minnesota in 1893. John was having a hard time; the Panic of 1893 that swept the country found him among the unemployed. He, with some friends, batched in a cabin on the shores of a lake, where they fished, hunted, trapped, and somehow survived. When he found work, the going wage was $1.00 a day, which seemed to him an inadequate return for his efforts after leaving his homeland for the promised land of America. The gold mining boom in the West beckoned. He left Ely to explore the possibilities for the good life in Telluride, Colorado. Did he send a letter for Ida Maria to join him? Or did Ida Maria's uncle Matts Leander, who also met her at the train station, arrange this marriage?

Clergyman J. C. Rollins solemnized the rites of matrimony between Ida Maria Wikstrom and John L. Sundquist on the sixteenth day of March 1895 in the County of San Miguel in the State of Colorado. Witnesses to the marriage were J. Forstrom and Ida Maria's uncle Leander Hästö. The marriage certificate was filed with the County Clerk on 19 March 1895.

Their wedding portrait was taken in a studio setting adorned with flowers and ferns. The name Erickson, Telluride, Colo. appears as the studio logo on the photograph. The bride and groom appear as solemn as the words printed on their marriage certificate. Ida Maria stood apart from John, openly facing the camera. John's right arm reached in front of him to grasp Ida Maria's outstretched right hand, which wore a white fingerless glove. Her left hand by her side reveals two wide bands on her third finger.

Other wedding photographs from the period show the groom seated and the bride standing beside him. Did standing together in the portrait suggest a more egalitarian relationship between John and Ida, or was the pose simply the photographer's style and not of a period or trend? In the manner of most late nineteenth-century portraits, their posture and faces give little clue to their emotions. They appear, from their stance, as if merely waiting. John's gaze is fixed somewhere in the distance. Ida Maria stares soberly and passively into the camera's lens.

Or do we detect the bewildered look of a young girl not yet ready for the vows she had just sworn?

The groom was handsomely costumed in a long, black, cutaway jacket buttoned at the top with a white bow tie. He sported a boutonnière of flowers in his left lapel, a white handkerchief tucked in his breast pocket, and a gold Hamilton watch he had purchased after arriving in Telluride. His uncreased trousers draped over one shoe, while his other shoe remained hidden under white tufted carpet.

Ida Maria's elegant white, full-fashioned floor-length gown had leg-o'-mutton sleeves, the pointed lace at the edge of her skirt drawn up by two white satin bows. The bride's full floral corsage pinned on the left side of her ruffled bosom repeated the wax orange blossoms on her headdress. She wore a single-strand pearl choker and a jeweled broach at the neck of her dress. Had Ida Maria packed her beautiful white floor-length wedding gown in the large cloth satchel she was carrying when she stepped off the train in Telluride? Who helped her adjust the delicate tulle veil that fell to the floor from her flower-bedecked headdress? And who buttoned the dozens of white satin-covered buttons on the sleeves of her gown?

The young couple was legally wed, but in the eyes of the Lutheran church in Finland, a marriage abroad was not automatically considered legal in Finland. When Sweden surrendered Finland to Russia in 1809, the Czar allowed Finland to retain the *Sveriges Rikes Lag* Swedish law of 1734 as the law of the autonomous Grand Duchy. *Giftermålsbalken* The Marriage Code section established that marriages had to be made in the church and stipulated that a valid marriage occurred only when the couple voluntarily informed the church authority of their plans and banns were read in the church. While some sections were amended, the Law of 1734 remained in force well into the independency and thus was active at the time of Ida Maria's marriage. Even if the marriage were to take place abroad, under the law in Finland, the bride must inform her church of the couple's plans to marry. Sections of the 1734 revision are still in force in Sweden and Finland today, although paragraphs have been revised over the years. While there may have been people who continued to follow the old tradition of gathering their belongings under the same roof without benefit of clergy, it was not until 1917 that provisions were made by civil law for those who did not want to be married in church.

The proclamation of the intent to marry, called *lysning*, sometimes referred to as banns, must be announced on three consecutive Sundays prior to the wedding in the church in the parish where the bride had her proper home to ensure that the persons to be married have fulfilled all legal conditions for marriage. If there were no objections, the couple could be married. An entry 20 December 1895 in the Kronoby church communion book about Ida Maria: *Lysning* to marriage with *torparesonen* crofter's son J.L. Sundquist from Nykarleby. In the banns registry 20 December 1895: *Lysningsdagar*, the days of the reading of the *lysningen* 22 December 1895, 29 December 1895 and 5 January 1896 *torparesonen* Johan Leonard Sundqvist och *bondedottern* farmer's daughter Ida Maria Andersdotter Lillbroända. *Fästmannens hinderlöshetsbetyg* attest to the groom's lack of encumbrance issued by Nykarleby pastor E. Kovero 16 December 1895. *Lysningen* taken out by the bride's father, farmer Anders Lillbroända.

LIFE AND TIMES OF THE SUNDQUISTS IN TELLURIDE

While her husband continued to work in the mine, Ida Maria established and managed a *bårdinghus* Sundquist Boarding House at 461 West Pacific Avenue in South Telluride. She recognized that their countrymen needed a place where they could stay and a place to store their belongings. The newly arrived emigrants from Finland preferred to become "boarders" with a family, perhaps from the same parish in Finland. Some of the miners needed only temporary room and board as they stayed at mining camps in primitive company-built dwellings for protracted periods. Among the recent arrivals from Ostrobothnia, some were married men who had come to Telluride to work until they could send for their wives and families in Finland; others were unmarried. The Sundquists' daughter Leona Marie Sundquist later recalled their experiences in Telluride:

My earliest memories centered around the activities
of a boarding house, which Mother managed while Father
worked in the mines. Since the mines were located high in the

mountains, the miners were required to live there while working and only came to town at intervals. The boarding house became the home for the Swedish-Finnish miners when they were in town.

Mother was a good manager and had definite standards for life in that boarding house. I recall the large ledger in which she kept financial records of the small enterprise. Mother demanded that anyone living at her place when they came down from the hills had first to clean up, get a bath, shave, and haircut, dress in respectable clothes, make a deposit for room and board, send money home to Finland to their dependent families or make payments on loans which they had contracted for passage to this country. Then she allowed them a sum for their pleasures in town. By that time they were so subdued that drunkenness was at a minimum, and frowned upon.

What happened to the ledger? What tales it would tell! The tattered pages of an 800-page reference book testify to its use: *Svensk-Amerikansk Uppslagsbok*. Swedish-American Reference Book by Fred Lonnkvist, published by John C. Winston & Co. 1889. Its topics cover a wide range, but it is the section on bookkeeping, debit and credit, daybook and ledger that would have been most helpful to Ida Maria in handling the affairs of fellow emigrants. A third of the book is Swedish-English dictionary with keys to pronunciation, and its table of contents indicates the practical aspects of this book for an uneducated immigrant.

Besides keeping a good set of records, Ida Maria had a family to look after, and there were boarders to be fed. When the men came down from the mines, the rooms of the boardinghouse were filled to capacity. When the miners left for days at a time, she sent with them a supply of her meat pies made with cubes of beef, potato, and onion mounded on thick rolled-out pastry crust, topped with dabs of butter and gravy, folded over, and slow-baked. Ida Maria's famous meat pies traveled well in a knapsack and were just as good eaten cold as hot. Ida Maria's tasks were endless—baking, cooking hearty meals, housekeeping, soap-making, washing laundry using a scrub board, ironing with a sadiron heated on top of the wood-burning stove, darning socks with a well-worn wood darning egg, mending clothing, and tending her chickens in the backyard, that provided eggs and meat for their table and were used for barter.

The Finland Swedes brought their cultural food traditions to America, and it was most important that there should always be *fil-bunk* in the cupboard. Ida Maria hand-carried a "starter" for *fil* when she left her homeland. She soaked a clean white cloth in *fil* and dried it in the open air. In America, she soaked the cloth in warm milk in a dark cupboard and within a few days the rich creamy *fil* was ready to eat. Various bacteria "worked" to thicken the milk into a thick, stringy kind of yogurt. A teaspoon of *fil* "starter" was reserved from one batch to start the next.

John encouraged his siblings in Nykarleby to come to America. Earlier, he sent money to his brother Herman, who found work in the mine. As the young couple was soon to welcome their first child, John sent for his sister. Maria Sofia Danielsdotter Sundquist received the appropriate emigration paper to leave Nykarleby parish on 23 January 1896, and she departed Finland 24 January 1896 for Telluride to work at the Sundquist Boarding House. The extended family welcomed John and Ida Maria's first-born daughter Leonia Maria 19 April 1896. That summer, the family celebrated the marriage of Maria Sofia Sundquist and Ida Maria's uncle Leander Hästö 21 August 1896. Axel Hästö was witness to their marriage. The newlyweds lived next door to John and Ida and welcomed their first-born child Signe Maria on 16 March 1897. Axel Hästö and Brita Johnson were witnesses to her baptism 9 May 1897 by Adolph Riippa, Evangelical Lutheran Pastor of Suomi Synod. That same day Leonia (Leona) was also baptized at her parents' home, witnessed by Leonard Käänta and his wife Sanna, Matts Leander Hästö and his wife Maria.

The few years in Telluride were years of alternating joy and sorrow for the young Sundquist family, mixed with the challenges of operating a boardinghouse. The following two years, two girls were born, but both became ill and died. There were no inscribed words celebrating Heldur Hildegard and Ida Elvira's arrival in this world, but there were words appropriate for the babies whose lives ended too soon. An ornately

decorated gessoed and hand-painted frame holds the scroll that commemorates the girls' short lives in Telluride, Colorado. Across the top
of the plaque, a white dove in flight on a black background carries in its
beak a white ribbon with the words: "Gone but not forgotten." White
morning glory flowers frame the epitaph: "In loving Remembrance of
our Little Darlings, Heldur H. Sundquist and Ida E. Sundquist." And a
poem appears at the bottom of the plaque, author unknown:

> These little lips so sweet to kiss
> Are closed forever now.
> Those sparkling eyes that shone so bright
> Beneath that pearly brow.
> That little heart that beat so high,
> Free from all care and gloom,
> Is hidden now from those he loved.
> Beneath the silent tomb.

Heldur Hildegard born January 1897, lived one year and two months
and died 31 March 1898. Four months later, Ida Elvira was born in August
1898. She lived only six months and died 8 February 1899. Baby Leander
Edwin, born to John's sister Marie Sofia and Matts Leander Hästö, died
11 September 1898 and was buried in the family plot in Block 216, Lot 4,
Lone Tree Cemetery on a mountain high above the town of Telluride—
another grave and dead to be mourned. The joy of possession and the
contrasting sense of loss were totally bewildering to a young Leona
Sundquist, as well as her grieving parents, when she wrote:

> Where have they gone? Heaven! Where is that? Maybe on
> the other side of the mountain."

John and Ida Maria agreed it would be good for Ida Maria to
have help. John sent $100 to another sister Anna Sofia Danielsdotter
Sundquist for her passage to America. His sister was on her own in
Finland at age fourteen after the death of her father and was hired out as
a housekeeper near Nykarleby. Their father Daniel Sundquist drowned
only a few months before she was born. His fishing boat capsized when
a storm suddenly arose in the Gulf of Bothnia.

Anna Sofia left Nykarleby 13 December 1898. She purchased a travel package and set out on her journey to America on the train from Nykarleby to Hangö, Finland. The ship that sailed from Hangö harbor to Hull, England took four days. In December, we must assume the ship was following an icebreaker vessel to depart from Hangö harbor into the Baltic Sea. Then another day by train from Hull to Liverpool where she boarded the ocean-going liner for New York. Fog delayed the departure from Liverpool, and she spent a lonely Christmas in a foreign setting. Anna Sofia recalled her voyage to America in an interview at ninety years old for *The Forum*, Nucla, Colorado in 1971:

> "Memories of that crossing are still vivid. I was not a bit frightened but was terribly seasick on the eight-day Atlantic crossing. We had such a storm we couldn't even get up on deck. It was so cold, children were crying. Passengers complained of frozen hands and overcrowded conditions."

Anna Sofia arrived in New York on New Year's Day and then, the long four-day train ride across snowy plains and through the Rocky Mountains to Telluride. She began work at the Sundquist Boarding House—cooking, waiting tables, housekeeping, and caring for Leona and her niece Signe, daughter of Maria and Leander Hästö. There she met Anders Johansson Mattjus Forsman (Andrew Forsman), a miner who emigrated from Purmo, Finland, and 29 September 1900, they were married. On 18 December 1900, the extended family happily welcomed John and Ida Maria's first-born son, Johan Vincent. Liander Hanson and Matts Ostman witnessed his baptism May 1901 by Pastor Frans O. Logren.

According to the 1900 United States Census records, the Sundquist family of four and boarders John Eastman, Fred Carlson, and Jakob Johnson, ore miners who emigrated from Finland, were all living in the house at 461 West Pacific Avenue, not to mention those who stayed there on a temporary basis. The boardinghouse became the gathering place and the center of social life for emigrants from the Swedish-speaking area of Ostrobothnia. There were always people coming and going; everyone shared news from home, and there built a circle of friends. This gave the individual a feeling of personal security and belonging.

As the immigrant population grew, it was within these boarding house "families" that they first discussed the need and possibility of an association of some kind for a better-organized social life and a place for meetings and social events. They organized *Nykterhetsförening* a temperance society. Typical of early Finland Swede mining communities in the Midwest, the organization not only emphasized aid and benefit for individual and families in times of illness, accident or death, but social and cultural activities were important parts of the functions of the local societies. In 1899, Telluride's Finland Swedes contributed to the construction and outfitting of the New Swedish Finn Temperance Hall at 472 West Pacific Avenue. Swede Finn Hall, as it was called, could accommodate meetings and cultural events.

Professor Anders Myrhman writes about the history of these organizations in his *Minneskrift* Memorabilia:

> "They were founded and nurtured by common immigrants who thereby tried to raise and secure their lives on a level above and beyond the hard struggle for their daily bread. These immigrants were without much education. But among them there were persons, out of concern for and with the support of their fellowmen, brought into being and fostered these organizations. The first benefit and temperance societies were organized among Finland Swede immigrants in the mining towns of northern Michigan in 1898 that initiated a movement to form not only new local societies, but also associations of societies that would lead to the founding of the Order of Runeberg nationwide in 1920."

During the Christmas holidays, *Finlandssvenskar* gathered for festivities at Swede Finn Hall. The evergreen tree was decorated with *Pepparkakor*. *Jultomte*, clad in his red and white costume, surprised the children and distributed his bag of presents. Everyone danced the familiar dances of their homeland to music played on the accordion.

Leona remembers the dances at Swede Finn Hall:

> My first memories of folk and social dancing. I recall being put to sleep, along with other young children and babies

on the benches along the wall while the young parents and miners were enjoying themselves. The waltzes were especially lovely. When the accordion player played polkas and schottisches, the place really began to bounce.

The tables were laden with traditional food—rye bread, cardamom bread, ham, *frukt soppa*, pickled trout, *lutfisk, och så vidare* and so on. And gallons of coffee cooked the Swedish way with a pound of ground coffee, two eggs, shell and all, boiled in three gallons of water for ten minutes. *Lutfisk* was a Scandinavian delicacy generally served in the late fall and at Christmas. The grocer kept an ample supply of dried codfish tied in long thin bundles. For nearly a month, Ida Maria would process the dried fish. She alternately soaked the fish in a lye solution, scrubbed the fish, and changed the water. Miraculously these sticks, that looked like tree branches hanging from the grocery store ceiling, were transformed into thick, tender white fish that was boiled in water. The Finland Swedes preferred their *lutfisk* served with white sauce gravy with ground allspice sprinkled on top.

Leona extolled the seasons in Telluride:

> Each Spring, when the willow bark glows with renewed life, I live again the memory of hiking trips along the mountain trails and the willow whistles Father would carve with his knife. Once he made a very long one with many holes. No flautist was ever more creative and more persistent. Day after day I practiced. But excellence was finally nipped in the bud; Mother's nervous endurance had its limitations. There were fishing expeditions to Trout Lake. There was the San Miguel River, just a narrow trickle of bubbling waters rushing off downhill. But where to? The other side of the mountain!

According to Nordic tradition, Midsummer Day—summer solstice—was celebrated with a picnic. To the lively accompaniment of violin music, children and adults participated in a "round dance" beneath a tall Maypole decorated with flowers and greenery. Finland Swedes had their picnic on one side of the hill at Bear Creek; the Finns on the other. After the picnic the Finland Swedes returned to town for a dance at their hall at 472 West Pacific Avenue. The Finns, too, had their gathering place called Finn Hall at 440 West Pacific in Finn Town.

On the 20th day of October 1900, John L. Sundquist stood before Judge of the County Court of San Miguel County J. M. Wardlaw at the Court House on Colorado Avenue and appealed to the court to become a naturalized citizen of the United States of America. He raised his right hand and took the oath to support the Constitution of the United States, whereby he renounced all allegiance and fidelity to every foreign prince, potentate, state and sovereignty whatever, and specifically to Nicholas the II, Czar of Russia whereof he was heretofore a subject.

The United States Congress passed the first law regulating naturalization in 1790. Generally, naturalization was a two-step process that took a minimum of five years. After residing in the United States for two years, an alien could file a "declaration of intent" to become a citizen. After three additional years, the alien could petition for naturalization. Mat Eastman and John Anderson, citizens of the United States, testified that John L. Sundquist "had resided within the limits and under the jurisdiction of the United States for at least five years, and at least one year within the State of Colorado, and during the whole of that time he had behaved himself as a man of good moral character, attached to the principles contained in the Constitution of the United States, and well disposed to the good order and happiness of the same and two years and upward having elapsed since John L. Sundquist reported himself and filed his Declaration of his Intention." Judge Wardlaw then ordered that John L. Sundquist be admitted to all and singular the rights, privileges and immunities of a naturalized citizen of the United States. Wardlaw certified the document, as he was also the ex-officio clerk of the county court.

Ida Maria Sundquist had more than one reason to celebrate: As an immigrant married to a naturalized citizen, she also became a United States citizen at the moment the judge's order naturalized her husband. From 1790 to 1922, wives of naturalized men automatically became citizens of the United States. This "derivative" citizenship was granted both to wives and minor children.

The act of February 10, 1855 was designed to benefit immigrant women. Under that act, "[a]ny woman who is now or may hereafter be married to a citizen of the United States, and who might herself be lawfully naturalized, shall be deemed a citizen." While one may find some courts that naturalized the wives of aliens, until 1922 the courts generally held that the alien wife of an alien husband could not herself be naturalized.

Names and biographical information about wives and children were rarely included in declarations or petitions filed before September 1906. The woman may or may not be mentioned on the record which actually granted her citizenship, and Ida Maria's name was not noted. Proof of her new American citizenship would be a combination of their marriage certificate and her husband's naturalization record.

ORE MINERS

Miners' conversations and activities gave color and zest to the spirit of the Sundquist boarding house as Leona wrote:

> They seemed to work in such exciting places—Pandora, Smuggler, Tomboy, Black Bear and Liberty Bell. I can still sense the excitement when they came home with especially rich specimens of ore, which were passed around and carefully examined. They all looked like any other rock to me. The sound of mortar and pestle still rings in my ears. But, I could never understand the glow of achievement when such a small sample of gold was recovered. Such effort for so little!
>
> A miner's union was organized. The earnestness and excitement of this undertaking left an undying impression upon my memory. Those early exposures to the workingman and his problems and my mother's intense interest in matters political gave direction to and influenced greatly my political orientation. Mother, at the time, had the right to vote in Colorado, which she took very seriously.

The miners worked eight-hour days and were paid $3.00 a day, as the union and management agreed upon, but a situation developed in 1899 that was headed for conflict.

With the arrival of new Italian immigrants, the mine owners recognized that the Italians were willing to work for less pay, so the Smuggler-

Union Mining Company changed the miner pay system. The Welshman, Arthur Collins, manager of the Smuggler-Union Mine, introduced a new piecework system that violated the spirit of the recently established eight-hour day. While other big mines in the area paid $3.00 a day, Collins attempted to institute a system whereby a miner would be paid $3.00 to remove an amount of ore 6 feet high by 6 feet deep and as wide as the vein. Since the veins in the region were wide, few mine workers could reach the normal daily wage of $3.00 unless they put in twelve to fourteen hours a day. If they worked eight hours, they averaged $1.84 day. Each day, workers became more indebted to the company store, as they could not earn enough money to meet their daily needs.

The workers protested. The mining company would not relent and said that those who weren't satisfied with the new system could leave. The miners went on strike 21 May 1901 demanding a return to the fixed-wage system. The mine closed for six weeks. Leona recalls:

> I remember well a miners' strike, the gathering at the boarding house, the earnest discussions, and the seriousness of all concerned. However, the large colorful miners' badges impressed me the most. I wished inordinately to possess one and to be able to strut around with it on my bosom.

The manager responded to the strikers by hiring non-union workers and curiously, the new employees were paid $3.00 per day, the pay that the strikers were attempting to achieve. The vice-president of Smuggler Mine, Harvard-educated Boston Brahmin, cabled that he would pull out and close Smuggler-Union mine rather than meet their demands.

On 3 July 1901, 250 angry union men, outfitted with weapons, marched up Tomboy Road to the Bullion Tunnel to persuade the strikebreakers to stop work. Despite the strikers' threat of trouble if work continued, the strikebreakers refused. One of the miners, John Bertills, Finland Swede emigrant from Ostrobothnia also known as John Barthell, had arrived in America 3 July 1893 along with Matts Simonson, Ida Maria's uncle. He stood upon a boulder and announced that all the strikebreakers were under arrest. One of the mine company guards opened fire. A heavy exchange of gunfire followed. Barthell was hit in the neck and collapsed upon the ground.

At Barthell's funeral services, W. C. Hunt of the Congregational Church reproached the miners during his sermon, denounced violence and lawlessness, the unnecessary deaths, and said that nothing could be gained by the methods they had employed. His words did not sit well with the miners, who considered Barthell a martyr to the cause. They boycotted the church and caused the resignation of the minister.

A thousand union miners marched to the windswept Lone Tree Cemetery high on the mountain to erect a monument at the gravesite of labor martyr John Barthell. Engraved on the monument were lines by poet Henry Wadsworth Longfellow:

> "In the world's broad field of battle,
> in the bivouac of life
> Be not the dumb driven cattle—
> Be a hero in the strife."

The pattern of separateness and closeness of each ethnic group in this cultural landscape was also reflected at Lone Tree Cemetery where the dead were buried among their own people.

After the shootout at Bullion, management backed off from its rigid stance and was forced to sign an agreement with the unionized workers under the watching eye of the Lieutenant Governor. Peace returned to Telluride after the turbulent summer of 1901, but only for a brief spell. By fall, it became explicitly apparent that the mining company was not following safety requirements and a rash of serious accidents occurred that claimed many lives. Twenty-four miners perished in the Smuggler-Union fire of November 10, 1901. John's sister Anna Sofia recalled in an oral interview that night when her husband didn't go to work at the mine:

> "Something told him he shouldn't go. His partner came
> over to the house and walked right in. I wondered what was
> the matter with him. When he saw Andrew lying on the bed,
> he was so relieved that he couldn't talk. Finally he told us what
> happened."

The constant threat of death or maiming from mine accidents hung over the town like the sullen clouds of a winter sky: collapsed or flooded tunnels, explosions, mine gas, a multitude of dangers. Leona recalls the hospital in Telluride:

> The hospital! That large and impressive building that we visited so often. In my childhood, that hospital housed many a miner who lived at our boarding house. Mine accidents, hospital beds, casts, slings, crutches, concerns and anxieties, frequent deaths, consultations, letters to relatives—all contributed to my early awareness of infirmity and death.

The miners, their wives, and families lived in fear of hearing the whistle blow that would signal a collapse in the mine. Ida Maria's Uncle Karl Simonsson died in 1888 in a mine explosion. Mining folklore considered rats to be mine sentinels: If rats abandoned a mine, that signaled danger. Rats knew better than so-called company experts when it was not safe. Rats could smell gas forming; they knew when a cave-in was imminent. Rats could hear supporting timbers creak from strain before miners' ears detected trouble.

From time to time, Ida Maria and John Sundquist had engaged in discussions about returning to Finland for a visit. Leona Sundquist also recalls discussions that took place in Telluride about not returning to America. John had worked in the mines for the past ten years; first in the Iron Mountain Range near Ely, Minnesota, a destination for many emigrants from Finland before the gold mining boom in the West beckoned. The couple knew firsthand that mining was a brutal occupation. And wages, hours, and safety concerns continued to be burning issues among the miners.

Considering the turbulent spring of 1901, the miners' strike, and the air of unease that still permeated the town, their conversation took on seriousness not before expressed. John suggested that they go to Finland so he could check on his widowed mother's well being. Ida Maria agreed. It would also be good to visit her parents and grandmother in Kronoby and to introduce their daughter Leona Marie and six-month-old John Vincent to their grandparents and great-grandmother. Ida Maria was frugal. She had successfully operated the boarding house for six years.

They owned their home free and clear, and she had managed to put some money aside. Together, they had enough money for the family to make the trip to Finland.

The handsome studio portrait taken in Telluride prior to their departure for their homeland and on the occasion of Vincent's baptism 13 May 1901 portrays a prosperous and stylish young family. Ida Maria's hair is beautifully coifed in tight curls, as is her daughter Leona's hair; Ida Maria's floor-length gown exudes elegance and style and appears to be a crinkled silk taffeta with decorated bodice. Vincent is wearing a christening gown; Leona has a corsage on the bodice of her long-sleeved white dress and she is wearing her mother's porcelain pendant with the wedding photo of her mother on one side, her father on the other. John's handsome tailored four-button suit is a vast contrast to the unpressed pants and jacket he wore at their marriage ceremony six years earlier in 1895. He is sporting gold nugget cuff links, a gold watch fob on a chain with a gold watch concealed in the vest pocket of his handsome three-piece suit.

They left by train, just as they had arrived, but this time they were together with two young children in tow. They stood with their bags at the train depot and looked at each other with some knowingness when the conductor stepped from the train and again called out the train's arrival in Telluride: "To hell you ride."

Thus far, it had been quite a journey.

Crickson EXTRA FINISH. TELLURIDE, COLO.

John and Ida Maria Sundquist, Telluride 1895

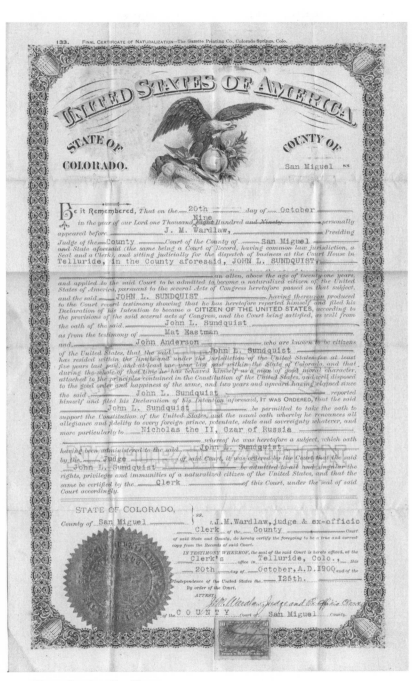

UNITED STATES OF AMERICA

STATE OF COLORADO.

COUNTY OF San Miguel ss

Be it Remembered, That on the 20th day of October in the year of our Lord one Thousand Nine Hundred and Ninety personally appeared before J. M. Wardlaw, Presiding Judge of the County Court of the County of San Miguel and State aforesaid (the same being a Court of Record, having common law jurisdiction, a Seal and a Clerk), and sitting judicially for the dispatch of business at the Court House in Telluride, in the County aforesaid, JOHN L. SUNDQUIST, an alien, above the age of twenty-one years, and applied to the said Court to be admitted to become a naturalized citizen of the United States of America, pursuant to the several Acts of Congress heretofore passed on that subject, and the said JOHN L. SUNDQUIST having thereupon produced to the Court record testimony showing that he has heretofore reported himself and filed his Declaration of his Intention to become a CITIZEN OF THE UNITED STATES, according to the provisions of the said several acts of Congress, and the Court being satisfied, as well from the oath of the said John L. Sundquist as from the testimony of Mat Eastman and John Anderson who are known to be citizens of the United States, that the said John L. Sundquist has resided within the limits and under the jurisdiction of the United States for at least five years last past, and at least one year last past within the State of Colorado, and that during the whole of that time he has behaved himself as a man of good moral character, attached to the principles contained in the Constitution of the United States, and well disposed to the good order and happiness of the same, and two years and upward having elapsed since the said John L. Sundquist reported himself and filed his Declaration of his Intention aforesaid, IT WAS ORDERED, that the said John L. Sundquist be permitted to take the oath to support the Constitution of the United States, and the usual oath whereby he renounces all allegiance and fidelity to every foreign prince, potentate, state and sovereignty whatever, and more particularly to Nicholas the II, Czar of Russia whereof he was heretofore a subject, which oath having been administered to the said John L. Sundquist by the Judge of said Court, it was ordered by the Court that the said John L. Sundquist be admitted to all and singular the rights, privileges and immunities of a naturalized citizen of the United States, and that the same be certified by the Clerk of this Court, under the seal of said Court accordingly.

STATE OF COLORADO,

County of San Miguel ss. I, J.M.Wardlaw, judge & ex-officio Clerk of the County Court of said State and County, do hereby certify the foregoing to be a true and correct copy from the Records of said Court.

IN TESTIMONY WHEREOF, the seal of the said Court is hereto affixed, at the Clerk's office in Telluride, Colo., this 20th day of October, A.D. 1900 and of the Independence of the United States the 125th.

By order of the Court,

ATTEST:

J.M.Wardlaw, Judge and Ex Officio Clerk of the COUNTY Court of San Miguel County.

1900 Naturalization Certificate

John, Ida, Leona and Johan Vincent 1901

Lone Tree Cemetery overlooking Telluride

Framed epitaph

Chapter 9

A Visit to the Homeland 1901

Summer of 1901 the *FÅA Finska Ångfartygs Aktiebolaget* ship entered Hangö harbor carrying among its passengers Ida Maria, her husband John, and their two young children, five-year-old Leona and six-month-old baby Johan Vincent. Eight years had passed since Ida Maria had left for America; John had departed Finland over ten years ago. This visit to their homeland would reaffirm the decision each had made years ago to emigrate from Finland.

They boarded the train for the journey to Soklot near Nykarleby where John's mother Greta Jakobsdotter Gertruds-Olin lived in a small cottage on Gertruds farm nr 19. One of the reasons for the trip was to be assured that John's mother was properly housed and cared for. She had been a widow since he was ten years old and one by one, six of her children left Finland and went to America. The chain of migration from Gertruds farm began with Greta's brother Jakob who went to Michigan and worked in the woods. Jakob later returned to Finland, and as an old man, he was still looked upon as a giant among men. The Olins were all strong, sturdy, and hard working people. Possibly Jakob Olin may have been the one to encourage his nephew John Sundquist to seek his fortune in the New World. John sent money at different intervals so that his brothers and sisters could purchase their passages to America. Herman found work in the mines; Maria Sofia and Anna worked for Ida Maria at the boarding house in Telluride.

Soklot

Gertruds farm nr 19 had been in John's maternal lineage for generations. As a matter of historical interest regarding farm ownership, the farm in Soklot was two separate farms in the 1600s and 1700s—the Jöns farm and the Gertruds farm, names derived from Jöns Jönsson, born ca. 1597 who was a farmer at the Jöns place 1627–1671, and the latter name derived from the widow Gertrud of Per Ericksson. He was a farmer 1619–1633; after his death, the farm was cultivated for thirty years by his wife, the widow Gertrud. In 1723, Matts Simonsson Ollila aka Matti Simonpoika, a farmer's son from Ollila, earlier a part of the Hyytiäinen farm in the village of Savo, Lappajärvi which lay about 60 kilometers southeast of Nykarleby, came to Gertruds and took over the deserted Gertruds homestead and half mantal of Jöns farm.

Following the devastation brought on by the wars with Russia known as the Great Wrath, the farm had been abandoned and lay in ruins and uninhabited for some years; the previous owners fled to Sweden as did many Finnish people at that time. The two farms were consolidated and became officially known as Jöns-Gertruds and designated farm number 19; unofficially called Ollila after Matts Simonsson Olilla who was the farmer at Jöns-Gertruds until 1734. His grandson Mickel was the first in the family to take the name Olin. The Gertruds farm was also called Ålila and Ålila-Sifriss. Ålila seems to be a Swedish form of the Finnish name Ollila, perhaps changed at the time to Swedish in the Swedish-speaking part of Finland.

John's mother, Greta Jakobsdotter Gertruds-Olin, born 25 December 1845 to Jakob Andersson and his wife Greta Sofia Andersdotter, lived her entire life at the farm, and the next generation including John and his siblings were born at the farm renamed Gertruds-Olin.

Anders Jakobsson Gertruds-Olin 1847–1921, a brother of Greta Jacobsdotter Gertruds-Olin, owned the farm in Soklot where both Greta and her husband, Daniel Mattsson Sundqvist, lived. Anders' daughter Sofia Alexandra Olin Holländer, who was married to August Holländer emigrated 20 August 1892 with her cousin Herman Sundquist to Ely, Minnesota. Sofia bought the Gertruds-Olin farm in 1912 for 5000 marks from her father Anders Jakobsson Gertruds Olin. The Holländers went to North America and settled in British Columbia, Canada across the border from Deming, Washington. When the Hollanders decided not to return to Finland, Gertruds-Olin farm was sold to Anders nephew Henrik Sundqvist, John's brother, who returned to Finland from America in 1922. The purchase included one horse and a carriage, one cow, the year's harvest, but no tools or furniture. Henrik's grandson Bengt Johannes Enqvist became owner of the farm.

John's father Daniel Mattsson Nabb Pörkenäs Sundqvist was born 28 July 1842 at nearby Pörkenäs. As a young man, Daniel went to Gertruds-Olin farm to work for the Olins as a *dräng* farmhand. There, he met Greta Jakobsdotter, and they married. At the time, it was considered that Greta had married below her class by marrying a farmhand. They lived in a small cottage at Gertruds-Olin and Daniel continued work on the farm as a crofter *torpare* and also fished. In the autumn of 1880, after selling a day's catch in Nykarleby village, he and other fishermen were on their way home when a storm suddenly arose on the Gulf of Bothnia. The wooden skiff sank near Åminne; Daniel drowned.

As an aside to this family tragedy: Years earlier when Greta was five or six years old, her mother sent her to deliver some freshly baked bread to an old lady in the village.

"Oh, poor child," the old lady had said, "You will be a widow with seven children when you grow up."

Greta was pregnant with Anna, their seventh child, when her husband Daniel died at sea. John Sundquist, the oldest son in the family of seven children, assumed the role of breadwinner at ten years of age to support his mother and siblings. As a young boy, he cooked for the fishermen, cleaned fish for market, mended nets, and took on odd jobs to support the fatherless family. He, too, went to sea at a young age before he had completed *Skriftskole* and narrowly escaped drowning. His four-year-old sister Johanna Wilhelmina went to live with her aunt Lovisa Nyholm, Greta Jakobsdotter Olin's sister.

John Sundquist's maternal grandmother Greta Sofia Andersdotter Kronholm-Skutnabba lived down the road from Gertruds-Olin farm in a well-kept farmhouse of some consequence. She was a great help to John's mother Greta and played an active role in his rearing. John had no formal schooling other than what the church required, but the grandmother supplied the boy John with knowledge of things, animate and inanimate, naturalistic and supernaturalistic, according to his daughter Leona. John's grandmother died 10 August 1890, two months before he left Finland to emigrate to America. Leona recalled that throughout John's life, he told numerous stories about this woman and her understanding of natural phenomena. Her predictions of natural events, weather phenomena, crops, pestilences, famines were unerring. Ailing children were brought to her for diagnosis and administration.

Upon examination of the symptoms, she would invariably hasten to some swamp, marsh, bog or roadside for herbs, roots, seeds, buds, inner bark of trees, etc. whereupon she would cook, stew or brew concoctions that, with the proper incantations, would be administered to the patient. If the child survived and recovered, she got the credit; if the child died, it was God's will. Adults and domestic animals were likewise given full treatment.

In the middle and late nineteenth century, rationalism had not yet rooted out mysticism and superstition from the rural community. John's aunt Lovisa Nyholm also had the ability to foretell the future. She lived until almost the century mark. There have been a few stories passed along, and as with the oral tradition of storytelling, there are often different slants to the story. Leona tells it thusly:

> One day Lovisa was walking along the road with a number of other people. Suddenly she saw, along the horizon silhouetted against the evening sky, a horse drawn hearse traveling at a very great speed. She recognized the horses as belonging to neighbors she knew, and commented that a death must have occurred in that family. The portend was correct; unbeknownst to her companions, someone in that family had died.

The other version of the story told by a cousin Vincent Erickson is that John Sundquist and his aunt *Moster* Lovisa were walking along a country road. Lovisa suddenly says to John, "Get out of the way and let the horse-drawn hearse pass!"

John does as he is told, but upon looking up and down the road he sees no one coming. "Where is the hearse, *Moster*?" John asked.

"Don't you see it? The horses are drawing the hearse, and they are traveling past right now. Someone in that family has died."

Upon returning home, they learned indeed that someone in that family had just died. How did she know that? She was an intelligent woman, and she was much alone for she tolerated no close friends unless they were according to her ideas of high morals and perfectionism. Perhaps this gave her the time to think more deeply and use another sense that most of us don't know we have or take the time to use. This family trait has not been lost over time. Leona tells of two instances of her occult power.

> The day my brother Dan died (I knew nothing about it) but I felt compelled to phone home to Dan's and Lillian's. (The "home" she speaks of is the old homestead, the farmhouse where Leona and her siblings grew up, that was passed on to the eldest living son, her brother Daniel.) I just felt I <u>had</u> to. Why? Not a thing to tell me why only that I was compelled to do it. I said to myself, "Why you and Lillian talked over the phone just the other day." Still I called. Lillian came to the phone. We didn't have too much of a conversation but I asked, "Well how is Dan?" Lillian says, "Why he's OK. He's sitting right here in the chair." I hung up the phone. A half hour later I got a phone call from Alice (her sister) saying "Dan has just died." I couldn't believe it. Now how do you explain that? I'll never forget it for I had such a compulsive feeling.

> The other queer experience was when mother died. Irene and I were on a trip to California. We had been driving down the Oregon Coast and were turning eastward to get to the main old 99 highway to go to central California. All of a sudden I said to Irene, "We are going back home." "Whatever for?" says she.

> All I could say was I must go home. I had not reason to give her. She was perturbed by me but I just had a compulsive feeling to go home. Which we did and when we got to Eva's in Vancouver, Eva came out and said that mother had died. I asked her when that happened and she told me and I figured that was when I had the urge to change our plans and go home. Those two experiences, they haunt me to this day.

Lovisa Nyholm had an extraordinary gift of reaching back into time to tell the oral history of our ancestors who lived, loved, struggled and died generations and generations ago. Yes, she knew details up to the 6th generation back. When Leona visited her aunt years later, she and her aunt strolled through the graveyard as *Moster* Nyholm told her stories. Leona sat down on graves whose crosses have rotted, rusted and crumbled into the ground and wrote a sketchy resume of genealogy from her father's side.

> There was *Moster*, old, wrinkled and partly stooped, pulling the grass aside so that I might see a small groove where once stood a cross designating the last resting place of some great, great grandmother or father I couldn't keep it all straight. There was also grandfather's grave, just a smooth mound – grass covered. Yes, the grass of all living plants is most kind. It covers all in it waving softness. Surely I have a horde of relatives still living in Finland, but truly there is a host of them which lie buried in the Nykarleby graveyard. A graveyard has come to mean something different to me now. Time of countless ages was represented in that graveyard and time alone, along with grass, smoothes the painful sorrows of the present. Yes, time brings measure of forgetfulness as events lose their cruel contour of the present and memories reshape themselves into a softer though possibly a fainter picture but a more comfortable one. There was *Moster* Nyholm – old, rugged with age and so conscious of its weakness and helplessness. To youth, death seems so harsh, so cruel, so merciless. Death to her seemed a deliverer – an agent of comfort and relief. Unknowing, she taught me so much.

It was summer when Ida Maria and John arrived at Gertruds-Olin farm. There was work to be done and all hands participated in the harvest. After John's father Daniel's death, John's mother Greta became a *torpare* crofter and was obligated to the owner of the land for a given number of hours of *dagsverke* daywork each year to pay for the small enclosed pasture by her cottage and hay for her two cows and sheep. Johanna, the youngest daughter, helped take care of her mother's obligations while she also worked for other farmers for wages. At harvest time, they tied rough sheaves of grain by hand and stacked hay over tall upright *aisor* wood poles with wood pitchforks. And they picked buckets of wild berries: blueberries, *lingon*, raspberries, currants, cloudberries, and *smultron*. Women's work carried on indoors, too where meals might consist of bread, the baked dark rye bread that hung on a pole across the ceiling of the kitchen, porridge and *stromming*.

Ida Maria dearly loved John's mother. Greta Jakobsdotter Gertruds-Olin was a remarkable woman who also inspired and was esteemed by her granddaughter. Leona Sundquist describes her visit with her grandmother in 1931:

> There she sat in the one chair in her home, her feet resting on a small *palla* and on her feet the leather *pjäcksona* which she wears, with their characteristic upturned pointed toes. I sat beside her on a bench. Dear old grandmother is very old (85 ½ years) and cannot stand up straight. She walks all bent over and when outside she walks with a long stick in her hand. Most of the time she just sits hunched up on the chair and thinks. As old as she is, it seems she has such down right good sense, and compared to younger ones, grandmother has a good bit of modernism in her, and in spite of a seriousness about her she has a spicy subtle quiet humor about her. And she laughs a great deal when we sit and talk and when she laughs she laughs with her whole face. She is so genuine. And as to her mind, old folks frequently get a bit absent-minded but grandmother has all her wits about her.
>
> I shall always draw strength and equanimity from the memories of my conversations with Grandmother. She is one of the most remarkable souls which I have ever met. There is a wealth of tolerance, patience and understanding and thoughtfulness there, which few souls possess. If, after a lifetime filled with opportunities and advantages undreamed of in her day and situation, I should approach my eternal destiny with the philosophical outlook and grace that she commanded, I would know that I had succeeded in living a satisfying and fulfilled life.

Lillbroända

In autumn, John, Ida Maria, and their children left Gertruds-Olin farm and boarded the train to Kronoby to visit Lillbroända. Ida Maria had not seen her parents, sisters, and grandmother for almost ten years since she left her homeland for America.

Across the narrow wood bridge, the traditional red painted house with white trim stood not far from the bank of the Kronoby River embraced by clusters of birch trees—the stately two-story house where Ida Maria spent her growing-up years at Lillbroända. Leona recalls the farmhouse:

> The kitchen and the living room were all one big room, and center of activities was the large corner fireplace designed with a raised hearth to make it easy to cook in the fireplace. The copper pot of hot coffee hovered above the fire from a metal arm that swung outward from the fireplace wall. There by the window was a small table always set for coffee. There were blue and white coffee cups and saucers, which were not large nor too small, but just right.
>
> I loved the "feel" of those cups. The spoons were very small. On the table was a large triangular loaf of sugar with appropriate chipping equipment. I became quite adept at using the equipment. Then you would take your cup over to the fireplace and there hung this copper coffee kettle. It was always hanging there, and always had coffee so that anyone who came in could go over there to get coffee.

Ida Maria set herself to weaving fabric while she was at Lillbroända. She sat on the wood bench in front of the floor loom, threw the thick shuttle of yarn between the tented warp threads and pounded the beam to tightly pack the threads, as she turned out yards upon yards of cloth and curtains to use when they returned to America. Her sisters Hilda Sofia and Wilhelmina sat carding piles of wool that their mother Kajsa Greta Simonsdotter Lillbroända spun into yarn as she pumped the pedal that turned the spinning wheel. Textile craft skills—weaving, knitting, tatting—were common among the country folk in Finland and every-one was expected to have some command of them.

John helped Ida's father Anders Andersson Lillbroända scrape and polish pieces of woodwork and repair harnesses. Ida Maria's grand-mother, her father's mother, Maria Kristoffersdotter Knif, who had lived with the family at Lillbroända since 1881, sat silently rocking in a small rocking chair, thoughtfully smoking her little homemade birch pipe. Leona described her visit:

> The bedroom where I slept had a tall cylindrical blue and white tiled stove which was constantly warm. My bed seemed more like an elevated chest with a bureau drawer opening at the top. I sank into this opening into a deep soft feather bed and fell sound asleep before I could figure how to get out.
>
> The magic of Christmas Eve at Lillbroända! Grandfather and I drove in a sleigh through the crunchy snow to collect boughs and branches, wood and cones. The horses had bells on their harnesses. I was tucked down in the sleigh, furs tucked over me, and then I would look up at the night sky and it was just beautiful, the stars, and the Northern Lights would come just shooting upward.
>
> The branches were placed here and there, especially in the entrance to the home. Twigs were caught up in curtains and corners. The huge fire cast flickering lights and shadows into the darker corners of the room. The pungent fragrances of evergreen spiced the odors of cooking and bakings. And finally, in a state of uncontrollable excitement, tempered by a bit of fear and uneasiness, a whistling, wailing, wind-like sound came from around the house corner. The door flew open and in sailed a huge sack of gifts and goodies from the *jultomte*, who careened off to other little girls and other places.

The Lutheran church required that the preacher periodically visit the parishioners: Läsförhör assured that everyone had a comprehensive knowledge of Luther's Little Catechism, chapters from the Bible, and could recite the Ten Commandments and Lord's Prayer. Children, too, from the youngest to those of confirmation age were required to attend.

> *Läsförhör!* Another occasion when the house was all "shined up." The preacher was coming to conduct the *Läsförhör*. It seems that the adult communicants of the church

were required to take part in an examination of their reading and understanding of the "written word" and their partici- pation in matters religious. So, therefore, a group of commu- nity folks assembled at Grandfather's house. Grandmother, proud of her "Amerikansk" daughter-in-law, wanted her to cook something special in an American way. She offered a hen to cook which Mother suspected was hatched before she left for America. I recall Mother's terrified expression and her quick recovery as she offered an alternative. Pie! Custard Pies! Pie is strictly an American dish, so there were no pie tins. Undaunted, Mother used huge milk pans. The heat in the huge brick oven at the side of the fireplace was uniform, so the pie turned out smooth and velvety. A miracle! All ate and remarked about the unusual fare. I especially recall the preacher in his black suit and funny white collar smacking his lips over the luscious morsels.

If anyone should wonder how the Finland Swede immigrants in America were so literate, there is no doubt that the requirements for learning imposed by the Lutheran church stimulated their life-long quests for education. Ida Maria had only three years of formal school education and John had no formal schooling. For centuries, national education requirements in the child's preparation for confirmation were in the hands of the church. The examinations in reading and scripture were held annually at *läsförhör*.

National education was established in the 16th century when the Finnish church went over from the Roman-Catholic to the Lutheran confession. The first book appeared in 1542–43 when Bishop Mikael Agricola published the alphabet. The church took energetic steps to teach the people to read. In 1686 it was enacted that priests were not to administer the Holy Sacrament nor marry persons who were unable to read. Consequently, as early as the beginning of the 18th century, the greater part of the younger generation in Finland could read, and a hundred years later reading was quite general in the country, though writing was less widespread. The agony of learning in order to be mar- ried is so well portrayed by Aleksi Kivi in his book the *Seven Brothers*.

While at Lillbroända, the conversation turned to stories about Putti Gubbe, the old man from Puutio, tales that had carried on through several generations of Ida Maria's ancestors. According to the mores of the time, John Sundquist was considered to have married above his station in life, while Ida Maria had married below hers. Not that that made any remarkable difference to them, but daughter Leona remembers that whenever an occasion arose about some peculiarity or irregularity, her father enjoyed subtly teasing Ida Maria regarding the association of Putti Gubbe with her side of the family, that invariably brought a reaction such as, "That's just a myth," or "It's just one of those folk tales."

While Putti Gubbe could fit the character in a folk tale, he was not exactly a myth as he appears in the family's history a generation or so predating Ida Maria, plus considerable hearsay regarding his activities as Leona related:

Puutio was an inland district inhabited largely by Finns and Tartars. I suspect maybe also gypsies since Putti Gubbe was a horse trader. Now, Grandfather did have a pair of spirited horses, and he was very proud of them. It is said that Putti Gubbe made his headquarters in Lillbroända when on his rounds of the community. Besides horse trading, he loaned money on interest and in writing. So, periodically he appeared to collect his interest. If people didn't have the cash, he just moved in with the family and had room and board until the interest was exhausted. He was very miserly, counted every penny and kopeck and kept very close records. In addition, though, he told many fabulous tales of incredible and astonishing achievements. I asked cousin Eugenie if she knew anything about Putti Gubbe. She said that when they later dismantled the house at Lillbroända, they found a fur-lined pouch in which Putti Gubbe had carried his cash. In it were a few pennies. My aunt Wilhelmina had remarked, "If Putti Gubbe knew about this, he would turn over in his narrow grave."

Indeed, it had been an auspicious time for Ida Maria to visit her family and her homeland. Winter arrived. After the buds for next year's growth were formed on the alder trees, they helped her father Anders Andersson Lillbroända cut the twigs and tied them in sheaves for the sheep in winter. The joy of homecoming turned to sorrow as Ida Maria's grandmother Maria Kristoffersdotter Björnvik Knif passed on 21 January 1902. She had lived at Lillbroända since the family moved there in 1881.

While there, the question about returning to America arose again. The turbulent times the miners experienced at Telluride prompted discussions about staying in Finland—not returning to America. And in Finland, there were opportunities to consider. Many Finland Swedes were colonizing in southern Russia in The Ukraine in the region of the Crimea where there was fertile land and the opportunity for the good life. It was John's dream as well as that of his countrymen to own a piece of land, to be free, to exult in achieving independence and the riches that he would bring forth from the land. In his home territory of Nykarleby, daughter Leona recalled that the estate of the poet Johan Ludvig Runeberg was offered for sale. John wanted to buy the home and land and settle there. He would have been quite happy to invest his hard-earned money in the Runeberg farm in *Österbotten*. Daughter Leona recalls that "mother would have none of it."

Father was inclined to make his home in Finland, but Mother finally laid down the ultimatum. She would return with her two children to America—come what may. Knowing Mother, she would have done just that. I shall always be deeply grateful to my mother for her intuition and decisiveness.

Ida Maria was a renaissance woman—a woman who has a range of accomplishments, resilient, strong, and assertive—with a goal in mind and "a mind of her own," her daughter Esther wrote years later in a college thesis. She recalled her mother's lovely Swedish accent emphasising each spoken word: "No, ve vill go to America."

My parents' decision not to stay in Finland but to return to America was the point which would determine the rest of our lives. Mother was instrumental in this turn of decision. She was determined not to stay in the 'old country.' She is rather headstrong and influenced dad's return.

Ida Maria had made her decision nine years earlier when she left Finland bent on her destination—America. And that decision had been reinforced by the return visit to her homeland. Around her she saw life that seemed preordained at birth—the child stepped right into the fetters of traditions and customs of the past and there he/she stood shackled for life and it hardly ever occurred to rebel or to change it. That kind of life would not be hers.

Her firsthand knowledge of opportunities for women in America fortified her thoughts and action when reviewing her earlier decision to emigrate. She was seventeen when she left, accustomed to living and working in an agrarian society. Now years had passed, she was married with two children, and two babies she birthed lay buried in Lone Tree Cemetery atop a hill in Telluride, Colorado. While in America, she had a responsible position of authority in running the boarding house in Telluride while John was at the mine. She collected a portion of the boarders' mining wages, which she helped them allot to their families in Finland and tended to her chickens, which were important in a barter economy—all while raising a young family. Perhaps she found that relatives and friends in her homeland were unable to fathom her hard-won maturity or could they relate to the nature of her achievements that would have been foreign to most rural women in the late 1890s. Although men and women worked side by side, the women's role was subservient to their husband. Perhaps there was no one who would or could understand the person she had become.

Author Anders Myrhman addressed the "conflict of attachment" felt by many of the emigrants: The uprooted experience located between the desire for the future and the memories of the past, that settled itself uneasily within the physical and conscious self. Ida Maria now belonged to two countries—her homeland Finland and America—and two different cultural landscapes. But the new country had contributed to her current personage. Did she think that staying in her homeland would diminish the achievements she had made? Was her growth and accomplishments in America not something that could have been translated into a good life in her homeland? But Ida had made up her mind. She had traversed the North American continent; she had seen unlimited opportunities for women in America. There would be free education for her children Leona Marie, Johan Vincent, and the baby she was now carrying. A young and growing country would offer more advantages for a young and growing family.

Ida Maria spoke up: "No, to America we go."

Ida Maria packed her travel bag and included therein the root and branch of a small-leaf evergreen myrtle. In Finland, a bride might wear a wreath of myrtle in her headdress at her wedding to denote virginity. And a maiden in America might wish to include the shrub's small, white delicate flowers in her headdress. We can be almost certain that Ida Maria carried another cloth soaked in *fil* so she would again have a starter from her homeland for *fillibunki* when she reached America.

We do not know if Ida Maria attended to the following matter regarding the church while in Finland, but from information recorded in the Kronoby church records 10 February 1902, two days after the family sailed on the SS Polaris, Ida Maria was officially moved to her husband John Sundquist's Nykarleby parish. I earlier cited that while their marriage in the United States was legally performed, the union was not automatically accepted in Finland because of the 1734 Lutheran Church law that required that the bride inform her church of the couple's plans to marry—even if the marriage took place abroad. The reading of the *lysningen*, taken out by Ida Maria's father Anders Lillbroanda took place at Kronoby church 22 December 1895, 29 December 1895 and 5 January 1896, and duly recorded in the banns registry. Specifically the law requires that the proclamation must be read in the parish where the bride had her proper home. If the priest did not announce in the appropriate place, he could be stripped of priestly privileges and functions. The move to a new parish may have created a clerical issue, as I found in the Nykarleby church book the dates 22 December 1905, 29 December 1905, and 5 January 1906; *Förelysta i* Kronoby. Was additional action deemed necessary by the pastor to comply with church law regarding *lysning* because Ida Maria's official parish was now Nykarleby as noted in the Kronoby church records, or merely confirmation in her new parish of a marriage entered into in America?

The family boarded the train in Kronoby to begin the first leg of their return trip to America. The train stopped at the railway depot near Nykarleby where John's brother Henrik August Sundquist, nineteen-year-old cousin Johannes Olin, and John's brother-in-law Henrik Sunnell boarded the train for Helsingfors. They had taken to heart the stories that John and his brother Henrik had told about riches to be found in the New World. Considering the economics of the time in Finland, it was hopelessness on the one hand and hope on the other.

Henrik Edvard Johansson Sunnell from Sorvist, a thirty-year-old married man with family joined the group going to America. Sunnell leased his property in Finland to a family friend with option to purchase should he not want to return. His wife, John's sister Johanna, and four children Helga, Edward, Bertha and Elvera moved to Soklot to live with the widow Greta Sundquist in her small cottage.

Henrik Sundquist had been to Seattle in 1898.

"By Golly," he would exclaim in his favorite American slang, "Those giant trees in the state of Washington would never have been cut if I had not been there with my saw."

His wife Sofia would not leave Soklot for "the land of glory," as she called America. Nothing could persuade her to leave her homeland. To the Sundquist family's great surprise, John's mother Greta was there, too, on the depot platform with a huge bulging basket filled with food for the trip—*limpa, kaffebröd, smör, ost, korv, syltad sill, lingon, och så vidare.*

There were undisclosed problems that delayed them in Helsingfors; then the "boat train" to Hangö where they would board the SS Polaris for England. They waited in a cold, barren, dark room crowded with passengers and their valises, while the ice-breaker cleared passage for the SS Polaris, a passenger steamer built by Gourlay Bros. & Co., Dundee for *Finska Ångfartygs Aktiebolaget*, Helsinki.

The steamships SS Polaris and SS Arcturus were put on line in 1899. At a length of 84.20 meter x 11.40 meter breadth, the Polaris was equipped with a triple steam engine and made 13.5 knots. She was designed to accommodate eighty first-class passengers, eighteen second-class and 167 third-class passengers. However, it was not unlikely that there might be up to 700 emigrants crowded on the deck despite the fact that there was cabinspace for less than 200. The Hangö-Hull line was the principal

emigrant line. The ships would also carry cargo, especially Finnish butter, to England. From Hull on the southeast coast of England, they would
again travel by train to the port of Liverpool to board Cunard Line's
ocean-going SS Campania.

On 8 February 1902, the day before Ida Maria's twenty-sixth birthday, the family looked back at their homeland for the last time—but not
without the dramatic enactment of her stealth plan.

Greta Olin Sundqvist courtesy Inger Sandvik, Finland

Greta Olin Sundqvist's home at Soklot courtesy Inger Sandvik

Fireplace in Greta Olin Sundqvist's home

Haying at Soklot. Johanna Sundqvist Sunnell with rake, left; Bertha Sunnell, far right

Ida's home at Lillbroända

Chapter *10*

Return to America 1902 —
A Stealth Plan

Leona Marie Sundquist, Professor Emeritus Western Washington University, leaned forward and looked intently at my husband and me sitting across from her at the polished mahogany table in her dining room overlooking Bellingham Bay. My aunt, now 90 years of age, was not quite six years old when she traveled to Finland in 1901 with her parents and brother John Vincent, but the events of the trip were firmly ingrained in her memory. Decades later, with an illustrious career behind her, she recalled events from the past.

"There is something you should know," she began.

The afternoon sunlight reflected off Bellingham Bay and highlighted one side of her beautifully lined face. On her head sat the usual toque, as she called it, a small close-fitting blue knitted cap that she always wore even inside the house. She had interrupted her story to thrust her arm across the table to hand me a sturdy envelope chock-full of negatives of photographs she had taken in the early decades of the 20th century. Besides being an honored marine biologist, she had a passion for photography and documented the life and times of the Sundquist family with her Leica camera in the early 20th century.

"Someday you may want to write about our family history," she said as her blue eyes fixed on mine. "You should have these."

In retrospect, I wonder if at the moment she handed me the envelope, the torch was passed, and I was destined to be a family storyteller as the eldest daughter of the succeeding generation, although it would be years later that I would tell this story.

Now that people are allowed to travel into Russia, there are some things you should know. And some of the details would be better left consigned to family oral history. My father left

Finland for many reasons, however, the manner of his emigration or the continued Russian rule over Finland seemingly presented a problem when plans were made to return to the United States in 1902 after our eight-month visit.

When Ida Maria and John emigrated from Finland, each was issued a passport to leave the country. In the lists of Rural Police District of Kokkola (Gamlakarleby) from year 1893, there is a note that on 6 May 1893 farmer's daughter Ida Maria Lillbroända, born 1876, home place Kronoby, was issued a five-year passport.

The National Archives of Finland contains lists of emigrants from Parish Records Offices, Administrative Courts. The researcher for National Archives of Finland found farmer's son Johan Leonard Danielsson Sundqvist, born 1870, Nykarleby, among the list of people who left the Province of Vasa to America in 1890. The Emigrant Register at the Institute of Migration in Åbo, Finland reported from passport information in the National Archives in Helsinki that Sundquist received a one-year passport issued in Vasa Province on 17 October 1890. According to family lore, Sundquist and his Uncle Anders Olin rowed a boat across the Gulf of Bothnia from the coast of Finland to Sweden, and passenger records reveal that he traveled from Goteborg, Sweden by ship 24 October 1890 to Hull, England. Then he would have traveled overland to Liverpool where on 30 October 1890, he boarded the ocean-going SS Corean for Quebec, Canada. The final destination noted on the Finnish Migration Passport list: Ely, Minnesota, USA.

My aunt Leona continued to carefully lay out the background:

> Father left Finland in 1890 with a passport, but in 1901 when we visited Finland, the country was still under Russian rule as an autonomous Grand Duchy.

From 1809 to 1878, Finland was exempt from Russian military conscriptions. The Imperial Finnish Societe inaugurated a law establishing a Finnish Defence Force. *Finska militären,* the Finnish national army, was formally Finnish based on Finnish legislation (1878 Act); the officers would be Finnish, the command language Russian. It was supervised by the Russian Governor General in Finland as well as by Russian Ministry of Military Affairs. Enrollment would be by draft. In the spring of 1890, John may have been required to attend the *kutsunnat* drafting event or lottery. A minority of young men who drew a small lot number would begin their service time of three years; the remainder (majority) would fulfill 90 days training during the three following summers (45+30+15 days). If he had drawn a lot with a small number, he would then be bound to join the Vasa Rifle Battalion the same year on 1 November 1890 and start his three-year service obligation. If he had attended elementary school, his obligation would have been two years, but John had no formal schooling. It may be coincidental, but John Sundquist boarded an ocean-going vessel in Liverpool, England on 30 October 1890 bound for Canada.

The Finnish Diet in 1898 considered illegal a law proposed that Finnish men would be eligible for service in the Russian Army, since it had not been prepared in accordance with the Finnish Constitution, but in 1901 the Czar issued a new law concerning military service despite the resistance of the Finnish Diet. The Finnish nation reacted by implementing a draft strike, while many communities refused to form the conscription boards that the law prescribed. As a result, Russian authorities elected not to enforce the law. No Finnish males were ever conscripted to the Russian army, but rumors flew about to the contrary, a common misconception still in 1916 prior to Finland's independence, prompting many to flee.

This national unrest was occurring at the same time as John and Ida Maria's visit in 1901. Once again there was turmoil, but they had made the decision to return to America. They began to make plans for the voyage, but they became concerned about leaving Finland. And their concern was not about their transport following the icebreaker ship to leave Finnish waters. They had heard that along with a passport, the authorities portside may ask for a certificate showing military fulfillment before a man could leave the country. Leona continued her story:

> In theory, there should not have been a problem. All of
> us were American citizens in 1902: My brother and I were
> American citizens born in Telluride, Colorado. My father

(John Sundquist) had renounced his allegiance to Nicholas the II, Czar of Russia, who ruled over Finland when he became a naturalized citizen of the United States of America in 1900. Under United States law at the time, the wife of a naturalized citizen was automatically granted citizenship. But that was in America.

My parents had presented their United States naturalization paper at the clerk's office in Gamlakarleby before our departure, and it was appropriately stamped. However, Mother apparently surmised they could run into a problem at the dock when they boarded the ship. She was determined about returning to America with her family intact, and toward that end, she had a premeditated plan. She was not about to take any chance or allow any unknown happenstance to interfere with our leaving the country. This trip, we would all greet the New World by arriving in New York.

We sat spellbound as she continued with her story:

We took the train to Hangö, and there we sat in a cold, barren, crowded dark room awaiting the icebreaker to clear a passage for the ship. Watching over the crowd were the ubiquitous Russian Cossack soldiers with their boots, tunics, and fur caps. Finally, the crowd dispersed out into the cold, crisp air. My brother and I began our climb up the gangway between the pier and the ship with Mother close beside us and Father a step or two ahead. As we neared the end of the narrow rope-lined gangway and Mother was assured that the officers checking passenger documents were looking in her direction, she gasped aloud and fell face down on the rough wood planks of the gangway. The officers saw her collapse and rushed to her aid. They bent over her inert body, as Father quickly and silently slipped through the crowd of emigrants that gathered at the railing to see what had happened, and he boarded the ship. The guards helped my pregnant Mother to a sitting position. I was terrified, and when my brother and I saw blood oozing from a cut in her lip, we began screaming and crying. Mother cautiously and unsteadily arose as to further assure them of her incapability and handed her document to the officers who had come to her aid. The document she presented was not the singular paper the American naturalized citizens carried with them when they left the United States that bore the name of John Sundquist; she handed them a Finnish passport.

The Finnish passport that she handed to the officer would not have been the passport that Ida Maria Lillbroända had been issued 6 May 1893 prior to her emigration from Finland, as that five-year passport would have expired. I finally located on the Finland Institute of Migration website a record of her 1902 Finnish passport. Actually, I stumbled across it quite by chance when I was researching Finnish passport records under "L" hopeful of finding Ida Maria under her farm or place name Lillbroända, and I discovered an Ida Lundqvist, Kronoby, with the correct birthdate. Why was the 1902 passport listed in the Finland migration records under the name Lundqvist, not Sundquist, her married name? Was that intentional or a typo on the part of the transcriber of old documents? Perhaps a young clerk had mistaken the handwritten 19th century script S to be an L because of its similarity. I was stunned to find that she had been issued a Finnish passport 1 February 1902, only days before their departure.

But why had she felt it necessary to apply for a Finnish passport seven days before their departure from Hangö when in fact, she was an American citizen? On the back of John Sundquist's naturalization certificate, there is an official stamp and in writing *Uppvist I Gamlakarleby den 1 februari 1902*. She had presented the United States naturalization certificate to the authorities in Gamlakarleby. Why was that not sufficient? Did Finnish authorities not understand that she was a naturalized American citizen at the time of her husband John Sundquist's naturalization in 1900, as United States law at that time deemed a spouse automatically became a United States citizen at the moment of her husband's naturalization. The spouse name however was not included on the naturalization paper. As was customary, only the applicant name— John L. Sundquist.

Was she concerned that she had forgotten to bring the marriage license with her to prove her relationship and her citizenship? Or did she think that her status as a naturalized American citizen would be a moot point if John were arrested? We know that either John or Ida Maria was carrying the naturalization paper, as we see the same data recorded on each of the family's passenger arrival cards filled out upon their arrival in New York—"Paper of John Sundquist Co Court of Law Miguel Co Col. Telluride Col. Oct. 20 1900." Did she procure a Finnish passport as assurance or insurance, if you will, that if her husband should be detained, she could again leave Finland and return to America with her children? Leona was aware of the uncertainties and her mother's distress:

> I shall never forget my parents' relief as we finally left port
> with the ice chunks grinding against the sides of the ship.

Together, they watched the circling beam of light from Russarö Lighthouse on an island some five kilometers south of Hangö harbor until it faded into the distance. A last parting fare-thee-well from their native country.

Passenger List/Page		Port	Depart Finland	Ship from Finland
28/7	Johan Sundqvist (31)	Hanko to New York	8.02.02	Polaris, Cunard Line
	MK Johan, Ida ja Leona			
28/7	Ida (25)	Hanko to New York	8.02.02	Polaris, Cunard Line
	MK Johan, Leona ja Johan			
28/7	Johan (3M) infant boy	Hanko to New York	8.02.02	Polaris, Cunard Line
	MK Ida, Leona ja Johan Sundqvist			
28/7	Leona, age 5	Hanko to New York	8.02.02	Polaris, Cunard Line
	MK Johan, Ida, ja Johan Sundqvist			
28/7	Henrik Sundqvist (23)	Hanko to New York	8.02.02	Polaris, Cunard Line

Traveling on the same vessel was Sundqvist's brother Henrik, brother-in-law Henrik Sunnell and cousin Johannes Olin, age 19.

Chapter *11*

Journey Toward Home

The Sundquist family arrived in New York Harbor 24 February 1902 aboard the Cunard Line SS Campania from Liverpool, England. Contrary to their first entry into North America as immigrants over ten years ago, beside their names on the passenger manifest was stamped the letters: CIT. DISCH. ON PIER. The American citizens disembarked at the Citizen Pier. Can those of us born to later generations, complacent about our freedom in America, possibly imagine the Sundquist family's exuberance as the Statue of Liberty came into view to greet the young family? The ultimate satisfaction may have been when the U.S. Immigration Service officer pounded his circular stamp on John Sundquist's United States Naturalization Certificate at 3 PM, 25 February 1902.

Over two weeks had passed since they embarked on their long journey back to America 8 February 1902 on the SS Polaris from Finland to Hull, England, then the train to Liverpool, followed by a prolonged wait before they boarded the SS Campania that sailed from Liverpool 15 February 1902.

Another long journey lay ahead, across the vast North American continent to the edge of the Pacific Northwest in Washington State. John Sundquist had penciled a name and address on the back of the naturalization certificate. Their destination: the Lindstrom home at First Avenue South, Seattle, Washington. Ida Maria, John, and their young children Leona and John Vincent boarded the Canadian Pacific Railroad Line headed West. The colonial coach, part of a long train carrying passengers and freight, provided housekeeping with stoves for cooking, counters, and other amenities for food preparation. Leona wrote later:

It seemed that we were eternally crossing the great plains. Then, oh joy! There were the mountains again! Huge mountains! Tunnels, steep canyons and rushing water, sights and sounds so reminiscent of Telluride. Surely we'll soon be home. We changed trains at the border at Sumas, Washington, and boarded The Northern Pacific that took us to Seattle.

The Lindstrom family welcomed them at their home in a community called Ballard located on Salmon Bay about five miles north of Seattle's business district, a municipality incorporated in 1889, that was largely populated by Scandinavian immigrants.

Father built a house at the end of Second Avenue—the last house to the left at the entrance to Salmon Bay Park. Beyond their home was forest, except for a few scraggly clearings where gypsies camped in their tents.

The region had suffered in the national depression known as "Panic of 1893," but by the late 1890s, the depression was over and Northwest Washington embarked on an unprecedented period of economic growth. At the edge of Puget Sound, Salmon Bay hosted a bustling center of businesses that grew out of the burgeoning lumber industry— shipbuilding, lumber, wood products, sashes and doors. "Shingletown, USA" was a name attached to the town, as it became the world's leading producer of Western Red Cedar shingles.

The first mills were established on the shores of Salmon Bay in 1888. The forest line from tidewater up into the interior valleys and lowlands was in steady retreat as lumber mills and shingle mills hummed with the sounds of saws ripping through the logs and the sweet smells of pitch and inner bark arose from the still-living wood. From surrounding forests, enormous Western Red cedar, Sitka spruce six-feet through, and Douglas fir trees were felled with two-man crosscut saws, their branches lopped off and the trunks cut into lengths the mill could handle. Too heavy to be hauled by wagon, "skid roads" that reached back into the woods were constructed by placing small logs crosswise eight to ten feet apart across the trail, a notch in the center of each crosswise log acted as a guide. Enormous trunks of trees were dragged down the skid road by teams of oxen. The logs spilled into Salmon Bay and were herded in between long boomsticks and chained together. Then a tug hitched a cable to the boom and towed the raft to the mill.

The greater Seattle area was a new fast-growing city; there were more carpenters than members of any other trade. The Finland Swedes brought with them their innate talent of working with the wood, whether it was employed as a shipwright or a builder. John continued to build houses in the area around Salmon Bay in Ballard and on Queen Ann Hill. He teamed up with Abraham Löfquist, a contractor. They bought adjoining lots on Boren Avenue in Seattle not far from the Gethsemane Lutheran Church, and together, they built houses on these lots. The Löfquists lived in their house; John rented his newly built house. City of Seattle Building Permit #18360 signed by John Sundquist permitted a structure at 1929 Boren Avenue.

Dressed in their Sunday best, the family would board the streetcar for excursions around Seattle to Pioneer Square in the center of town, a thrilling ride on the cable car to Madison and Leschi Parks, and to Woodland Park, as the streetcar passed through forests and around Green Lake. On a trip to Ravenna Park, they spotted through the trees Denny Hall and other buildings on the University of Washington campus.

The family's social life centered around the Runeberg Society, named after Johan Ludvig Runeberg, Finland's national poet. John and Ida Maria were associated with the early beginnings of the temperance society "Sveaborg" organized 2 June 1903; Henry Lillsjo was an active leader in the organization in Seattle. The Society's activities included music, folk dancing, food, and camaraderie. At a picnic in Ravenna Park, standing on top of a huge stump, Leona recited in Swedish a poem by Runeberg:

> Säg mig du lilla fågel
> Där mellan almens blad.
> Hur kan du ständigt sjunga
> Och ständigt vara glad?
> Jag hör din röst var morgon,
> Jag hör den varje kväll.
> Men lika ren är stämman
> Och tonen lika säll.

> Little bird among the elm tree's leaves,
> How can you incessantly sing and remain so cheerful?
> I hear thy voice each morning; I hear it every eve,
> Still ever so clear is thy voice and thy tone so gay.
>   (Translated by Gunnar Damstrom)

John Vincent was an active toddler; Leona reluctantly had begun her schooling:

> I found myself being ushered to the public school, that institution so highly touted by my Mother as the reason for our return to America, free education for all children. I was placed in kindergarten, perhaps because I was just starting school, or maybe because I couldn't speak or understand English. I didn't like it. The children were all babies. I towered over all of them. I was much older, and surely, I thought I was much wiser.

Six months after their return from the visit to Finland, Ida Elvira was born at Salmon Bay 13 September 1902, the day forest fires raged in the vicinity.

> Lamps were lit at midday to assist the doctor as he attended my mother. She was very ill. I shall never forget Father's concern and that dark red disk of a sun in the thickening sky.

It would be the second time we have seen the name Ida Elvira, as Ida Maria birthed a daughter in Telluride with the same name. The first child named Ida Elvira had lived for only six months, and it was not uncommon in Finland for parents to name a succeeding child with the same name of a deceased child, so they again chose to name the new baby Ida Elvira. Ida Elvira was baptized 19 October 1902 by Martin L. Larson, Evangelical Lutheran Pastor, witnessed by Abraham Löfquist and Britta L. Löfquist.

From the clear blue Colorado skies in Telluride to the burdensome grey of low-hanging rain clouds over almost impenetrable forests interlocked with tangles of salal, Oregon grape, vine maple, salmonberry, huckleberry, and blackberry, the environment surrounding the Salish Sea was a geographical change that one cannot ignore.

Ida Maria at 27 years old reflected on her life. Ten years before, she had left her homeland to be a part of the American Dream. She had traveled the North American continent – twice. While willingly looking forward to the opportunities in America, it must have taken immense courage for her to again leave her homeland in 1902 and never look back. The years in Telluride had further supported her resolve to bring her dream to fruition. She had birthed four children and she suffered the loss of two babies who lay buried in Lone Tree Cemetery high on a mountain overlooking the San Miguel River valley. She had developed a responsible position of authority in successfully managing the family affairs and running the boarding house. She was the one who held things together in the home and community while her husband John was away at the mine sites. She kept the books herself while she also collected some of the boarders' money from their mine wages, which she helped them allot and send to their families in Finland. With the wide range of skills she developed, she had been a significant partner in the management and operation of the boarding house and raising the children.

But Ida Maria was not content. She had always set her direction, and she became increasingly restless, as she felt like a passive participant in her American dream. Her daughter Esther later confirmed:

> "She wished to be doing something for the ultimate good of the family and wanted to see her efforts involved in this struggle to develop in the new land."

John, too, was not satisfied with the city life. The young and restless immigrants reviewed their shared dream that was explicitly to own land, to farm, and to be their own boss. To romanticize the "freedom" of farm life would be the luxury of someone who has not farmed, especially a dairy farm where the farmer and his wife are obligated and constrained to the animals' well being, but their goal was not to be dependent on others and to be in charge of their own destiny. Owning land was the ultimate symbol of freedom, security, and independence. And the freedom of space: to be embraced by the universe and the four directions

159

when walking one's land, to recreate family roots in the new land were all part of the dream. Some believe that one must be on the land four generations for roots to establish. With nineteen generations of family roots firmly entrenched in Ostrobothnia, it was only natural that they would yearn to plant and nurture roots in the New World, hopefully for generations hence.

To hasten the fulfillment of their dream to own land, John left for Alaska spring of 1903 to "try his luck" placer mining at Council near Nome. The Alaska Gold Rush kicked off in 1897 when gold was discovered in the Klondike. And another wave of hope and opportunity beckoned in the spring of 1900 with the news that gold had been found near Nome on the coast of the Seward Peninsula, the great arrowhead-shaped landmass in Northwestern Alaska nearest to the Old World. One can look across the Bering Strait and see the dim outline of Asia; along the coast, moss-covered tundra extends to the mountains. Watercourses are numerous and gold-producing creeks even more so. Fifteen thousand people landed on the Nome beach during the great Nome stampede of 1900 and a city of white tents sprang up as if by magic. The number of gold-producing creeks was increasing exponentially as miners were digging into the benches and finding old channels. The total value of gold taken out of Seward Peninsula since the first discovery of commercial importance was estimated to be $18,500,000. The Ophir creek region near Council in 1902 produced $5,000,000 in gold alone in ten months, more gold than any other creek.

These statistics would certainly whet a man's appetite for instant riches. John had worked in the iron mines in Minnesota, then five years in the mines of Telluride. He was not averse to hard physical labor, and he knew a little about mining for gold. However, rather than toiling within mine tunnels, placer mining occurs beside the rivers or streams where gold nuggets have been found among deposits of sand and gravel in the stream beds. Panning for gold by hand depends largely on water for washing and separating the gold. By vigorously swirling water in a large metal pan, gold particles separate from the gravel and being of higher density, settle to the bottom, while sand and gravel are washed over the side of the pan. Once a placer deposit is located by gold panning, the miner then might use equipment that can process volumes of sand and gravel more quickly and efficiently, such as a sluice or dredging.

John Sundquist assembled his gear at a Seattle outfitter, including a small pick hammer and a circular heavy metal pan with a portion of the rim folded inward to allow for a better grip. He sailed out of Seattle to reach the Alaskan coast when the ice melted in the Bering Sea and broke loose from the shore. *The Hand Book of Seward Peninsula* 1903 reported that year that the ice did not start to move out until June 8th. It covered the sea for miles and not a vessel was in sight. Once disembarked in Council, The Council City & Solomon River Railroad ran from tidewater at Solomon City to Council City. This railroad made accessible and opened up the richest mining section known in the world. He panned for gold until the latest sailing date in November for his return to Seattle before the ice came back in. The days were long and arduous. There was no darkness; the sun goes down in the far north an hour or two before midnight and rises three or four hours later. The miners had to "make hay while the sun shines" and that they did. John brought home a few shiny nuggets in his overalls and tall tales of men, places and activities.

John returned home from Alaska with enough money to go north of Seattle to look at land. John Sundquist and his friend and fellow carpenter Victor Lillquist had worked together building houses around Salmon Bay and on Queen Ann Hill. Later, Lillquist worked as a carpenter for Great Northern Railroad and became interested in Skagit County when he was repairing railroad bridges there. He told John that Leander Palm, a Finland Swede from Terjärv who had settled in Cedardale in the mid 1890s, knew of available land for sale. John's younger brother Henrik had also learned firsthand of land opportunities in the rich alluvial flood plain near the town of Mt. Vernon in Skagit County. Henrik had joined the Sundquist family on their return trip to America in 1902 and found employment only a few miles from Skagit Valley at English Logging Camp I amid heavily forested land in the foothills of the Cascade Mountains south and east of Conway.

Conversations among the Finland Swedes would gravitate toward the opportunity of purchasing rich farmland in Skagit County sixty miles north of Seattle. They talked about the geophysical characteristics of the area as if they were describing the fertile floodplains of Ostrobothnia, the land where they were born. The flat Skagit Delta stretched toward saltwater Puget Sound. The Skagit River meandered through the coastal plain created by alluvial deposits, and forests of evergreen trees stood

161

where land was still uncleared. This area resembled their homeland, but rather than having to face harsh, cold winters, Western Washington was in a temperate climate zone.

On a crisp autumn day in October 1903, the two emigrants from Ostrobothnia boarded the Great Northern Railroad in Seattle and headed north to look for land. Their destination: Mount Vernon, the county seat of Skagit County. They passed through Everett where steam and smoke rose from sawmills and lumber mills that stood at the edge of Puget Sound. At Conway station, some Norwegian-speaking immigrants disembarked. The foothills that arose from the valley's eastern edge were blanketed with dense deep green forests that melded into the backdrop of dramatic peaks and crags of the North Cascade Mountains. In the clear air, the magical presence of snow-covered Mt. Baker in the Cascade Mountain Range loomed large over the valley from its height of 10,778 feet elevation. More than a hundred years earlier in April 1792 when the English explorer Captain George Vancouver entered the inland waters of the Pacific Northwest in his exploratory voyage, he was overcome by the beauty of a distant mountain peak as he sailed through the Strait of Juan de Fuca. He described Mt. Baker as "masses of glowing opal, a detached island separated by a line of mist, floating above the dark forest."

Indeed the secret was out. There was rich alluvial land available for farming in the flood plain of the Skagit River. Decades before Skagit County's resources were on display at the 1909 Alaska-Yukon-Pacific Exposition in Seattle, the region's first world's fair that highlighted the Northwest's growing prosperity and importance as a trade and shipping portal to Alaska and Pacific Rim countries, people had become aware of the rich delta land. Frank Wilkeson, a columnist for *The New York Times,* traveled West and put Skagit County on the map when he wrote an article in 1891 that brought national attention to the region that split from Whatcom County in 1884 and became Skagit County. He extolled the area's rich resources and in part described its terrain:

> Skagit River area is the most resourceful in the United
> States, if not on earth. In this valley sufficient food to feed
> a million persons can be produced. No need for commer-

cial manure here! In my opinion it is the most productive
agricultural land in the temperate zone.

East of Swinomish slough are the delta lands of the Skagit,
lands that have been made of silt gouged by glaciers out of the
Cascades' rugged flanks and carried by annually-recurring
floods to Puget Sound and there deposited. This filling-in process is still in progress. Reeds and aquatic plants took root until
there were extensive grassy flats, which were never water-cov-
ered save at exceptionally high tides. To the east a towering line
of dark-green fir trees marked the boundary of the delta land.
Today this delta is reclaimed from the sea by dikes.

On its alluvial lands stand sufficient Douglas fir and red
cedar to replace the wooden ships that compose the mer-
chant marine fleet, if met by disaster. Forests so dense, the sun
couldn't pierce, and trunks of trees that are from four to eight
feet in diameter.

The alluvial lands of the Skagit are enormously productive,
and they fetch more money after they have been thoroughly
logged than they will with the timber standing on them.

Selling land was like a "piece of cake" for real estate promoters, as
one-mile square "Sections" of 640 acres were sliced into geometric land
parcels of 20, 40, 80 acres or more. The Federal Land Ordinance of
1785 declared that all land had to be surveyed before it could be offered
for sale because of conflicting property claims and lack of information
about the frontier. The rectangular survey had no relationship to the
geography. The national government survey method neatly outlined
land into townships of 36 square miles, which were cut into one-mile
square sections, with the exception of the thirteen colonies, Texas, and
parts of the country too rough for surveyors. The grid began at the western border of Pennsylvania and eventually covered almost seventy percent of the 48 continental states at that time. The method was designed
to create a checkerboard of identical squares covering a given area,
rather than identifying property by specifying the shape and boundary
dimensions of a parcel and following geographical land characteristics.
The right angle became king.

On 31 October 1903, John Sundquist and John V. Lillquist signed a Real Estate Contract to purchase forty acres for $2000.00 (fifty dollars per acre with $200 paid as earnest and 8% interest on the balance) from John L. Downs and his wife Leonia M. Downs. The property was located on an old skid road where tree trunks were dragged from forest to river by teams of oxen. Some of the land had been cleared, but there were still acres covered by virgin forest. The woodlands and the nearby Skagit River that flowed into the Salish Sea reminded them of their homeland. The legal description of the property: (SW 1/4 of SE ¼) of Section Thirty one (31) in Township Thirty four (34) North Range Four (4) East of Willamette Meridian. At fifty dollars per acre in 1903, the price per acre of property in Cedardale, south of Mt. Vernon, had already doubled in a year's time. As the story goes, on one-half of the forty acres was a nice sort of house and some outbuildings. Who would get the land with the building? So they drew straws. Lillquist got the house part and Sundquist got the other part.

The Sundquist family moved north to Cedardale in the autumn of 1904—John, seven-month pregnant Ida Maria, Leona, John Vincent, and two-year-old Ida Elvira. They left behind a rapidly growing city where that year Seattle boasted its tallest and first steel-framed skyscraper—the fourteen-story Alaska building at Second Street and Cherry.

Leona, Ida Elvira, and John Vincent Sundquist, Salmon Bay

Skagit Valley from Little Mountain

Real Estate Contract

It is Hereby Mutually Agreed, By and between John L. Downs and Leonia M. Downs < husband and wife > of Skagit County Washington parties of the first part and John Sundquist and Victor Lillquist the parties of the second part, that said parties of the first part will sell to said parties of the second part, their heirs or assigns and said parties of the second part will purchase of said parties of the first part, their heirs, executors or administrators, the following described lot tract or parcel of land, situated in Skagit County, State of Washington, to wit: The South West quarter of South East quarter (SW¼ of SE¼) of Section Thirty one (31) in Township Thirty four (34) North Range Four (4) East of Willamette Meridian, with the appurtinances

626

thereunto belonging, on the following terms:- 1st. The purchase price for said land is Two Thousand (#2000.00) Dollars of which the sum of Two Hundred (#200.00) Dollars has this day been paid as earnest, the receipt whereof is hereby acknowledged by said parties of the first part, and the further sum of One Thousand eight hundred Dollars to be paid on or before the 31st day of October A.D. 1908 with interest thereon from this date until paid at the rate of Eight per cent per annum, said interest to be paid annually, and if not so paid shall be added to the principal and bear like interest. 2nd. Said land to be conveyed by a good and sufficient deed to said parties of the second part when said purchase price shall have been fully paid together with all taxes and assessments levied upon or against said land during the continuance of this contract. 3rd. Time is of the essence of this contract. 4th. If said parties of the second part fail to pay the whole of said purchase price and interest and taxes when due and before delinquency within the time above specified, then the said parties of the first part may, if they so elect, rescind this contract, and in that case all payments made by said second parties shall be forfited. Witness our hands and seals in duplicate this 31st day of October A.D. 1903.

Signed, Sealed and Delivered
in the Presence of
Fred G. Pickering
H.P. Downs
State of Washington
County of Skagit } SS

John L. Downs   (Seal)
Leonia M. Downs (Seal)
John Sundquist   (Seal)
John V. Lillquist (Seal)

Real estate contract

Cedardale Road

Chapter *12*

A Place to Call Home
in Skagit Valley

While they cleared the land and John built their home, the Sundquist family of five lived for two months with the John Holmquist family, whose home was on adjoining acreage to the east. With the help of neighbors Lillquist and Holmquist, the Sundquist home was ready for the birth of Eva on 28 December 1904. Leona described the task of clearing the land:

> Besides the cedars, there were Douglas firs, Sitka spruce, a very large cottonwood tree, alders, elderberry, vine maple, and a jungle of impenetrable undergrowth. Father cleared the land by hand with horses and cables. What possesses man to induce him to tackle such a formidable job? Clearing meant the use of ax, saw, brush hook, shovel, horses, block and tackle, spar trees, stump piles and bonfires, bonfires, bonfires. The two horses, two old mares, Fanny and Tubby, were our prized possessions. Without them to pull and haul, jerk loose stumps, and drag logs we never could have cleared that land. Every member of the family bent his back to the task, pulling, hauling, cutting, grubbing, tending the fires. Best of all, we roasted quantities of corn and potatoes in the embers, following the sparks skyward into the night. Darkness and firelight! There seemed no end to this clearing of land. Black stumps, mud, mud, mud (*gyttja*) and the chaotic criss-cross of logs, twigs, and branches seemed to persist eternally.

As soon as the building site for their home had been cleared, Ida Maria surrounded her new habitat with botanical reminders of her homeland—flora that held meaning to the young family in America as reflected in the trees and bushes she planted, many of which survived for several generations.

By the entrance gate, a mountain ash tree: The hardy ornamental tree bears clusters of white flowers followed by brilliant red berries. The common European mountain ash or rowan tree *Sorbus aucuparia* is one of the most revered plants in Nordic folklore. From early times in Finland, the mountain ash has been considered a tree of spiritual significance, planted to protect the home and keep travelers safe from harm when they ventured from home. The rowan tree is referenced in *The Kalevala*, a collection of Nordic oral history and folk tales assembled by Elias Lönnrot from interviews with the peasantry in Eastern Finland in the 1800s.

In the farmyard, a short distance from the house: a white-barked birch. The birch tree's light green foliage and bright white trunk are prominent features of the Ostrobothnian landscape. The ubiquitous birch has held powerful connotations in the lives of Finnish people back to ancient times. The rural Finnish culture of centuries past was often referred to as the "birch-bark culture," and for good reason, as the birch tree provided well: birch bark was used for roofing, baskets, shoes; leafy branches were cut and dried for winter fodder for the cattle and used to bind sauna whisks. Birch is important in Finland as firewood, as many homes are heated with birch logs, not to mention most of the saunas at Finland's popular summer cottages. The birch tree is the national tree of Finland.

Beside the porch steps to the back door of the farmhouse Ida planted the lovely lily-of-the-valley *Convallaria majalis* that blooms early in the spring. It has a powerful sophisticated aroma. Significantly, the popular flower would in later years be honored as the official flower of the Ostrobothnia region and the national flower of Finland.

Their new land provided ample natural resources as Douglas firs and Western red cedars were transformed into farm buildings. Wood is abundant in Finland and has always been the traditional building material. The original farmhouse replicated the Ostrobothnian vernacular building tradition—the long, narrow two-story farmhouse with end-gables, both sides with the same pitch. The architectural design is striking in its simplicity of form and lack of Victorian-era embellishment and ornamentation. One notable difference, the traditional two-story farmhouse structures found in Ostrobothnia in Western Finland commonly use vertical board and batten exterior siding rather than the horizontal siding or clapboard typical of American farmhouse construction.

The structure was built on an elevated poured-concrete foundation wall about four feet above ground level. This allowed for a crawl space under the house, but essentially, as with other homes built in the flood-prone alluvial plain, the raised elevation was calculated so that the main floor would be above flood-water level in the event the Skagit River spilled over the dikes at flood stage or a ruptured dike caused flooding. Three miles south, all the homes in the village of Conway were greatly elevated so that steps cascaded ten feet or more above ground level. Below-ground basements were never a consideration. These elevated foundations serve as reminders that the land claimed as our own is not really ours. Everything ultimately belongs to Nature.

The farmhouses in Cedardale are scattered at some distance from each other and surrounded by cleared fields and patches of forests; the majority of the homeowners built quite near the road, albeit the location of each was relative to the acreage of the parcel. Leona described her parents' farmhouse:

> The original dwelling stood in the middle of a cleared spot in the surrounding thicket. It was a simple house, two rooms downstairs and two rooms upstairs. The door from the porch opened onto the kitchen. There stood a black, wood-burning Monarch range with a huge oven below and two warming units above and a hot water reservoir at the far end. Next to the reservoir was a sink with an outlet for wastewater to the outside. There was no running water in the house. A pump with a charcoal filter barrel was located on the porch. A stairway led from the kitchen to the bedrooms upstairs. The front room was a living-dining room with a dining table along the south end. A sewing machine stood under the east window. A folding bed, in which I slept, occupied the north corner and wall and opened up along the west wall. A glass-enclosed dish cupboard separated the kitchen from the dining room. Home-woven curtains graced the windows and likewise

171

home-woven carpets on the floors. In the south and east windows were pots of pelargonium, Kristi Tår fuchsia, Christmas cactus and a small-leaved evergreen myrtle, the start of which was obtained when we were in Finland. These plants were invariably found in the neighbors' homes.

At this time, many supplies were stored in root cellars, low elongated affairs partly above and partly below ground. Earth covered the entire structure. A passageway separated the bins along the two sides. Here were stored apples of various kinds, potatoes, carrots, table beets, and parsnips, after the first frost had sweetened them. Squash and pumpkins were piled at the far end. The atmosphere and smells were magnificent. This took care of storage until we built the tank house.

At the north end of the house, John added a two-room lean-to structure. One room contained a bed and living arrangements for John's brother Henrik Sundquist from Soklot and Ida Maria's uncle Victor Vikstrom from Kronoby, when they came down from the logging camps at times of forest fire, shut-downs, and holidays. The other room below became the dairy room, with shelves for huge milk pans, until a milkhouse was built next to a larger barn. John constructed a floor loom from vertical grain fir that was set up in the lean-to for Ida Maria who wove carpets, curtains, bedspreads and household linens.

John's talent for carpentry was well put to use as he designed and built the first of many buildings around the periphery of the vast central farmyard that would make up the farm compound. The first small barn, hayshed, stanchions and stalls for two brown cows, Coora and Darky, were built with rough-hewn cedar board and batten construction.

From huge fallen Western red cedar trees, they split cedar to use as roofing for the barn and sheds and cut pickets for the pig pen and fences. All hands that could wield a hammer, male and female, climbed up on the roof to help nail cedar shakes to the roofing frame. Some of those shake roofs were still in existence seventy-five years later.

John and Ida Maria added Holstein cows to the herd. Dairying was a commitment to cows. There was no day off for the milk cows or for the milkers. Cows must be milked by hand twice a day and on a regular time schedule; otherwise the cow's milk would dry up or worse, health problems could ensue for the animal. All the family participated in milking before school in the morning and in the evening. The chores continued in the dairy room where the milk and cream would be separated. The wide shelves accommodated huge milk pans. Ida Maria and the girls skimmed thick cream from the pans and churned into butter, and the skim milk fed to the calves. Later a hand-driven cream separator would be installed. When daughter Eva left home for college, John purchased a milking machine, and she would later boast that her milking skill was irreplaceable, except by a machine.

Building by building, the number of structures grew. Each building had its own character and attention paid to architectural design. The square tankhouse was designed so its width decreased as it towered upward from its wide base. Next to the tall tankhouse, the garage boasted a square façade in front of its pitched roof remindful of the New Swedish Finn Temperance Hall in Telluride that John had helped build in 1899. Then he built the large end-gabled woodshed, granary, and storage sheds. The connected-farm architecture was a Finnish farm concept that came to America along with the Finnish concept of log houses. The silo was constructed of clear Douglas fir. The two-by-six inch tongue and groove forty-feet-long boards were not flat, they were chamfered—slightly curved when milled to conform to the circumference of the circular structure. All in all, to the eye, the farm buildings that encircle a vast farmyard speak to the Sundquist's well-thought-out architectural planning and design from the circular silo, square pump house, square façade on garage, to gabled buildings of various sizes, form accommodating function, such as the later addition of a small gabled milk house juxtaposed against the large milking barn.

The two-story house for the chickens deserves further explanation. The Plymouth Rock chickens were Ida Maria's. They were also used for barter. She welcomed this responsibility and considered this new venture not only as a business but a means for her to contribute to the family's welfare. As we have noted, it was her nature to be involved in their destiny, evidenced by Ida Maria's first business experience as manager of the boarding house in Telluride, from which she had managed to save money.

Before John could build a proper chicken house, the chickens ran wild and at night would roost in a rough-hewn lean-to. To find their eggs, Ida Maria and the children would search for their deposits among nooks and crannies around the tree stumps. The chicken house that John later built was an architecturally pleasing design, notwithstanding that the other farm buildings were aesthetically and appropriately designed to their function. Thick, rough plank stairs butted against the end wall accessed the second floor where Ida Maria's chickens roosted in luxury in their separated compartments. It was a long, narrow two-story building with an offset pitched roof, precursor to some late twentieth-century contemporary residential architecture. Beneath the higher gable was a row of small clerestory windows; on the main floor, a row of south-facing windows, all framed in white against the traditional earthy red-ochre pigment commonly seen in Finnish farm buildings.

Dozens of Leghorn chickens came later, and the increased egg production provided a more lucrative income. Daughter Leona would carry a bucket of eggs on the ferry that crossed the Skagit River. Otto Larson operated the cable that guided the ferry between Skagit City on Fir Island and the mainland. Leona would sell or trade the eggs at Gage's General Merchandise Store in Skagit City, for a variety of goods ranging from a wedge cut from a huge wheel of cheese to gingham cloth, buttons, sewing thread, and lace. In addition, Gage's store had clothing, shoes, boots, harnesses, and hardware. A large red coffee mill on the counter and a wood pickle barrel on the floor contributed to the aromatic atmosphere at the general store. Leona described progress at the Sundquist farm:

> As trees were cut and homes, sheds and barns were built, stumpage and uncleared land encouraged the growth of the wild blackberry (*Rubus ursinus*), the delicious small blackberry. As children we spotted the best berry patches and staked claims to them. We were rather careful in honoring the established claims. Gallons upon gallons of berries were picked and canned. Rows upon rows of quart jars stood on the shelves. They were eaten as sauce, in pies and especially with thin, crisp Swedish pancakes.
>
> During the early period on the farm, protein foods were often limited to eggs and chickens. However, we did have veal whenever a bull calf was born. And there were times that I felt

there were a disproportionate number of bull calves born, as I wearied of eating veal. My parents discouraged the eating of pork, unless it was very well cooked, a direct consequence of old country experiences with parasites.

Fish was a common item in our diet—salmon and trout from the nearby Skagit River. Trips to the river for fish were fun. Father would saddle Fanny, who was as broad as she was long. A gunnysack and rope were tied around the pommel. And a dime and a quarter were tied in my "hankie." Off I rode to the river, then north for a mile or more to Mr. Stein's where I crossed the dike and there on the riverbank would be a row of fish. If the salmon run was good, the price posted on the stump was ten cents; if not, the price was twenty-five cents. I took my pick of fish and placed a dime or quarter in a tobacco can nailed to a stump. These fish from Mr. Steins were large. I became adept at picking out the best female salmon. I cleaned the fish, cut pieces for immediate consumption and the roe I liked very much with rye bread and buttermilk. The excess parts were usually salted; sometimes, we would smoke them in Mr. Holmquist's smokehouse.

Ida Maria and her husband John were now able to see and realize the fruits of their own labor and share those joys with a growing family. If Nature and climate affect the spirit and sensibility of the people who live in a place, the Finland Swedes from a similar geographical and rural landscape in Finland made themselves known in their new territory. Indeed, they were a hardy bunch, shaped by their environment.

Shingling the barn roof

Coffeetime, Daniel playing harmonica

Ida tending her flock

Stacking wood

Ida harvesting rhubarb

Chapter 13

Sundquist Farm 1905

The Sundquist farm began as a beehive of activity that never let up. The new farmhouse was not large, but, as Ida Maria's daughters would relate: "People were always coming and going." She had been accustomed to a house full of people at her boarding house in Telluride, and the family welcomed visitors as they always brought news from outside the Cedardale community.

Ida Maria put the boiler kettle on the black, wood-burning Monarch range to prepare hot water for baths. John's younger sister Johanna Sundquist Sunnell and four children had just arrived by horse and carriage from the railway station in Mt. Vernon, the last leg of her long journey from Finland with children ranging in age between three and ten years. Snowdrifts were still above the fence posts in Ostrobothnia when they left Soklot by sleigh to Nykarleby where they boarded the train to Hangö. The first ship took them to Hull, then they traveled by train across England to board the ocean-going vessel at Liverpool. They were stranded in ice and fog near Greenland before they finally disembarked at Halifax, Nova Scotia, and boarded the Canadian Pacific train headed west across Canada. Johanna was not without some support as three Olin cousins, Hendrik, Sander, and John also were traveling with her. John Olin's knowledge of English language was helpful to the travelers until they reached Calgary where he changed trains for the railway to Colorado where he would return to the mine.

Johanna kept her eye on the map she carried with her, but when the train arrived at Sumas on the Canadian border of Washington State, she hustled her four children off the train to board another train headed south to Seattle, thinking there was a stop in Mt. Vernon, but alas, she painfully discovered at the first stop at Sedro that there was no westward connection to Mt. Vernon. They were on the wrong train. The station attendant pointed to the map to show they were on the Seattle,

Lakeshore & Eastern line from Sumas through Sedro and the valley of the lakes to Seattle. As the crow flies, Sedro-Woolley and Mount Vernon are only about thirteen miles apart, but in 1905, the only transportation between the Skagit River communities was by packhorse or the occasional riverboat. Johanna and the children were put off at Sedro and told to take the next northbound train back to Sumas and continue on to New Westminster, British Columbia to board the Great Northern train that would pass through Mount Vernon. How do you explain this mistake to a weary traveler, who spoke no English and had four small children clinging to her skirts?

At the Sundquist farm, the children were delighted to welcome playmates. Johanna's daughter Agnes Sunnell would later relate:

> "Let's pretend" was our favorite form of child's play:
> There were huge cedar trees with knotty roots bending
> upward out of the ground and covered with green moss. This
> formed a circular area that, with some imagination, became
> our living room. The cedar tree's curvaceous roots protruding
> from the ground became chairs and sofas to sit upon. Broken
> pieces of crockery, glass, and other things from the kitchen
> were our play dishes. Now that we had dishes and furniture
> for our living room, we decided to give a party. Our guests
> knocked on the trunk of the tree just as if they were entering
> our house. We entertained by pretending that we had coffee,
> cookies, and coffeebread.

The Sunnell family stayed at the Sundquist farmhouse while John Sundquist and John Holmquist helped Henrik Sunnell build their house. Sundquists had stayed with Holmquists when they built the farmhouse. That was just the way it was. People reached out to help each other. They were the American Dreambuilders; they all had a common goal of assimilating into a new culture and reaping the rewards of the new land. Together, they would realize their dreams. And together, they helped each other in times of need. Leona relates an incident shortly after the birth of her sister Alice:

Whooping cough had hit the family. Alice was scarcely a month old when she too became a victim. Whooping cough was serious enough for the older children, but extremely so when the infant daughter began to whoop. She would get into a whooping spell and turn blue. Father and Mother became alarmed and were sure she would die. In alarm they realized that she had not been baptized and all the associated religious implications. Father philosophically thought the good Lord would, in his infinite wisdom and compassion, take good care of the matter. But Mother wasn't so sure. Rules were rules, and she knew there had been provided an emergency clause that a layman could baptize an infant if no clergy were available.

Mr. Holmquist, our next-door neighbor, would be the person to contact, as he was our Sunday school teacher and considered himself knowledgeable in religious matters. I was told to get the lantern and go fetch Mr. Holmquist, and to tell him to come immediately, as the situation was critical!

So off into the black night I ran, through the front gate, jumping the mud puddles down the road, through their gate and on to their house. I pounded on their locked door. They were forever opening it. There was Mrs. Holmquist, a saint of a woman. Mother loved her. I managed somehow to convey the message and its urgency. Mr. Holmquist became frightened at the thought of the undertaking. "But the child is dying!" Mrs. Holmquist got the necessary book, marked the page and said, "Now be off."

So off went a child with a light and an old man with a book down a muddy road in the blackness of night to baptize an infant.

The necessary basin of water and a home-woven linen towel had been assembled. All was in readiness. In the midst of the ritual, the baby began to cough. Mr. Holmquist panicked, and Mother shouted, but Father quietly took the book, pointed to the place, and softly told Mr. Holmquist to proceed.

And so Alice was baptized.

Washington Territory began attracting Finnish immigrants. Charles Tollber (Karl Tollberg) was one of the first to homestead in Skagit Valley on Fir Island in 1869. The Kamb brothers, Oscar and John, seed growers and dairymen, were early settlers in Mt. Vernon area. John emigrated in 1886 and Oscar, 1895. Alma Elizabeth Adin born in 1876, emigrated in 1899 and married Oscar Kamb in 1900. She will be remembered as "Myran" from her verses and articles published in *Finska Amerikanaren, Norden* and *Ledstjärnan* newspapers. Oscar and Alma were from Yttermark/Närpes.

The boundaries of the Finland Swede cultural landscape in Cedardale expanded as families continued to migrate toward this rich valley farmland. The Leander Palms were perhaps the first Finland Swedes to settle south of Mount Vernon. Sofie (Anna) Palm from Leplax arrived in Skagit County in 1893, the year she married Leander who emigrated from Terjärv. Their son Roy was born on the farm in 1896. The Palms were of great assistance to later Swedish-speaking persons who moved into the Cedardale community.

Two miles south of Mt. Vernon on Cedardale Road (later renamed Hickox Road) lived several Finland Swede families: Ida Maria and John Sundquist from Kronoby and Soklot/Nykarleby, John Victor Lillquist and his wife Emma from Pedersöre, and John Holmquist and his wife Marie who came from Pedersöre in the early 1900s. Across the road from Holmquists lived Sam Erickson from Vörå and his wife Anna from Keskis/ Vörå. Matt Semell and wife Ida Sofia Gustafson came from Nedervetil in the early 1900s, Emil and Hilda West, and Jack Andersons from Oravais. Other Finland Swedish emigrants from Ostrobothnia who settled in Cedardale: Sofia and Gustaf Jackson, Gustaf from Forsby/ Pedersöre; Sofia from Soklot/Nykarleby, sister of Jack Olin and cousin of John Sundquist. Following Sofia's death in 1928, Gust married Henry Sunnell's widow, Hannah, who was John Sundquist's sister from Soklot/ Nykarleby. Jack Olin from Soklot/Nykarleby and his wife, Hanna Wik emigrated in 1900 and married in 1910, arriving in Cedardale about 1915. They had three daughters, Toine, Judith, and Miriam.

On Cedardale Road east of the railroad lived Herman and Fanny Stahl from Kronoby, and their son Lasse; Andrew Hanson from Kronoby, whose father was Hans Hästö, married Hilda, Fanny Stahl's sister from Kronoby; Henry Gust Mattson and his wife Ida M. Mattson, and Oscar and Anna Mattson. Gust and Oscar were brothers from Terjärv; Anna from Lovisa; Mattias and Edla Eriksdotter Holmström from Oravais, and William and Anna Westlund from Munsala. Isaac and Anna Bergström, Isaac from Kvelax; Anna from Munsula. Sofia Johnson, from Munsula, lived with her sister Anna Bergstrom. Edward Bergstrom and his wife Marie lived on River Road, Marie from Mona/Munsala, Edward from Kvelax; Marie's brother Einar Alskog lived next to them; Elsa and Gust Holm.

Henry Sunnell family: Henry from Sorvist/Nykarleby; Hannah Sundquist Sunnell, John Sundquist's sister from Soklot/Nykarleby. Four of their children, John Edward, Helga, Bertha, and Elvera born in Soklot, emigrated with their mother in 1905. Jacob and Lovisa Nyholm, John Sundquist's aunt.

Mr. and Mrs. Peter Olson; Peter from Sweden, his wife from Finland. Mary Anderson emigrated in 1902 and married Alfred Anderson from Sweden. Alfred and Mary had one daughter, Elin. Louisa Markuson from Munsala married Andrew Markuson.

On the hillside above the Hill Ditch, also known as Carpenter's Creek, lived two sisters, Wendla (sister to Charles Tollberg) and Peter Johnson, an ethnic Swede, and her sister Marie and John Olin, a Finn from Borgå. Wendla Tollberg emigrated in 1883, one of the first Finland Swedes to arrive in Lower Cedardale in 1885.

Another factor that bound Finland Swedes together in their own cultural landscape was their language. When Ida Maria and John lived in Telluride, they spoke Finland-Swedish dialect among friends and relatives who had settled in the same community on West Pacific Avenue. The adults tended to do the same in Cedardale, while school-age children began learning English. Finland Swedes spoke the Swedish language, but the Swedish dialects spoken by emigrants from various parts of Ostrobothnia—Kronoby, Terjärv, Vörå—were difficult for their neighbors, the emigrants from Sweden, to understand. There is a remarkable difference between the Swedish dialects spoken in Ostrobothnia and the Finnish south coast.

The Swedish dialect spoken by Finland Swedes was considered strange even by Swedish-speaking people from Sweden, and they faced negative reactions and misunderstandings by people outside their own community. Carol Semell Stieger spoke of her mother's problem:

> "My mother's mother-in-law had lots of Swede-Finn
> friends and when she visited with them, Mom didn't under-
> stand what they were saying, even though my Mom spoke
> Swedish."

Finland Swedish children were subject to teasing and taunt-
ing by their Swedish playmates, as Helga Sunnell Erickson Danielson
described:

> Most of the children were from Swedish speaking families
> from Sweden. There was only one Norwegian family and one
> English speaking family. The families from Sweden had been in
> the United States longer and their children knew some English,
> but the language of the schoolyard was Swedish. The Swedish
> children snubbed us Finland Swedish children. We were not
> included in their games. We were foreigners and not accepted.

Hulda Lillquist, who lived next door to Sundquists, was teased in
school about her accent: "Swedish, Swedish, struck a straw. Can't say
nothing but yaw, yaw, yaw."

Finland-Swedish language was never encouraged or introduced to
the generation born in America, nor to their grandchildren. The language spoken in the household would be English. As a child, I urged
my grandmother to speak Swedish, but she would respond: "We are
Americans now. We speak English." Grandmother had become self-
conscious of her dialect and protective of her family, which were good
enough reasons for her not to teach the next generation her dialect.
Further, there was little said about the "Old Country." We know that
the Sundquists sent funds to help finance building Soklot *Ungdomshus*,
a place where young people could meet for concerts or dances, as was
noted in the newspaper *Finska Amerikanaren* 21 October 1909. Few letters, if any, had crossed the ocean in the early part of the twentieth
century between the relatives in Finland and those in America. The
lack of communication between the family in America and those in the
homeland prompted a seemingly chastising letter to Ida Maria from her
daughter, written during Leona's visit to Finland in 1931, holding her
mother responsible for lack of communication:

Dearest Mother,

I have always felt that you have never been very closely bound to your old home, family and relations in Finland. It has seemed to me that you have simply picked up your things and left them. Yes, you have thought of them but have not been particularly vitally concerned about them, I may be wrong in this but such has been my impression. You have become more Americanized than the rank and file of folks who have left this country for America. I have often, so often, wondered about you in this past and still do. In many ways you are a puzzle to me and yet I seem to grasp an understanding of your inveterate spunk and spirit that has driven you ever onward and forward and consequently away and utterly away from your birth place. So consequently your home and childhood background and relationships have been left as a faint blur.

Leona.

Throughout the country, the prevailing paradigm among immigrants was the concept of total assimilation into the American society and each family worked diligently to achieve success and acceptance. Did Ida Maria's daughter not understand or perhaps Leona could not fathom until decades later the courage her mother had shown and the personal and physical journey she had undertaken as a young girl, and for what? Her children's future.

The dominant Anglo Saxon population promoted the idea that America was a "melting pot" in which all racial and ethnic groups must shed their heritages in order to be Americans. Considering the social insecurity of the newly arrived immigrants, they bought into the concept, as the welfare of their families in America was most important. The young Sundquist family, recent arrivals into a new social sphere, was anxious to prove they belonged. And for them, a mastery of Standard English was the ticket to cultural admission. They understood this must be accomplished as quickly as possible to become good American citizens and be successful in the New World.

Besides, it had not escaped the immigrants' attention that at this same period in early twentieth-century America, assimilation was being physically and emotionally forced upon the children of native people who were hustled off to boarding schools far from their homes where they would not be allowed to speak their language. According to the dictates of the dominant population at the time, everyone must shed their heritage.

All groups were affected whose languages were different from the American majority, not solely Nordic immigrants. No doubt this brought to mind the language strife created in Finland when the 19th century National Romanticism movement in Europe found its way there.

Skagit County schools were typical of those throughout the country in encouraging children to reject the Old World heritage of foreign-born parents. The Melting Pot concept was rampant throughout America. The young Sundquist family recognized that it was absolutely essential to their ability to seize the opportunities in the new country and ultimately for their success in America to be assimilated as quickly as possible into the American society. Education was the way to accomplish that, and Leona was the first to attend school. She described the setting:

> Meadow School was located on Lee's property by the river, about two miles from home. We donned our hats and carried lunch in a Wild Rose Brand Pure Lard tin pail with a wire handle. It was a one-room school with rows of double-seated desks; teacher's desk was on a raised platform in front; recitation bench below; black pot-bellied stove in the middle of the room; water bucket and dipper on a bench in the rear; also a wash basin and roller towel nearby, and a row of lunch buckets.
>
> I was absent from school a great deal of the time during that first year due to inclement weather; snow and icy conditions added to the muddy roads and the long trek along the dike. So the next year, the children along our road were sent to the one-room Upper Cedardale School, eastward on the hill. It was not in our district, but much nearer home. Also, the road conditions were better after we crossed the railroad. At Cedardale School we associated with more "American" children; the Meadow School consisted largely of Scandinavian children—Swedes, Norwegians, and Finnish Swedes. We attended the one room Cedardale School for

more than a year until a new two-room Meadow School
was built which was more centrally located in the district
and only about one mile from home. In the two years at the
Cedardale School we had two men teachers: Mr. Carson, a
young Spanish-American war veteran and Mr. Ratterman,
who introduced me to Dutch ball and the boys to football. At recess and noon he wore cleated football shoes, and
we thought he was mighty fine. While in the fourth grade I
discovered geography. The large geography book not only
served to hide our chewing of gum, (dried pitch gathered
from spruce trees) but also led to the discovery of maps and
their meaning.

There were new orchards to exploit on the way home from
the Upper Cedardale School. Mr. Hickox had an old orchard
which offered a variety of apples and a garden with moss rose
bushes and lilacs. Thompsons' across the road from the Hickox
was a large place. They had horses. Maud Thompson galloped
her spirited horse up and down the Cedardale Road, passing
our place to and from her Garland cousins.

Victor Lillquist and John Sundquist built the new Meadow School
and a year later, the Lincoln School in Cedardale. Leona Sundquist
described her enthusiasm:

> The new two-room Meadow School (1907) was located
> on the river road about one mile from home. It had an entry-
> way with two cloakrooms and a bell tower overhead. I loved
> that bell. It not only rang for school purposes, but also for
> the announcement of unusual events, such as deaths, etc. We
> always entered the building by marching, one line for the
> lower grades and another line for upper grades. I was now in
> the fifth grade; brother Vincent was in lower grade line. The
> teacher either beat on a triangle or clapped her hands to keep
> time to our marching. Rows of single desks filled the major
> part of the room. Each morning Mr. Hammock read a chap-
> ter from the Bible. We sang a song, saluted the flag, and went
> to work.

Blackboards, on two sides of the room, were constantly in use. At the beginning of each week a new Memory Gem or Quotation was written on the top of the front blackboard. Monday morning this was read and discussed, and then supposedly contemplated throughout the week. Our names were also listed, and as the week progressed, gold and/or silver stars were posted dependent upon the perfection and tidiness of papers presented.

A stove and an organ in the far front corner of the room became a social center. There was music and much singing. The Paulson girls (Norwegian) sang something called soprano and alto and Mr. Hammock, our teacher, sang something lower. I liked this alto stuff, and tried hard to achieve it. It turned out to be soprano on a lower level. I couldn't figure out the complexity; seems that it had something to do with "notes." I did much better with spelling and ciphering matches at the blackboard.

Just across the road from the schools was a dike which kept the river in bounds. The stern wheeler named "The Skagit Queen" plied the waters of the Skagit. At times of high tides and high water the stern wheel with its threshing water and the bulk of the boat seemed verily to ride level with the top of the dike.

We had a wonderful playground on the other side of the dike for hide-and-seek and run-sheep-run. Trees, bushes, ferns, wild flowers, birds, especially bluebirds, squirrels, chipmunks, etc. etc. constituted a perfect field laboratory, had the teacher been prepared and had science teaching been in vogue. Right near the school was the Skagit City Ferry run on a cable by Mr. Larson from Skagit Island. Skagit City consisted of Gage's General Merchandise Store, the Methodist Church and parsonage. At noon when any of us were flush with money, a penny or two, we would take the ferry across the river to Gage's store. Here big investments were made in candy hearts, licorice whips, and jawbreakers.

To get to the school was a frightening experience. I never liked the distance between our place and Lillquists' and Semells'. I was alone and the road was narrow and muddy, squeezed in between tall, dark, towering trees. With relief I joined the neighboring children, Hulda and Hjalmar Lillquist, Hilda and Ted Semell. From their place to the river we walked through a more open stretch of terrain to the river and another good mile southward along the top of the dike to the school.

That a child should fear walking alone on a lonely road through the forest would not be uncommon, but what is remarkable is that Leona's sister Esther writes about her fear of that same stretch of road no more than an eighth of a mile, and a generation later, I experienced the same. I can only wonder what happened in the past on Cedardale Road or at an earlier time on the Skid Road. Something alarming must have occurred there that caused this disturbing memory to remain embedded in the land.

The Finland Swede immigrants, raised under the teachings of the state Lutheran Church in Finland, recognized the need for religious instruction for their children. Immigrants from Sweden had established a Swedish Baptist mission in the community, and the children from our road sometimes attended Sunday School at the Methodist church across the river in Skagit City, but Finland Swede parents were adamant about their children being brought up in the Lutheran faith and decided to organize a Lutheran religious group.

At first, church services and youth Sunday School were held in the adjoining neighbor John Holmquist's home with Holmquist as Sunday School teacher, and later, Henry Sunnell taught Sunday School at Leander Palm's place as they had an organ. Church services were held twice a month. The Reverend Anderson from the Pleasant Ridge Lutheran Church was the pastor. After his morning service, he would drive from Pleasant Ridge in horse and rig for an afternoon service in one of our homes. Hot coffee and some food awaited his arrival. This simple service was quite a contrast to those I had experienced in the old country, with altar, pews, organ music and high mass services.

Sy-förening Ladies Aid Society associated with the religious organization was organized in 1906 and met once a month. The "Martha" group was devoted to crafts, sewing, needlework, and conversation that carried on through the afternoon's visit over the clicking of knitting needles with a brief respite for drinking coffee and enjoying cardamom coffeebread and cookies. The society served a very important function in the lives of the womenfolk, whose daily routines were restricted to place and demands.

On 13 November 1907, The Swedish-Finnish Evangelical Bethesda Congregation was inaugurated in Cedardale with the assistance of Pastors G. A. Anderson of the Swedish Evangelical Lutheran Bethsaida Church and N. J. W. Nelson of Pleasant Ridge near LaConner. The Bethsaida Church located at Pleasant Ridge was the first Lutheran congregation organized in 1881. The pastors came once a month to preach a sermon in Swedish and baptize babies. *Sionsbladet* newspaper March 1909 reported the Cedardale congregation numbered twenty-four communicants. Deacons: Gust Jackson, John Holmquist and Henry Sunnell; church wardens: J. E. Bergstrom, John Sundquist, and Leander Palm. Sunday school superintendent was John Holmquist; earlier superintendents included Henry Sunnell and Oscar Mattson.

As more Finland Swede emigrants arrived in Cedardale, they began to make plans for a community meeting place. Isak Bergstrom, Leander Palm, and John Sundquist were elected as building committee. It was agreed upon that a building could be constructed on a plot of ground belonging to Mr. Ole N. Lee and his wife Anna Egtvedt on Stackpole Road east of the highway. However, it was stipulated by the Lees that there would be no social dancing. The Lees, of Norwegian heritage, were members of *Den Evangeliske Lutherske Menighed* of Skagit, a member of the Old Synod located at Fir.

Leona recalls that the Cedardale Community Hall served not only as a place for religious services but also as a social center. As the young people grew in number, there was a demand for a center for social dancing. Another hall was built just north of the Brittons' home.

There were programs at holiday times, basket socials
to raise money for some project or need, folk- and square

dancing. Social dancing was prohibited by the Lees; however, we had a wonderful time dancing *"Gustav Skål,"* 'Tra, la, la, så gore vi så,' 'Skip to my Loo my darling,' among others. Music was mainly provided by someone playing the accordian or violin.

The women raised money to buy lumber for the building by holding bake sales, selling fancy work and aprons, and basket socials. By June 1909 the members completed the hall. Cost of materials was $330.33 and all the work was donated. John Sundquist and Victor Lillquist were knowledgeable carpenters who helped plan and managed the work. The hall was heated with a wood stove, and the kitchen had a wood range. The men made the tables and benches; the ladies curtained and decorated the inside with the best of their artistic ability. A wood altar faced with five handcarved spiraling columns was inscribed with the words: *Jesus Wår Frälsare* Jesus Our Saviour. A pump organ added to the spirit of a hall of worship.

In 1913, the settlers in Cedardale along with the Lutherans from Pleasant Ridge near La Conner agreed that they would unite with a new Lutheran church in Mt. Vernon and the Augustana Lutheran Synod. Seventeen confirmed members of the Cedardale church became charter members of the Swedish Salem Lutheran Church: Mr. and Mrs. Leander Palm, Roy Axel Palm, Mr. and Mrs. Oscar Mattson, Mr. and Mrs. John L. Sundquist, Mr. and Mrs. Gustaf Jackson, Mr. and Mrs. Henry E. Sunell, John Sunell, Helga Sunell, Mr. and Ms. William Westlund, Mr. and Mrs. Mattias Holmstrom.

The Cedardale hall continued to serve the Finland Swede community for several years. Leona recalls community activities:

As the land was cleared, fields grew larger, and a larger barn was needed. Tall straight trees were selected, cut, and fashioned into the main upright columns, cross beams and other supporting structures. These were piled in appropriate groups so as to hasten the work of the day when the neighbors gathered for the barn-raising bee. Such activity! They were well organized. Everyone seemed to know just what he had to do, so before nightfall the main structural skeleton had taken shape. The one frightening moment for me was to see Father walking the ridgepole securing the hay track to the beam.

Community-organized labor was characteristic, not only in barn raising, but also at harvest time. Mr. Gildersleeve had a threshing machine run by a wood-burning steam donkey and a long, swaying belt connecting the two. Neighboring farmers would come with wagons and pitchforks, and neighbor ladies helped Ida Maria prepare the meals for the threshing crew. Each family would try to outdo the other in the quality of meals served.

Most of the work on the farms in the community was done by exchanging labor, use of horses and equipment. Father kept careful records of these transactions. I recall a tradition developed that the annual summation of these records took place during the Christmas holidays. The neighbors would meet at our house for this annual business meeting. Money was rarely, if ever, exchanged. Notations were made as to how many hours of work one person owed another.

I recall especially the early morning breakfasts; the wagons arriving through the thick fog; the men, cold and chilly, coming into the warm, smelly kitchen and on into the dining room; the steaming bowls of oatmeal; the platters of bacon, eggs and sausage; milk, cream, and coffee, coffee, coffee. I would just as soon forget the eternal dish washing and scouring of kettles and pans.

The women, too, were busy. In the yard, long tables were loaded with steaming dishes of food, pitchers of milk and coffee, coffee, coffee. There were choices of pies--apple, cherry, and mincemeat --and rice custard pudding. Then Father passed cigars. Father never smoked, but whenever we had company for dinner and after every Sunday dinner, company or not, he would fetch his box of cigars.

Skagit County was divided into five Rural Free Delivery areas. Letters, packages, and magazines addressed to the Sundquist family R.F.D. #5, Mt. Vernon, were delivered by a horse-drawn mail wagon to the large mailbox installed on a cedar post alongside the milkstand on Cedardale Road. No longer would they have to go by ferry to the post office at Gage's Mercantile Store across the Skagit River in Skagit City.

In 1909, John increased the size of the farm to include land that he had been leasing for grazing. He purchased a parcel of twelve acres "commencing at the northeast corner of Section 6 on the east side of the Seattle & Montana Railway for $2400 gold coin of the United States paid in hand to H. I. Leake." Each morning after milking, Leona would drive the small herd of cows down the road and over the tracks to the pasture, before she left for school. Much of the land was standing water, swampy, and a natural habitat for water birds, mallard ducks, trumpeter swans and other birds resting on the migratory flyway. There were countless flocks of swans and white snowgeese which literally covered the skies in those early days. Hawks, eagles, and owls, even the huge snowy owl. Long-legged herons stalked their hesitant way through the marshes, along the sloughs and in wet cut-over land.

The farm was at the edge of the Skagit delta, so ditches were dug to drain water from the fields—along the road, in the fields, next to the railroad. As time went on, a drainage district was organized, and the men with shovels, horses and scrapers dug huge ditches to carry the water to the river outlet near Conway. Since the land was near sea level, there was poor drainage, so pumps had to be installed at the outlet to pump the water out into the Sound.

Leona recalls the discussion she heard among the neighbors about getting a water pump:

> "Well," Father said, "Nothing doing; we're not using gasoline to run the pump. We're going to get electricity out here. An electric pump." And of course, somebody interjected, "but there's no electricity around here." And Father replied, "Well, let's just induce somebody to get the electricity down here, you know—money making proposition." The electric company was interested, but Father said, "On one condition, and that is, that we get electricity to our farms. If you don't do that, we'll get a gasoline pump." And that's how electricity came to south of Mt. Vernon. And Father became a Dike District Commissioner.

Floods were a continuing threat even after the formation of Districts to maintain ditches and dikes. The South Fork of the Skagit tended to overflow its banks and inundate the countryside, so the opening into the North Fork was enlarged to relieve flood conditions. When Mr. Hammock was forced to move from his place at the junction of the two forks of the river, he invited Sundquists and others to his place to dig and salvage sacks full of Daffodil bulbs that would ultimately be inundated.

The emigrant settlers continued their battle to harness Nature. In the late fall, when Chinook winds blew following an early snowfall, the warm air was the forbearer of impending danger. One could feel it in the air. The fresh snowpack in the North Cascade Mountains quickly melted and the Skagit River flowed at flood stage, that eerie heaving and fast-moving glacial green water creeping higher on the dikes far from the river's natural bank. And again in the spring, there might be a rapid spring thaw. Leona recalls the trek one night up the road to the river with food and coffee for the men sandbagging the dikes. The floods remained imprinted in her mind:

> The rush and roar of the swirling water was frightening. One time a team of horses pulling a scraper disappeared in the water-soaked dike. The men were saved. In spite of their efforts, the river would often have its own way and burst through the dike, covering the farmlands far and wide. Then there was a rush to collect the cattle, get them into barns or to higher ground, which meant herding them a half mile to upper Cedardale Road near the hill. When the larger barn was built, Father had the flooring constructed so that it would rise and fall with the water.
>
> During one flood, Father stretched a rope from the kitchen porch to the barn. Then Mother and Father, with milk pails and lantern in hand, disappeared on a raft into the night. Hand over hand on the rope John pulled the raft through the swirling water to the barn. I was left in charge of the children and the house. We seemed very alone!

While her father often admonished his family when they gathered around the kitchen table, "Everyone is talking but no one is listening," an incident that surely commanded everyone's attention for many evenings was Leona's encounter while fetching the cows for milking time and the eventual outcome:

> One evening, as I was coming home with the cows on Highway 99, the cows flushed a strange man out of the ditch. He covered his face with his arm and walked hastily away. I was frightened and took refuge behind my cows until he had gotten some distance away. Then I had to get some order with my cows. After that episode I never went alone with the cows.

October 26, 1908, *The Skagit News Herald* front-page emblazoned in bold headlines followed by a lengthy detailed story: ENGLISH IS KIDNAPPED! Lone Highwayman Stops Him While On His Way Home this Evening. $5,000.00 IS DEMANDED. Details Are Arranged Beforehand By Party Who Evidently Kept Informed Of His Movements.

> "This evening word was telephoned in from Cedardale of the narrow escape of E. G. English from a lone kidnapper. This (Monday) evening as he was coming from his logging camp at Conway, Mr. English was accosted below the Cedardale road, and made to drive to a lonesome place near Little Mountain, and write a note to his wife for a ransom for his release, prior to being tied up in a hollow stump: "Dear Wife—I am kidnapped for $5,000.00 (Five Thousand Dollars). Don't attempt to resist, as I am threatened with having my ears cut off if it is not forthcoming by tomorrow noon. For God's sake make all haste. Show this to Mr. Hannay and solicit his aid. "E. G. ENGLISH."

A note attached by the highwayman further asked for direct obedience:

"And now by the blackest curse that human anatomy can endure, we faithfully promise to "express" our captive's ears to his nearest relatives if the ransom is not forthcoming by tomorrow noon, 12:00 at first (railroad) tressle. XXXO"

The bold kidnapper was finally captured November 16, 1908 in Seattle and brought to Mt. Vernon on the evening flyer. Nearly all the population was at the train station to get a glimpse. The *Skagit News Herald* headlines on February 8, 1909 reported BEZMER TRIAL Is Now the Leading Event of the Court Term. One hundred witnesses were summoned, including Leona Sundquist:

> To follow up this incident, some days later an officer of the law came to school to question me regarding this occurrence. It seems that later that evening, as was his custom, Mr. English, of the English Logging Company, who lived in Mt. Vernon, was coming home in his horse and rig from his Camp One, which was located in the hills south and east of Conway. He became the victim of a hold-up along this lonely stretch of road where I had been with my cows. I was the only person to vouch for the presence of a man at about that time of the evening in this particular part of the road. So I became a witness in this hold-up case. This became an interesting first-hand experience with the law, the court, the judge, the jury, the trial, the lawyers, cross-examination, etc.

February 22, 1909, *The Skagit News Herald* headline reported COUNTY ATTORNEY WINS HARD CASE. The list of witnesses reveals Leona Sundford, not Sundquist, so there must have been some degree of disappointment expressed by the family regarding the misspelling and the revelation that the news or names in the news may not always be accurate.

> The trial took a number of days, for which I got paid. What to do with all this money! Mother took charge of the matter. The bulk of it went for goods for a dress and shoes. The rest I could spend however I wished, provided it was

wisely spent. I asked my teacher for ideas as to a good book or books. She suggested *Little Women* by Louisa May Alcott, among other possibilities. So forthwith I went to town. Mr. William Bowers Ropes owned the bookstore in a little house at the foot of the Mt. Vernon viaduct. I bought *Little Women* which Mother and I just devoured. I read it again and again. For Father, I purchased Gray's *History of the Pacific Northwest*, and then to be sensible I bought a secondhand black-covered Webster's Dictionary for one dollar and ten cents.

The ditch along the road in front of the farmhouse was always full of water. There was a small bridge of three long cedar slabs across the ditch to reach the road. To reach the iron front gate, John's brother Henrik hauled a five-feet-wide Western Red Cedar plank from the sawmill up Cedardale way, that would span the ditch and contain a cartwheel, as daughter Esther recalled.

That plank was from a single old growth cedar, a goodly solid ten inches thick, thicker than I could grip in the span of my thumb and pinky and wide enough to lay crosswise and barely hang over head and feet. On the far side of the ditch, Father carved out a slot in the dry sand of the Skagit bottomland gauging the depth and breadth sufficient to hold that plank with as much care as cutting a tongue and groove for a fine piece of cherrywood chest of drawers. That plank—cut from a single old-growth cedar, a good solid, fragrant cedar, fresh cut, aromatic, warm scented in the sun—spanned the ditch, of sufficient length to contain my cartwheel.

An incident at the ditch foreshadowed an impending tragedy concerning water. Little Eva had just learned to walk and somehow she had managed to get through the iron front gate and had fallen into the ditch. Her brother Vincent, just four years older than Eva, saw her going through the gate, ran after her, jumped into the ditch, and saved her from certain death. He stood with water up to his shoulders, holding the young child and screaming for help, as he too was slipping lower and lower into the water. Ida Maria ran to rescue her young children. Vincent had saved his sister's life.

While ditches were dug and dredged for practical use, they became a source of pleasure and play as well as Nature's classroom. The delicate tufts on pussywillow branches along its banks and the appearance of salmonberry shoots were the harbingers of spring. When the new growth was about a foot high, I would hunker down beside the ditch to peel and eat the crisp, delicious salmonberry shoots.

Ditches have an ecology of their own. A ditch becomes a natural laboratory for the study of plants, animals, tadpoles and frogs, creepy living things, bees, insects, and awesome damselflies and dragonflies. As a young child, I too, laid across those cedar planks that spanned the ditch at the entry to the farmyard and scooped tadpoles into a bucket of water. In the summer, the bank that abuts the hay field was beautifully arrayed in clusters of tall grasses, salmonberry stalks and pink wild roses. The rich green broad leaves of wild raspberry bushes nearly concealed the split wood posts and barbed wire fencing. Monarch butterflies settled quietly on milkweed as white moths flitted about. Bristly sandrushes lined the roadside edge of the ditch punctuated by enormous molehills of rich dark brown earth. Frog songs became an evening lullaby.

Milking time: Ida, Vivian, Leona and Daniel Sundquist (ca. 1920)

Milkstand and cart

Binding oats and coffeetime in the field

Ida Elvira driving Case tractor; Daniel on the plow

At the Skagit County Fair

Ida Maria driving 1917 Model T Ford

Chapter *14*

The American Dream Fulfilled 1920s

The farm had increased in size since Ida Maria, John and three children moved into the original farmhouse in 1904 in time for the birth of Eva. The herd expanded and so did the outbuildings as another barn was built to shelter the animals and hold straw in the loft from the oat harvest, straw that would be spread in the barnyard where the cows gathered before milking. The tall silo was constructed with clear Douglas fir 2 x 6 boards, forty feet in length. The chamfered tongue and groove boards were slightly beveled when milled, so that the boards were tightly fitted. Investments were made in a Case tractor and improved agricultural machinery, which reduced man-hours of labor. The local poultry industry was rapidly developing, and Ida Maria's increasing flock was now being hatched in incubators and housed in a modern and enlarged chicken house. The increased egg production rapidly added to the family income.

The family also increased in size: Daniel was born 1906, Alice 1910, Esther 1912, and Vivian 1916. Viola and Violet, born 1914, died in infancy. Within the span of twenty years of marriage, Ida Marie had birthed thirteen children. The expanded family strained the existing farmhouse and thoughts turned to planning an addition to the original building. The house in rural America was the ultimate signal of success and prosperity, and it appears that nothing was spared in transforming the original farmhouse into one of the finest structures in the Skagit Valley with the addition of a two-story extension to the original two-story dwelling.

Farmhouses in an agrarian society were burgeoning throughout America, and there was no isolation from the mainstream of architectural ideas in the rest of the country. During the late 19th century, agricultural societies offered prizes for farmhouse designs; winning plans were displayed at county fairs and published in farm journals.

Both men and women sketched practical plans for houses and barns. Since Ida Maria had always participated in the direction of the family, it would be no surprise to find the two of them sketching simple practical plans for the farmhouse, perhaps too the barns and outbuildings that John had added to the farm. By 1918 when the farmhouse addition was completed, the family included seven children.

Who could interpret the family's needs better than the homemaker? The architect, perhaps, but women have always played a role in the design of a home. Some architectural historians posit that the most livable homes, including the American farmhouse, were designed by forgotten women of the 19th and early 20th centuries. Designed for efficiency and flexibility to accommodate large families, the most noteworthy feature in the early American farmhouse was the dominant large kitchen which in today's definition would be a combination kitchen/ family room—a room that not only accommodated meal preparation and dining, but with adequate space for feeding large threshing and haying crews, for preserving fruits and vegetables, for tending a baby's crib, churning butter, conducting farm business and studying by kerosene lamp around that same kitchen table. Who but a woman would be mindful of designing a home with a first-floor bedroom, whose initial purpose was the birthing room? There might be separate quarters for farm hands and porches—a front entry porch, a cool porch on the east side, summer kitchen on the back porch.

John's workmanship was superior and his building expertise had been greatly enhanced during the time he worked as a carpenter building fine homes in the rapidly growing community of Ballard, the Queen Anne Hill neighborhood, and on Boren Avenue in Seattle with Abraham Löfquist. Illustrated architectural brochures appeared that year such as *Seattle Architecturally*, Seattle, 1902; individual publications by practitioners and plan books including the E. Ellsworth Green Practical Plan Book, Seattle, 1912; and Voorhees' *Western Home Builder*, Seattle, 1911. At the turn of the century there were more carpenters than any other trade in the Seattle area. John had been building two-story houses in Ballard and in Seattle before they moved to Skagit County so he looked forward to the grandeur of his own dwelling, which would also bear witness to their success in America. Architecture is often a distinctive defining legacy and myriad architectural features speak clearly of lifestyle.

The original Sundquist structure began as a simple unembellished two-story structure reminiscent of the simplicity of a two-story Finnish farmhouse, but during their time in America, Ida Maria had seen the stately homes in Duluth, where she first arrived in America to work as a maid. In Seattle, neighborhoods were developing with their particular style of architecture, and in Skagit Valley other successful immigrant farmers were building large dwellings nearby. Ida Maria gleaned her ideas no doubt from accumulative learning and keen awareness of her surroundings wherever she lived.

The emphasis of their multi-gabled farmhouse design was on pattern and line, a stately home with design integrity, solidly constructed sans ornamentation or embellishments such as brackets under the eaves or spindlework seen in the late 19th century Victoria architecture. Architectural detail included wide front and side gables, creating triangular forms on the sloping roofline, bay windows upstairs and down beneath the side gables, and quintessentially American porches. The spacious formal front entry porch, as wide as the house, took on a classic appearance with four substantial square porch columns that supported a balcony above, complemented by white-painted railing and balusters. A side porch became an extension of the farmhouse kitchen activities, a shaded respite on a warm afternoon, and a retreat after supper to sit on the porch and enjoy a delightful summer evening. Because of the Nordic immigrants' innate sense of working with wood, that was the favored material. The roofing material was cedar shingles, and the exterior clad with cedar beveled siding painted white. Every corner of the structure, the cedar siding is joined together by mitering, which adds to its elegant simplicity. It would have been cost effective to have corner boards rather than mitered corners, but with this level of skilled workmanship, the structure exudes a craftsman elegance, purposely not ornamental.

Indeed, the workmanship and design were exquisite. John did all the carpentry; the function and practical details of the interior design of the dwelling clearly had Ida Maria's signature: A glass-enclosed dish cupboard separated the kitchen pantry from the dining room. The spacious cupboard was convenient from the kitchen through a hands-free swinging door and to setting the dining table. On display through leaded glass doors were Ida Elvira's handpainted porcelain trays and dinner plates she designated for each person in the family. In the spacious kitchen pantry were large pullout storage bins for sacks of flour, ceiling-high cupboards for storing canned fruits and vegetables, and a preparation counter. Features were included that John and Ida had seen in Seattle's stately residences, such as wainscoting with cap molding. Two square stained wood columns acted as a visual divider between the grand entry foyer and parlor, the public room where guests were entertained. Visible from the parlor were beautiful turned-wood balusters, and the polished sculpted railing highlighted the staircase that ascended to the first landing and curved gracefully upward to the second level. In the parlor, a formal settee with carved wood frame and side chairs were upholstered in the same plush checkered cutout velvet. An exquisite kerosene table lamp sat on the table in front of the curtained window, its light illuminated the handpainted floral pattern on the soft green glass globes. A massive wood-paneled sliding door retreated into the wall and closed off the parlor when it was not being used.

The original structure built in 1904 in turn became the spacious farmhouse kitchen with an attached sewing room and a washroom and access to the upstairs via the back stairway. The new structure included a spacious dining room finished with five-feet-high vertical dark stained wood-paneled wainscoting with cap molding. The ten and a half feet high stained wood ceiling was finished with molding. A grate in the ceiling allowed heat to rise from the first floor wood-burning tile furnace into the upstairs bedrooms. Upstairs, one long vestibule accommodated Ida Maria's floor loom and a wire strung lengthwise held clothing and dresses. There were three large bedrooms and the smaller bedroom in the original structure and bathroom with toilet, porcelain washbowl and clawfoot tub installed February 1918. Daniel's large bedroom at the south end of the second floor included extra beds for farmhands or visitors. Daniel was twelve years old when he inscribed his name on one of the rafters in the new construction. The girls enjoyed one bedroom for dressing and clothes storage. However, the small closet would not be considered sufficient for a family of girls so the shelves in the cedar-lined closet in the parents' bedroom held undergarments and such. There, they could dress in the warmth radiating from the brick chimney that rose upward through the closet. A screened sleeping porch as wide as the house accommodated several beds where Ida Maria and the children slept every night. They slept there even throughout the winters, as Ida Maria held to the concept that fresh air and lots of it was important to one's health. "My mother would be called a health nut today," remarked her daughter Esther.

To Esther, it seemed like there was always someone staying at the farmhouse. Ida Maria welcomed family and friends: Uncles Vikstrom and Henrik Sundquist from Finland, two women friends visiting from India, Bertha Sunnell, a cousin and school teacher who couldn't reach home during a flood. Their news and stories added to the eclectic mix of subjects discussed around the dining room table.

One night almost ended in double disasters when someone yelled that the barn was on fire on the adjacent Holmquist farm. Uncle Henrik raced down the back stairs, not remembering that there was a fence temporarily constructed at the bottom to discourage baby Vivian from crawling up the stairs. He hurdled over the obstacle and fell to the floor.

An amusing story concerns the golden oak cabinet that held a pull-down bed. One evening when Mr. Holmquist visited the Sundquists from his home some distance to the north, he was invited to spend the night and crawled into the pull-down bed upstairs. It so happened that Ida Elvira came home from the university late that night and not wishing to wake anyone, she crept quietly upstairs and silently crawled into the same bed—she thought with her sister. But to her utter dismay, when she awoke the next morning, she bolted out of bed when she discovered the person sleeping next to her was not her blonde sister, but the silver-bearded Mr. Holmquist. The story still elicited laughter to tears when it was related by her sister decades later.

Appointments belonging to place give clues to the owners' aesthetic taste, economic situation and values and hold memories within their physical form—memories and stories that bind the present with the past and for future generations to ponder. While the Sundquists may have determined the unique form or style of their house according to regional dictates of the time coupled with John's previous home building experience, its unique style is an amalgamation of influences, Finnish culture, and the American experience.

Architecture set the stage; it embodied the events in itself, and it was where the news of the day was discussed—events that occurred at home or at some distance when the family scattered. Esther recalled the evenings the family gathered in the dining room:

> The huge sliding door is closed, the hall door shut and everything is cozy. We listen to Amos and Andy, and then the evening goes on in conversation and story telling. There are naturally exceptions to some evenings when daughter is out on a "date," brother "stepping out," the whole family out for the evening, dad away at a school board meeting, etc. But as a rule the evenings are spent in quiet manner.
>
> The children's stories comprise endless sessions of what has occurred during the while they have been away at school. Often times dishes go undone and fires untended while with elbows on the dinner table the family sits (and as dad puts it) "everyone talks and nobody listens."

No sooner had the farmhouse undergone its grand transition, when the Influenza Pandemic of 1918 reached Skagit Valley, and the family was beset with illness and tragedy. The "Spanish Flu" or "La Grippe" raged across the world and took an estimated forty million lives. In Telluride, John's sister Maria Sofia Sundquist Hästö died from the flu. John became ill, then the hired farmhand John who also lived at the farmhouse. Ida Maria hired another hand and an older neighbor boy. One of the upstairs bedrooms took on another role and was designated the "Pest Room," the name pest in Swedish and English meaning pestilence or contagious infectious disease, where the sick would be confined so as not to infect others. Daughter Esther recalled:

> Mother cut up an old sheet, and we all had to wear a triangle over our mouths. Our father did not get well fast and so toward spring, I accompanied him on the train to Soap Lake. I wore a new plush red coat, the only purchased coat I had. I had a tiny bed in his room. Dad had mud baths and had to drink lots of water. When we returned home, the hired man had also recovered.

Leona Sundquist, the eldest daughter, successfully passed eighth grade examinations and was eligible to attend Mt. Vernon Union High School, a few blocks east of the viaduct in Mt. Vernon:

> No one of our nationality and status in life had ever attended high school or was expected to do so. But after all, Mother had insisted on our returning to America where there were educational opportunities, so I was to attend high school. The neighborhood shook its collective head in misgivings. "What are those Sundquists thinking of, sending their daughter to high school! She'll come to no good end. High toned ideas!" I worked hard to be successful, as I knew that to attend high school was a special privilege. Also, I must not disappoint my parents, and I must not allow the neighborhood to say, "I told you so."
>
> I had my chores to do each morning and evening, milking cows, feeding calves and chickens and collecting eggs. I usually walked to school on the railroad track. I rode my bicycle whenever the path at the side of the railroad track was not too muddy. The highway was too muddy to negotiate under any circumstances. The time spent in walking was used to study Latin and, later, German vocabularies. Time had to be used effectively, as I didn't have much time at home for study, and besides, I was too tired by nightfall. I used to get up early to study an hour or so before milking time.
>
> In the summer between my sophomore and junior years, courses in domestic science for girls and manual training for boys were to be introduced for the juniors. This was announced and elaborately discussed in the local newspaper. Mother announced one day, "Leoni, I tink yoo beter täk dis Mystic Science, it mey kum in hendy som dey." So I took "domestic science." But my course had already been determined when I entered high school, and that was the sciences.

Leona Sundquist was the first to fulfill her mother's dream of education for all her children. She graduated with honors from Mt. Vernon High School in 1914 at the top of her class. With great pride and satisfaction, Ida Maria and John Sundquist attended their daughter's graduation ceremony. A quote in *The Skagina*, the 6th annual classbook publication of Mt. Vernon High School, describes Leona: "She points upward to the clear Sunny heights of her own atmosphere."

My parents were so proud. I had succeeded; the world was mine. After high school graduation, I had hoped that I would attend the University of Washington. Roy Palm was going. Ann Gerriets and Jane Good were going. Father, from time to time, had expressed interest in the University. During the AYP (Alaska, Yukon Pacific Exposition, 1909) that was located on the University grounds, Father had explored the University buildings and environment. Mother was expecting something more practical in the educational process. So suddenly one day she announced that she was going to Bellingham to visit the Wilson's Business College, whose brochures had flooded the mailbox, to see if it would be appropriate for me to go there and learn something of a more practical character and where I might begin to earn an income sooner. So off she went and all alone, an unheard of event. Wilson's Business College was located in the "Old Town" section of Bellingham. It was near the railroad depot and the various industries located at the waterfront. And besides, there were nearby saloons and other unsavory-appearing structures. She concluded this was no place for her daughter. And so it transpired that I went to the University.

In the late summer of 1914, Father took me to Seattle to enroll me at the University. I well remember the moment we got off the streetcar at 14th and 40th Streets and entered the main entrance to the University. We paused at the statue of Washington. We read the descriptive materials and then found our way to the administration offices. Father arranged for my matriculation and payment for a room at Clark Hall, the women's dormitory.

Indeed, Leona and cousin Helga, the oldest children in the Sundquist and Sunnell families, set the pace as their younger sisters followed the path they had cut to higher education. Helga Sunnell was the first student from adjoining Cedardale School District to graduate from high school in 1917.

That year President Woodrow Wilson and the United States Congress declared war against Germany 6 April 1917. The United States originally pursued a policy of isolationism and had only a small army, but it drafted four million men to fight in this "War to End All Wars." By summer 1918, 10,000 fresh soldiers were sent to France every day. The United States Federal Government required "civilian" registration for the draft of all men born between 1872 and 1900. Daniel, born 1906, was not old enough to register; John again avoided military service as he was born in 1870. Aliens were also required to register, as did John's brother Henrik Sundquist from Finland, who was living intermittently at the Sundquist farmhouse; however, he was not drafted.

Leona was the first in her family to graduate from the University of Washington. She graduated in 1918 with a major in German. However, World War I was still raging, and high schools were eliminating German language from their curricula as "un-American." Because of the nationalistic fervor accompanying the United States' involvement in the war, people speaking a foreign language that sounded like German were suspect. The physics and geology courses that were university elective courses gave Leona the edge in securing a teaching position at the high school in Nooksack, Washington where she also taught botany for three years. During the summers, she attended the Puget Sound Biological Station at Friday Harbor, Washington, accumulating a rich background of field and laboratory experiences in the biological sciences that prompted her decision to return to the University to get her Master's Degree in physiological botany.

Leona described a scene at home on the farm:

> The youngest daughter Vivian had joined the Girl Scouts, a youth organization for girls in the United States, and she had on this lovely outfit. She was a handsome kid with her gorgeous hair and very intense dark blue eyes. She came walking down the back stairs and said, "Mama, how do I look?" And her mother replied, 'A gypsie!' Her father quickly retorted, 'Putti Gubbe will out. He not only lives by us but left some

genes around, sprinkled here and there.' Oh, I will never forget that. My father was quite a tease.

The name Putti Gubbe had again surfaced, recalling a conversation on the visit to Finland in 1901. The old man from Puutio was not only a horse trader, but a trader who went as far as southern Europe and traveled up into Finland with spices and then back with furs. If people didn't have the cash to pay for spices, he moved in with the family for room and board until the charges were paid. At times, when Putti Gubbe came to Kronoby, he stayed at the ancestral home Lillbroända in Finland, albeit several generations predating Ida.

Anytime an irregularity appeared in the family, John would tease Ida Maria that it was because of her genetic background. On this occasion, it was the beautiful Vivian with her intense blue eyes and olive skin as had occurred in other generations of Ida Maria's family. Ida Maria also had a swarthy skin complexion. Was this unusual characteristic in a *finlandssvensk* family derived from Putti Gubbe's prolonged visits to Lillbroända generations ago, as John would teasingly imply? A variation in skin color might bring to mind the story of Putti Gubbe, but certainly variations would be possible from a heritage that has a sizeable number of Finnish, not to say possibly Sami ancestry, which may have conveniently been ignored. And centuries ago during the great Nordic War, Finland was occupied by Russian Cossacks for ten years 1711–1721, which may have contributed to the "different complexion."

Within the glass doors of the golden oak Craftsman-style bookcase that Daniel handcrafted were some of the books read by the Sundquist family in America in the early 1900s. At first books were few and mostly in Swedish, but as children went to school, literary books in English made their appearance. Most of the books are now in author Arlene Sundquist's library:

Selections from The Poetical Works of Robert Browning –
  Second Series. Boston: Joseph Knight Company 1894.
Young's *Book of Secrets*, a portion thereof.
Augsburg's Drawing – Book II. A Text Book of Drawing
  Designed for Use in the Fourth, Fifth, Sixth, Seventh and

Eighth Grades by D.R. Augsburg. Educational Publishing
Company 1901

SöndagsSkolbok. Liturgi och Sånger for Söndagsskolan. Rock
Island, Ill. Augustana Book Concern. 1903. (Inscribed
Sundquist)

Finlands Historia, by M.G. Schybergson, Vols. 1 and 2, 1903,
Helsingfors.

The Poems of Rudyard Kipling. By Henry Ketcham. A. L. Burt
Company, Publishers, 1900. Inscribed Leona Sundquist

The Light That Failed by Rudyard Kipling. New York:
Doubleday, Page & Company. 1908. Inscribed Leona
Sundquist

Departmental Ditties, Barrack-Room Ballads, and Other Verses
by Rudyard Kipling. New York: Hurst & Company

The Dramatic Works of Friedrich Schiller. Wallenstein
and Wilhelm Tell. London: G. Bell and Sons, Ltd. 1914
Inscribed Leona Sundquist U. of W.

Ben Hur: A Tale of the Christ. By Lew Wallace. New York:
Harper & Brothers Publishers.1908.

Poor People by Fiodor Dostoyevsky. New York: Boni Liveright,
Inc. 1917

War – What For? by George R. Kirkpatrick. 1913

Sadhana: The Realisation of Life by Rabindranath Tagore. New
York: The MacMillan Company 1915. Inscribed Leona
Sundquist

The Holy Bible inscribed to Ida Elvira Sundquist, 1917.

Representative Short Stories Collected by Nina Hart, A.M.
(Columbia) and Edna M. Perry, A.M. (Columbia. New
York: The Macmillan Company 1920. Inscribed Daniel
Sundquist

Girl Neighbors; or, the Old Fashion and the New by Sarah
Tytler. Inscribed Leona Sundquist

Poetical Works of Thomas Moore. Edited by A. D. Godley.
New York: Oxford University Press 1910 Inscribed Leona
Sundquist

Poems of Edgar Allan Poe. New York: Thomas Y Crowell
Company. 1902. Inscribed Leona Sundquist

Poems of James Russell Lowell. New York: Thomas Y Crowell &
Co. 1892,1898. Inscribed Leona Sundquist June 9, 1914.

*Tennyson: Idylls of the King: Selections: Gareth and Lynette,
Lancelot and Elaine, and The Passing of Arthur.* Edited by
Willis Boughton, Ph.D. Boston: The Athenaeum Press:
Ginn & Company 1903. Inscribed by Leona Sundquist,
Member of Class of '14, Mt. V.H.S. The 1903 Preface
notes: "The three idylls included in this volume are those
selected as a substitute for *The Princess* for the College
Entrance Examinations of 1906 and thereafter."

The Princess: A Dream of Fair Women And Other Poems by
Alfred Tennyson. New York: Hurst & Company. Inscribed
Leona Sundquist, Sixth Grade (ca. 1908). Meadow School.
Compliments of Mrs. V. C. Blackburn.

The Vicar of Wakefield by Oliver Goldsmith. New York: The
Macmillan Company. 1913. Inscribed Leona Sundquist
April 1914.

The Iliad of Homer translated by Alexander Pope. New
York. The MacMillan Company 1911. Inscribed Leonia
Sundquist 1914.

Shakespeare's *Julius Caesar* Edited by William Allan Neilson,
Ph.D. Chicago: Scott, Foreman and Company. 1901.
Inscribed Sold to Daniel Sundquist 1924.

The Purgatorio of Dante Alighieri. Translated by Thomas Okey.
New York: E.P. Dutton & Co. Inscribed Leona Sundquist
University of Washington.

*Carlyle's Essay on Burns with The Cotter's Saturday Night and
Other Poems from Burns.* Edited by Willard C. Gore.
New York: The MacMillan Company. 1918 Inscribed Ida
Sundquist

History of English Literature. By Rueben Post Halleck, M.A.
New York: American Book Company. 1900. Inscribed
Leona Sundquist, Senior Class of 1914 and Ida Sundquist

Treasure Island by Robert Louis Stevenson. New York: The
Macmillan Company. 1917.

"Father would sit for hours reading," Leona wrote. *Ny och Fullständig Förenta Staternas Historia* (New and Complete United States History) is now a tattered 800-page book. Written in Swedish, the book informed Ida Maria and John of everything they needed to know in America. In addition to United States history (42 states) and important persons, there were phrases, slang, how to write a letter, dealing with United States money, farming, typical American foods, and more. Decrepit and worn with some pages lost forever, the book's condition attests to his attention and perhaps some mishandling of generations hence.

Svensk-Amerikansk Uppslagsbok Swedish-American Reference Book by Fred Lonnkvist, published by John C. Winston & Co. 1889. A well-worn 800 pages used to advantage. Its contents indicate the practical aspects of this reference book for an uneducated immigrant. A third of the book is Swedish-English dictionary with keys to pronunciation. Its topics cover everything one needs to know relative to social and business, home medical care, handbook for farmers, songs and literature, writing, and cooking. And a well-worn publication of historical biblical events: *Den Sköna historien: Gyllne perlor af religiösa tankar.*

Another well-used tome entitled *What To Do and How To Do It* published in English (ca. 1905). The Compiler writes in the Preface: "With the increase of public intelligence have come also many new and complicated conditions of life, demanding greater condensation of knowledge and practical intelligence of judgment. This work is intended to be an everyday hand-book of comprehensive, important and practical information, of public utility and of special service to the housewife and the farmer." From construction to kitchen to farming to health and a chapter on "Things Worth Remembering," every aspect of life was covered in the 500-page book.

Within schoolbooks, formerly blank pages are fully inscribed with doodles, drawings, and penciled poetry. Whether the poems are original or plagiarized is left to history. In any case, it appears that *Plane Geometry*, inscribed by Ida Sundquist and Eva Sundquist, was not exactly what the aspiring poets had in mind when they wrote the following:

In the shade of the old Geomtree
There is no sense in the leaves I can see
For the finals we had sent
me clear to the back
And D- was all I could see
You could hear the dull . .
   of the cheats
As they wiggled and squirmed
in their seats.
Now its all a haze
My mind is in a blaze
In the shade of the old
   Geom-e-tree.

Stevenson's Treasure Island passed through many hands as the inside cover pages were inscribed Eva Sundquist, Year of 1918; A.D.S bold lettering; Daniel Sundquist, Class of '24, Union High School Mt. Vernon, Washington; Vivian Sundquist. Opposite the title page, Daniel wrote:

Do not steal this book for fear of shame.
For in it lies the owners name.
When you die the Lord will say;
where is the book you stole away.
Then you'll say; I Don't Know,
Then he'll send you Down Below
   Signed A.D.S. ~

Daniel Sundquist graduated from high school in 1924. He inherited the woodworking talents of his father as well as his apprenticeship in the building of the new farmhouse addition in 1918. Daniel built oak furniture in the style of the well-known furniture designer Gustav Stickley. Stickley who achieved success in the early 1900s as the leader of the Arts & Crafts Movement in America created the first truly American furniture, known throughout the world as Craftsman.

Alice Sundquist graduated with honors as salutatorian of the class of 1927 Mt. Vernon Union High School. She was Girls Club President, and that year the first Mother-Daughter banquet was held 9 May 1927 to honor mothers. The Mt. Vernon newspaper reported:

> Alice Sundquist was presented with the Women of Rotary award, a handsome gold wristwatch, at the commencement exercises held in the high school auditorium. A faculty committee chooses a student to receive this gift basing the decision on scholarship, leadership, character, and general good influence among the students.

Leona had become a member of the faculty of the Washington State Normal School in Bellingham, Washington, and she was able to offer money to her sister to continue her education. Each daughter, as she graduated and became employed, helped the next. That's just the way it was with the first generation in America. Alice, too, went on to the Normal School in Bellingham and received her teaching certificate. After teaching, she received her B.A. and M.A. degrees in home economics education at Washington State University at Pullman.

Eva received a registered nurse's degree from California Lutheran Hospital School of Nursing in Los Angeles; Esther continued her education at the State Normal School in Bellingham, University of Washington, and trade school for cosmetology; Daniel went on to earn a degree at Automotive Technical School in Seattle, that would contribute to his future management of the Sundquist Farm.

Vivian, the youngest child born in 1916, pursued business education. Vivian was the one member of the family who became involved in business courses in high school and Skagit Valley Junior College that led to a position in the local office of the Federal Land Bank. Leona recalled that:

> Vivian became aware of the extensive loans that were made to farms that we had always considered so very affluent. Problems had overtaken many farms. There had been a tendency on the part of the early pioneers who homesteaded along the river and out on the Skagit Flats to grow oats year after year. The soil was fertile and the crops lush. Many of the

older farms in our vicinity were later taken over by tenant farmers who further exhausted the soil.

It would have been an interesting project to have kept data on this change in ecological succession of plant communities in response to changes in the physical and organic conditions of the soil and the associated economic return to the farmers which had ultimately led them to the Federal Land Bank for loans. This is one of many examples in our country of "go west young man": exploit the natural resources, leave behind a ravaged environment, and then finally the Federal government must be called upon for rescue.

In a letter written to her younger sister Esther at college, Leona muses about individual responsibility, and that "what one does or attempts to do which is not right conventionally or traditionally is all right if you're willing to face the consequences of society's criticism and if one only had just oneself to consider, but who is free to do that?"

I marvel at the good sense – common sense – Mother and Dad have used with us. Yes, they give us free rein and we can hang ourselves in it if we wish – if we are that selfish – or we can use that freedom to enjoy life sanely and with digressions, which will bring satisfaction to ourselves and bring happiness instead of sorrow upon the very parents who have allowed us freedom. Yes, let children use their heads, but not against stone walls. The longer I live and the more I see, the more I appreciate my mother and Dad and all folks at home. There are few like them in this old world of ours and we're mighty lucky.

Historian and writer James Truslow Adams coined the phrase "American Dream" in his book *Epic of America*:

"The American Dream is that dream of a land in which life should be better and richer and fuller for everyone, with opportunity for each according to ability."

For Ida Maria, her American Dream was fulfilled. The children had responded to parental efforts that they would be educated in the American society; her daughters were able to weave their way through the perceived and known barriers. With their academic achievements and accomplishments in music, drama, student government, choir, and sports, each of her six daughters and a son who attained adulthood made their mother proud and satisfied with her lifeway decision.

Imagine the excitement generated when the first motor car appeared on the farm, a 1917 Model T Ford touring car with a cloth roof and curtains, parked for protection under a shed roof. Then came a 1923 Model T Ford license number WN X23 64474 and a double garage also to accommodate the Ford. With this new mode of transportation, the family traveled to picnics by the Salish Sea and longer trips to Clearbrook near the Canadian border to see their former neighbors Holmquists who sold the adjoining farm to Sundquists and moved on.

Subsequently, another automobile drove into the farmyard: Leona's 1925 Model T Ford Coupe license WN X-25 that she purchased after joining the teaching staff at the Normal School in Bellingham, and then a new family vehicle, a four-door 1926 Buick automobile Washington license X26 56-733. Dressed in their finest costumes, the girls took turns photographing so everyone could be seen standing beside the shiny new black car. Considering there were Ida, John and seven children at home plus a family guest all posing inside or standing beside the car and sitting on the running board, the vehicle itself was barely visible in the photograph except for the dashing appointments: spoke wheels and a gleaming sculptural metal cap on the hood.

In August 1928, the Board of Regents of The University of Washington awarded Ida Elvera Sundquist a Life Diploma to teach her major subjects, General Science and Home Economics in the High Schools or to supervise or superintend Public Schools in the State for the period of her natural life. But it was not a year later, 26 May 1929, when "the period of her natural life" came abruptly to an end. Ida Elvera had almost finished her first year of teaching Home Economics at Vancouver High School in Vancouver, Washington; she and her finance made plans to marry in the summer, but it was not to be. Ten years earlier, it was the telephone that had serendipitously brought the news of John Vincent's drowning in the Skagit River when Ida Maria picked up the earpiece to place a call and heard someone on the party line say, "The Sundquist and Lillquist boys just drowned in the river." The horrific news of Ida Elvira's tragic death stunned the family when a telegram was delivered to the farmhouse early Monday morning, the day following her death.

While her grief-filled parents were informed by telegram only of the fact, the news media expounded on the gruesome details of their daughter's death. The front-page headline of Monday's *Mount Vernon Daily Herald* blared in inch-high bold letters:

DAUGHTER OF LOCAL FARMER KILLED IN AUTOMOBILE WRECK.

Ida Elvera was decapitated Sunday when an automobile in which she was riding with H.W. Durose, her fiancé, was struck by Great Northern train No. 548. The investigation revealed that Durose had crossed the track behind one train and met another coming in the opposite direction. The train dragged the auto 200 feet. Miss Sundquist was thrown from the automobile and killed, but Durose was in the wreckage of the machine. The tragedy seems especially sad in that Miss Sundquist was to have been married this summer to Fred Durose, who is attending dental college in Portland, Oregon.

Fred Durose, Miss Sundquist's fiancé, who is still very ill in a hospital in Centralia, has not recovered sufficiently to stand the shock of having the loss of his sweetheart imparted to him. He has only recovered consciousness for a few minutes, then lapses back again into a state of coma. He has shown greater improvement during the last two days, and his physicians feel now that he will recover.

The funeral services in the Salem Lutheran church were touted by the "Herald" newspaper to be one of the largest ever held in this community:

"Accident Victim Buried While Fiancé Fights For Life Not Aware That Sweetheart Is Dead."

The altar, in front of which the casket, laden with flowers, rested was abloom with summer flowers, bespeaking the sorrow of scores of Skagit friends at the early death of Miss Sundquist. Among those who mourned, there were many young friends. A quartet of young girls, composed of Miss Ellen Linquist, Miss Mable Roseland, Miss Ruth Wersen and Miss Arletha Johnson, contributed two selections. The burial was in the local cemetery; a long concourse of sorrowing friends following the remains from the church to the cemetery.

The death of a family member has an untold effect; the depth of intense, deep, and profound sorrow cannot be measured. We only know of Leona's grief that strained her health and surfaced in letters written during her time at Columbia University (September 1930—June 1931). And again in a letter written while traveling abroad in September 1931 to her parents at home:

> There is much of misery and want in a big city but there is also much else, which may be but froth in the realities of life, but they do serve to take your mind away from yourself a moment. That is what I felt in Berlin, a relief from—yes, I must also say, that as tough as New York was and as much as I disliked it & in fact hated it, yet it (sic) there was something there that occupied your thoughts & time & it helped a bit to relieve the ever present strain of sorrow, that I was submerged in.

Ida Elvera's black photograph album holds the only physical evidence of a life well lived, albeit cut short from our perspective. It is through Ida Elvera's album design with cryptic inscriptions, that we can know her, if only through her young life experiences. She was artistic with a personality that shines in the design of her album— vivacious, dramatic, and happy to be alive here and now as her arms thrust hither and thither in exuberant poses. I scanned her body posture, perused her clothing and hairstyle, and mused upon the setting that was selected to record that particular moment in time.

221

Albums preserved in their entirety are the legacy of the deceased and are treasured by those who never had the opportunity to physically touch them, hear their spoken words or know their presence on earth. Perhaps we place more meaning than was intended in the scant few words under a photograph or the moment captured forever on film. We are assimilating imagery and words from decades past with our own perspective, but it is the only evidence we have in our quest to know this blood relative as we pause to wonder what else she might have told us if we had had the opportunity for dialogue.

Social events in the early days on the farm were relatively simple, but genuine. At first they took place in various homes; the main events were singing and conversation. Leona recalls:

> Many of our friends were good singers, especially among the men, and Mrs. Oscar Mattson. Someone would always play the accordion. On one occasion, Father rented a phonograph, an Edison phonograph with a morning glory painted on the tin horn amplifier. Wound up with a hand crank, the phonograph played hollow black wax cylinders slipped onto the metal arm of the machine. We enjoyed this so much that Father finally bought the machine. Most of the recordings were in Swedish, among them being *Vårt Land; Du Gamla, du Fria, du Fjäll Höga Nord; Å Jänta å Jag; Modersmålet Sång; Suomis Sång.* There were few English records: The Star-Spangled Banner, America, The Old Folks at Home, and the Battle Hymn of the Republic. And there were a few humorous talking recordings featuring "Uncle Josh," such as Uncle Josh's Trip to Coney Island by Cal Stewart.

Music was a rich part of their lifeway. A magnificent highly polished upright grand piano from Bush & Lane Chicago graced the parlor; Daniel played the violin, Ida Elvera played mandolin. Ida Elvera and Leona were both accomplished pianists considering the 1922 and 1924 sheet music that has their names handwritten on the covers. The first generation born in America, while entertaining the family, carried on the music of their heritage with their performances of soul music—melodies from the homeland as musical landmarks of identity for the immigrants, evidenced by a tattered worn copy of *Finska Valsen För Piano Upptecknad* Af H. Wahlrot; *Hemlandssånger*: Utgifna af Augustana-Synoden, Augustana Book Concern: Rock Island, IL 1891; *Vårt Land, Sånger for Sopran, Alt, Tenor och Base*, by O. Vällane, 1891. The generation born in America learned and sang in Swedish the Finnish national and folk songs.

Sheet music published in Swedish by Dalkullan Publishing & Importing Co. and The Northern Book & Music Co., Chicago, Ills.; Aug. Södermann Century Music Publishing Company, New York, Pris 25 Cents, was purchased from O. Mattson Band instruments, Band & Orchestra Music 2218 1st Av. Seattle, WN:

Björneborgarnes Marsch Northern Edition .22 (Leona
     Sundquist 8/16/22)
Finska Valsen Arr. By H. P. Sather (Handwritten copy
     with words)
Friare-Valsen Bohuslänsk Skärgårdsvals
     Arrangerad för Piano Af David Hellström
Istorietta Opus 150, Théodore Lack, Copyright 1903 by Carl
     Fischer, New York
Jänta Å Ja!   För en röst med Piano   (Leona
     Sundquist 8/16/22)
Kläm I, Pojkar!   Hambo-Polska för Piano
Lill' Anna Marie   Folkvisa från Holstein För en röst med
     Piano
Lyckliga Jim Ballad Fred Bowers (handwritten)
Nya Fiskar-Valsen   Bohuslänsk Skärgårdsvals
     Arrangerad för Piano Af David Hellström
Nya Koster-Valsen   Bohuslänsk Skärgårdsvals
     Arrangerad för Piano Af David Hellström
O Night Of Peace & Stillness (Handwritten)
Swedish Wedding March   Aug. Södermann Century Music
     Publishing Company, New York. Primo and Segundo
Värmlandsnatt Frykdals-Polka Upptecknad Af J.G. Kjellberg
     Arrangerad för Piano

Daughter Esther reminisced about Sundays at home:

> Sundays have always been a real day of leisure. Church, Sunday dinner, gossiping, visiting, cards, games, anything to fill the afternoon, sometimes a hike up to Lake 10. On lovely afternoons dad gets out the car and we all get in and enjoy an afternoon ride.
>
> We have all attended Sunday School. The entire family is confirmed into the Lutheran Church. From early childhood we have each been taught prayers, the fundamentals of religion and a Christian attitude at home. Our religious training has not been "strict." As is the case in many farms where the work piles up during the weeks and the farmers feel they must work on Sunday in order to maintain an existence, this is not true of dad. He says, "You certainly won't get rich quick working on Sunday when you haven't gotten there all week."
>
> My father was Trustee of the local church for many years. His contribution to the church was not so much in the spiritual aspects as in the material aspects. His work has been in the financial foundation of the church. There, mother has not shone as brightly as she might have. That is one thing I hold against mother. For that church has (even though it has not been such a spiritual element in our lives) has certainly been a social element around which a greater part of our lives have evolved and through which we have formed our greatest contacts. However, as she says, she has done her part, but she might have done more in the same spirit as dad.

If we are to consider the comment that Ida Maria "has done her part," we might also consider elements of the church society at the time. Ida Maria occasionally joined the ladies of the church at the Ladies Aid Society as we see from photos of the group, but I sense that she would perhaps not acquiesce to the structure of the patriarchal church, considering her independent thinking.

The Ladies Aid Society met at the Cedardale homes of the church members, that is, the ladies and the pastor of the church. Why this social gathering of take-charge immigrant women, with like interests and language with the purpose of assembling for camaraderie and sharing news and letters from the homeland, should include the watchful eye of a pastor might have been beyond Ida Maria's acceptance. This group in the early 20th century represented capable strong women who had experienced leaving their homeland on a solo trip to North America or with small children in tow, traveling halfway around the globe to a new land, and successfully raising a family in the new world.

So why was a male pastor a participant in the ladies' gatherings? It would be unlikely an organized women's gathering would meet under the auspices of the church without having the leader of the flock there. When women banded/bonded together, who else but the pastor to support the patriarchal society and keep watch over the flock and conversations that might take place that would be detrimental to the patriarchy. His role was to read inspirational literature, offer a prayer, short sermon, then prayer/ devotional, all in Swedish. Consider that in the course of the time set aside from their daily household and farm duties, he had used up a good amount of their leisure time. Only then the women could discuss letters from the homeland, relate community gossip while drinking coffee, which undoubtedly would be the primary reason for getting together on a weekday afternoon usually once a month.

I recall the women of the church meeting at various homes. I found it puzzling and questioned why one man attended the ladies gathering, certainly women knew how to lead prayer and read from the Bible. My mother surely would have responded, "That's just the way it is." She was quick to affirm that the pastor was the one who looked after his flock. He was the obligatory guest at Ladies Aid. Could it be that women banding/bonding together might have been viewed as a presumed threat by the patriarchal dominated church and home? Men couldn't allow women to think on their own. That would only lead to trouble. And women were thinking.

What effect did a patriarchal religion have on my grandmother, on these women and the first generation born in America? These immigrant women were raised under the strict arm of the Lutheran Church in Finland where they could not marry until they were confirmed. No doubt their acceptance of the church in the New World would be varied. With the exception of Ida Maria's son Daniel who would marry a devout

Lutheran, few of the second-generation family in America continued their church experience. While I did not perceive all the implications at an early age, indeed I was aware of patriarchy. I knew then where I would encounter the Divine, and I have no doubt grandmother did also, considering her close ties with Nature and the comment by her daughter that "church has not been such a spiritual element in our lives."

It would be presumptuous to think that women didn't know about current women's issues in the Twenties just because they were down on the farm. Publications were delivered to the Sundquist rural mailbox and also received as early as 1902 in Salmon Bay: national weekly newspapers *Finska Amerikanaren-Norden*, Svenska *Posten*, *Svenska Amerikanaren*, and magazines *Kvinnan & Hemmet* Woman and the Home and *Ladies' Home Journal*. The Finland Swedish immigrants' children were off to high school, college and universities and were disseminating new information around the supper table. Leona Sundquist was the first to graduate high school in 1914. She attended University of Washington, Columbia University, and Harvard, and taught at Teachers College at Columbia and Stanford prior to 1923 when she began her extended career at Western Washington College to retire as Professor Emeritus. The Sundquist girls and their Sunnell cousins nearby surely delivered and discussed information among their families concerning the issues of the day, if in fact the parents had not already read of them in the newspapers and magazines.

In Sweden, Ellen Karolina Sofia Key's book and numerous publications concerning the issues of marriage, motherhood, and family life were translated into many languages in the early 20th century. Key, a Swedish feminist and writer, advanced ideas on sex, love and marriage and moral conduct in her book *Barnets Århundrade The Century of the Child* (1909) that made her world famous. She began lecture tours abroad in 1903. She also propagated her ideas through an enormous correspondence and influenced many young authors. Her liberal and radical opinions in most fields of cultural life, and especially on love and marriage, led to controversy. Daughter Esther wrote:

> "Sex has never, even in the family circle, been a tabooed topic of discussion. We have always felt free to discuss any matter with mother especially and with the older sisters."

There were issues concerning women's rights in the early part of the 20th century in America that culminated with new laws in the 1920s, including immigrant women's naturalization and women's right to vote. Down on the farm, they were aware that Finnish women were the first women in Europe to be granted equal right to vote in elections in 1906 and to run for parliament. Finnish women had attained political equality at a time when their society still retained many patriarchal features, but an agrarian society made it easier to accept the idea that equal political rights should be extended to women. Women and men in an agrarian society did not lead such different lives as they all worked together on the farms to accomplish whatever was needed. When Ida Maria was in Telluride, she was allowed to cast her vote. Colorado was the first state to enfranchise women by a vote of the male electorate passed in 1893, the major support from Populist ore miners. Even earlier in 1876, Colorado women had received voting privileges in school elections.

In Washington State on 8 November 1910, Washington's male electorate approved by a margin of two to one, ballot measure Amendment 6 to the state constitution that granted women the right to vote. Washington was the fifth state in the nation to enfranchise women. Washington's enactment of woman's suffrage opened the floodgate for other western states that quickly followed. Women in the east and southern states waited until 1920 when the right to vote for American women was codified in the Nineteenth Amendment to the Constitution.

Citizenship was an important issue for immigrant women. Prior to 1922, a woman's ability to naturalize was dependent upon her marital status. The act of February 10, 1855, was designed to benefit immigrant women. Under that act, "[a]ny woman who is now or may hereafter be married to a citizen of the United States, and who might herself be lawfully naturalized, shall be deemed a citizen." Under the 1855 law, an immigrant woman instantly became a United States citizen at the moment a judge's order naturalized her immigrant husband. If her husband were naturalized prior to 27 September 1906, the woman may or may not be mentioned on the record that actually granted her citizenship. As with Ida Maria Sundquist, the only proof of her United States citizenship was a combination of the marriage certificate and her husband's naturalization record, as she presented to the officials when she reentered the United States at the Port of New York in 1902. The Married Women's Act in 1922, also known as the Cable Act, gave each woman nationality of her own. Under the new law women became eligible to naturalize on (almost) the same terms as men.

Ida Maria was elated when she received a summons from the court to sit on the jury at a trial of an Indian who shot a white man. She exulted in the opportunity to serve her community and rode the milk truck to town each morning to report for jury duty.

Men were no doubt concerned and perhaps somewhat fearful of women gaining rights—taking matters in their own hands, so to speak, as change was in the air during the Twenties. At home, John was watchful of this new decade of flappers on the farm with flamboyant costumes and shorter skirts as hemlines rose to mid-calf during World War I. He expressed some concern as he openly opposed his daughters getting the new "bobbed" hairstyle in the Twenties. He said it was unbecoming. But bobbed hair was akin to making a statement by women attuned to matters beyond the farm. Daughter Esther recalls as she reflected on their new bobbed styles:

> "Mother had the deciding vote, and she could talk Father into the fact that this is the way it would be."

Ida Maria enjoyed a long history of being in command of events. Her daughters affirmed that she was a woman of strength and conviction, her speech was soft, she was careful to see that it appeared that John had the last word, but when Ida Maria spoke, it was in that tone of finality. And so it was that John Sundquist could only slightly resist when Ida Maria said, "There is nothing better than experience," as she and Ida Elvira strapped their duffel bags and valises to the sides and back of Leona's new Model T coupe for a road trip. They drove out of the farmyard and down the road on their way to California.

Ida Maria wanted to see where the lemon trees grew. There was no holding her back.

Farmhouse and addition (ca. 1918)

California, here we come!

Celebrating the family Buick 1926

Sundquist family 1926 Anderson Studio Mount Vernon
Esther, John, Ida Maria, Vivian; back, Alice, Eva, Daniel, Ida Elvira, and Leona.

The farmhouse

Ida on the kitchen porch

Chapter 15

Celebrating The Seasons

arm life is dictated by seasonal cycles, a lifeway that offers daily the closeness of living with Nature blessed by the sun, wind and rain. We feel the changing vibrations as each new season unfolds, experience the invisible bond that links Nature to all living creatures, and glean values imposed by cyclic time as Finnish author Topelius wrote:

> Country people, too, know time. In winter they often sleep ten or twelve hours a night, but in summer only three or four. Only amongst the gentry are there those who upturn the order of nature. On long winter nights they may stay awake with lamp or candle, but on light summer nights they sleep behind closed curtains. It is a pity to lose what is most beautiful in nature.

Finns exhibit a passion for Nature and innate understanding that body and soul are inordinately linked with the landscape and the seasons; no less today among many of their descendents in America, particularly in an agrarian society.

Summer harvest and coffeetime wrapped in a dishtowel

Ida Maria poured freshly brewed coffee into an empty Swift tin lard bucket and put on a fresh apron while the youngest daughters donned their fetching straw hats for the trek to the field. The older girls and son Daniel worked alongside their father in the field pitching hay with a wood-handled pitchfork into round stacks to dry in the field or shocking oats that were harvested with a binder. The binding machine, pulled by a team of horses, cut the oat stalks and bound them with twine into bundles, then four or five of the sheaves of grain were gathered by hand and stacked upright with the heads of the grain at the top so that they would dry before threshing. Depending on the harvest crop, nearby neighbors came to help also. The anticipated *kaffeedag* was of utmost importance during summer harvest, perhaps even more so while toiling in the field. Drinking hot coffee has a cooling effect from the hot sun and hard work of harvesting or threshing grains.

Ida Maria toted coffeetime accoutrements wrapped in a dishtowel handmade from colorfully patterned cotton sacks that contained milled flour. Four corners of the towel were tied together to create a sling to carry cups, saucers, and lump sugar. The girls carried pans of freshly baked cardamom-flavored *bullar,* slathered with churned butter and Everyday Cake, no doubt named because she made the scrumptious white cake almost every day. Or sometimes *rulltårta* with her luscious homemade loganberry jelly spiraling through each slice of the cake.

Why the saucers? John would pour his coffee from the cup into the saucer, and likely that Finland Swede neighbors who helped in the field did the same. The workers hunkered down in a minimum of shade among the hay or oat stubble, temporarily take off their straw hats or fedoras darkened from the stain of sweat, wipe their brow with a red or blue cotton patterned handkerchief, then enjoy their coffee poured into the saucer, sucking in the rich brew with a sugar lump tucked in their cheek. The family dog Gyp patiently waited nearby in a shady spot knowing he would get the last bite. Young Daniel carried his harmonica in his overalls breast pocket and might play a tune before they returned to work.

The first generation in America continued their traditional cultural celebrations and added some new American holidays as well. Midsummer Day marked the traditional summer solstice celebration that has its origins in pagan roots when cyclical events were celebrated. Summer solstice kicked off the season of summer picnics even as days began to shorten. Before the automobile, an area for a picnic center was cleared of forest and brush on the Lee's property east of Highway 99 in the northeast corner near the Matt Holmstrom home. Rope swings were attached to overhanging branches; a merry-go-round, teeter-totter, and horseshoe pits were constructed. A makeshift fireplace kept foods hot and the long wood picnic table was laden with food: Tiny creamed new potatoes dug from the garden along with green peas, potato salad, pickled herring, wild blackberry pie and berry juice pudding piled high with whipped cream. Wild berries that speak to the Skagit Valley's *terroir*, a special flavor that comes from the dirt—echoes of the earth derived from a combination of soil, climate, and weather that illumines our taste buds and our senses.

Between haying and harvest, community picnics occurred rather frequently, and when possible, children packed lunch pails and hiked the trail around nearby Little Mountain in the Cascade Mountain foothills to Lakes Ten and Sixteen, so named because of the Sections of land where they were located. The immigrants and their families celebrated *Fjärde Juli*, the Fourth of July holiday that observes America's Independence Day. With the advent of the new mode of transportation by automobile, picnic baskets laden with hot and cold prepared dishes were transported to various nearby places by the sea, the rocky coastline overlooking the archipelago reminiscent of the shores of the Gulf of Bothnia. The family later combined resources to purchase land beside the Salish Sea when John and Ida Maria, along with his sister Hanna Sunnell, purchased from The Similk Beach Development Company, Lot 3 in Block 5 of the Plat of Similk Beach, Skagit County, Washington, giving them easy access to Similk beach.

The long hot days of summer receded into memory; the Skagit flowed low and green—glacier green from melting glacial ice in the North Cascade Mountains.

Autumn's Tragic Message on the Party Line

The First Term at Meadow School began in the fall of 1910 on September 12, but the Daily Record of Attendance reveals that nine-year-old John Vincent and his sister Ida Elvira, age seven, were not in attendance the first day. His sister was marked absent the next day and a half as well, and on the third day, she carried home her brother Vincent's handmade wood pencil box with the sliding lid that he had from the time he started school in 1907 and that he was so very proud of.

The previous day Sunday, September 11th, was a golden warm autumn afternoon. Ida Maria was in the farmhouse kitchen tending three young children and preparing supper. The sweet aroma of cardamom bread baking in the oven of the woodstove permeated the two-story farm-house. Glass quart jars of freshly made Gravenstein applesauce lined the kitchen counter.

The older children, Leona and Ida Elvira, had gone to the barn with Pa to milk the herd of Holsteins—a twice-daily task that called for as many hands as possible. They milked cows by hand, filled the sturdy metal cans, hosed down the milk house, and pushed the heavy wood cart down the roadway to the raised platform where the milk wagon would pick up the cans next morning. After they finished their farm chores, the family looked forward to gathering around the wood kitchen table at suppertime.

Nine-year-old Vincent Sundquist and Hjalmar Lillquist, the boy who lived next door, ambled down the road after school and crossed the earthen dike west of the homeplace on their way to the Skagit River. Beyond the dike, another world beckoned: an enchanted forest, a secret place children were drawn to, although in later generations, there were copious warnings not to go near the water. The landscape on the other side of the dike changed dramatically from pastoral tilled fields to a scene of thick reedy grasses and ghostlike dead trees, their bare arms reaching out as if to snatch children away. Bleached roots of fallen Douglas fir trees protruded outward in their deathly repose; cedar trees sagged with the weight of dried grey silt that clung to the branches after the Skagit River had receded from flood stage. When the river ran silent, the foot-steps of mythic creatures magnified as they ran through the thicket and hid behind trees. It was a ghostly forest where children ran, not walked, to the edge of the river.

But this day was a day like no other. Mrs. Lillquist (the ladies were always referred to in the formal manner) slowly pushed baby Anna in the homemade buggy down the bumpy rutted road, attempting to find the path of least resistance on their way to the river. Four-year-old Selma walked alongside her mother with her hand clutching the edge of the carriage. They clambered up the narrow dirt path over the dike to the place neighbors tied their riverboats near the passenger ferry land-ing from Skagit City. Mrs. Lillquist strained as she pushed the buggy through the grassy area just before the rugged riverbank. When she looked up, she saw her son Hjalmar and Vincent Sundquist playfully run across the narrow planked gangway and leap over one rowboat to reach another. Then, she watched in horror as the boat overturned and both boys plunged into the murky glacial green water of the Skagit.

Mrs. Lillquist let go of the carriage and ran to the river. She waded into the muddy sand until the water was up to her chest, but by then, the boys were far beyond her outstretched arms. The strong, silent current of the Skagit River was carrying them away. Little Selma stood on the bank of the river and screamed, afraid that her mother would be taken away along with her brother and Vincent.

We can only imagine what thoughts ran through this woman's mind, as she frantically pushed the carriage a half-mile back up the rough dirt road to her home. She had been helpless to rescue her son and his friend.

The telephone.

Mrs. Lillquist rang for help. This part of the story is unclear. We do not know whom she called or when help may have come. In any case, it was already too late.

Down the road in the Sundquist farmhouse kitchen, Ida Maria lifted the telephone receiver off the hook to call out or was that her intention? It was a six-party line, serving six farmhouses on line—each house was assigned a different ring, but the rings were audible in all six farmhouses. It was not uncommon for neighbors to hear a private conversation if they lifted the earpiece from its hook to place an outgoing call. Ida Maria put the receiver to her ear, and she clearly heard the person on the line:

"The Lillquist and Sundquist boys drowned in the river."

That day the bell tolled at Meadow School to announce the boys' deaths. People from nearby farms gathered at the river and searched along its banks, but their efforts did not produce a clue. The Skagit had claimed the boys.

That the boys were never seen again might have been the end of the story, if not for the gift of clairvoyance known to run through generations of the Sundquist family. Before dawn the next day, John's sister Johanna Sundquist Sunnell, who lived nearby, lifted the telephone earpiece from its cradle and rang the Sundquist farmhouse. She told John she had a dream that night. She had seen Vincent about three miles downriver where the river forks.

At daybreak, John told Ida Maria he was going to the river. He pulled at the oars with the steady rhythm of his beating heart as he rowed his wood boat alone through the early morning fog hovering over the water. His deep thoughts surfaced to when he was a young boy of ten, and he had learned his father had drowned in the Gulf of Bothnia off the West Coast of Finland. Besides, he too, had a near-drowning experience at the same age. Now the Skagit River had taken their nine-year-old son. The situation was unfathomable. About three miles downstream, he found John Vincent's body entangled in a mass of branches and river debris—at the fork of the Skagit River.

September 28 was Anders Daniel Sundquist's birthday, the same day as his father John. "What would you like for your birthday dinner?" Ida Maria would ask, as each child was granted the meal of their choice on their birthday. She knew the answer before he loudly exclaimed, "Meat pie!" He always requested meat pie. Daniel didn't want sweet cake on his birthday. Perhaps because he was offered freshly baked cake almost every day.

During Ida Maria's boarding-house days in Telluride in the late 1890s, she baked meat pies, a favorite Finnish dish from her homeland, to put in the miners' lunchboxes. Meat pie became one of Ida Maria's kitchen staples and everyone's favorite meal. While it is basically a simple dish made with cubes of beefsteak and potatoes, diced onions, leftover beef roast gravy, and a thick hand-rolled crust, it is not created without some thought and loving preparation. The plan-ahead part is that the requisite to making meat pie: you must save a generous portion of rich gravy left over from beef roast cooked the day before. While Ida Maria used lard in the pie crust and constructed several pies for her large family, a recipe for one two-crust pie might consist of:

Two cups of flour; salt; 2/3 cup vegetable shortening cut into the flour by hand with a fork or wire pastry blender; then stir in 1/2 cup ice cold water. Divide the ball of dough in half and reshape into two balls. Place one on a floured board and roll out the piecrust a little thicker than one might normally roll out dough for dessert pies. Line the bottom and sides of a deep pie tin with one crust. Then add beef and russet potatoes cut into cubes and diced yellow onion. Sprinkle with salt and pepper. Pour leftover beef gravy on top of the meat/potato/onion mixture. Roll out the top piecrust and place over the dish. Pinch together the edges of the two crusts with thumb and index fingers around the rim of the pie tin. With a knife and fork create a simple signature design in the unbaked crust so the steam can escape.

Meat pie must be slow-baked for several hours. The intoxicating aroma permeated the farmhouse and tantalized the senses. Then, that moment of culinary delight as all savored the rich experience of Finnish meat pie.

Harvest Moon hovers over the Skagit
suspended in blue-grey twilight
announcing autumn's arrival. A tinge of
red preys upon vine maple leaves like
blush on a young girl's cheeks. Unlike
harbingers of spring that signal regeneration
autumn assigns change.

Like an artist mixing brilliant pigments
colors intensify to rich ruby red, medallion
gold magnified by sunlight. Bigleaf maples
punctuate the dark hillside, leaves clinging
like a showgirl's extravagant gold costume take center stage
against a backdrop of forest green fir.

Leaves languish as wind and time tickle
their presence, then drift slowly earthward
twisting, spiraling, settling. Swept into leafdrifts
by winter's first breath, only delicate skeletons
linger. The air takes on a hollow crispness
silence and greyness engulf the valley
autumn submits to the inevitability of winter.

In the Candlelight of Winter

The language of their homeland may have been replaced with the American language, but foods and holidays continued to reflect their Finnish Swedish cultural traditions. Tantalizing aromas competed for attention amidst preparations for the family's Christmas Eve feast. The heady fragrance of cardamom bread baking in the oven mingled with the scent of cedar boughs and the bouquet of *fruktsoppa* dried fruit simmering on the stove.

As was customary in Finland, *grankvistar* spruce boughs were placed at the entrance at Christmastime, and on the steps to the Sundquist farmhouse, cedar boughs were placed backside up, two or three branches deep, seemingly an invitation to trip and fall, but the tradition continued. I recall stepping with extreme care, strategically placing each foot among the cedar boughs. And it was magical. Each time the door opened, the fragrant aroma of cedar drifted into the house on the crisp air.

Daughter Alice explained somewhat in jest, "The cedar boughs were just a practical way to clean your shoes from dirty roads and paths before you entered the house!"

The oak dining room table was extended to its maximum length and covered with white store-bought damask cloths and napkins. Light from an abundance of flickering candles danced on china plates handpainted by daughter Ida Elvira. A silver basket held an array of traditional breads—Finnish *limpa*, rye *knäckebröd*, and crisp *flatbröd*. Bright red lingonberries glistened in a crystal dish. And pickled herring was a must. Ida Maria had skinned freshly caught herring and stuffed chunks of the fish into jars to be pickled in brine with colorful whole spices and herbs.

The much-celebrated dish at Christmas Eve supper was lutfisk served with boiled white potatoes and white cream sauce sprinkled with ground allspice. I recall that she wrapped chunks of lutfisk (processed cod) in a cotton flour-sack dishtowel and boiled 15 to 20 minutes in salted water in an uncovered kettle until the fish was tender but still firm. Which also brings to mind the uncommon odor of lutfisk cooking on the wood stove that permeated the entire farmhouse. For some, just looking at cooked lutfisk lying on a platter can be an equally disturbing experience; its appearance like an albinistic gelatinous blob that has the sluggish movement of an unearthly body. After that description, how can anyone believe that Christmas isn't Christmas without lutfisk, as glasses are raised to toast this fabulous fish.

Risgrynsgröt, a sweet baked rice pudding with cinnamon sprinkled on top or accompanied by *fruktsoppa* topped off the Christmas feast. The excited chatter among the older Sundquist girls signaled the presentation of the *risgrynsgröt* that held in the depths of this creamy dish a single almond. It was a Swedish custom, that whoever found the almond in their serving would be prosperous in the year ahead, but if a single person found the lucky almond, it would foretell his or her marriage in the next year. Whoever might suspect that Ida Maria had helped that event along with a hidden almond?

Some things never change and that applied to the order of the evening. Before gift packages were opened on Christmas Eve, everyone was sent to the kitchen to do the dishes after dinner; dishes were slowly washed and dried by hand, which for the children always seemed to take forever. It was a time of merriment and jesting, both in English and Swedish, as everyone gathered in the kitchen. Ida Maria sat on the wood box beside the kitchen stove—the warm box containing split wood. Everyone gathered around, as she began singing:

> Nu är det jul igen, ja, nu är det jul igen,
> och julen vara väl till påska!
> Men det var inte sant, ja, det var inte sant,
> för däremellan kommer fastan.

Aunts, uncles, and cousins joined in singing Christmas carols in Swedish *Stilla natt, heliga natt* and in English "Silent night, holy night" and a chorus or two of *Gubben Noah, Gubben Noah, var en hedersman. När han gick ur arken, plantera han på marken. Mycket vin, ja, mycket vin, ja, detta gjorde han.*

With everyone crowded together and the kitchen bursting with song and laughter, we barely heard the knocks at the door! The younger children ran to the door while everyone else loudly sang: *Jul bock knacka på vår dörr.* But no one was at the door. That was not the time to question who might have knocked; that was the signal to dash to the Christmas tree to open presents. The richly decorated fir tree reached to the ceiling, and the colorfully wrapped packages around the tree overflowed onto handwoven carpets on polished hardwood floors.

Following the evening's festivities, it was customary that the family, tired children and all, went to midnight Christmas Eve service at the Salem Lutheran Church in Mt. Vernon. Grandfather was a charter member, and he and my father Daniel Sundquist served as board members. "No complaining," my aunts would exclaim. "*We* had to *walk* over two miles to town after Christmas Eve festivities to be on time for Christmas *julotta* at six o'clock in the morning, and then we walked back home." That may be, but another aunt recalls the squeak and crunch of the runners on the snow, as they raced the neighbors' horses and sleighs to church.

Fortunately for us, traditions transform with technological advances. We drove to town that night in a warm car and returned to church the next morning, again by automobile for the 11 o'clock Christmas service. Aunt Alice recalled that each year Herman Ståhl, a neighbor and Finland Swede from Kronoby, Finland, sang "Hosianna" the triumphal late 18th century hymn that heralds the Christmas season.

Ida Maria was seventy years old the last Christmas she celebrated with her children, grandchildren, and her extended family. She was tired and frail; her health was failing. But her voice grew stronger as she again sang on Christmas Eve as always, seated on the woodbox beside the stove—*Nu är det jul ige*n. Now it is Christmas again.

Iridescence of Spring

1930 was a year of transition for Ida Maria and John, the first generation who founded the Sundquist farm. They had laid the groundwork for the remainder of their lives, as John retired from farming, and he and his son Daniel completed building a new two-story home on the northeast corner of the farmland. It was traditional in Finland that a farmer couple, when coming of that age, would deed the farm to one of their children, and one of the stipulations was that the parents for the rest of their lives would be entitled to live in an auxiliary building – *undantaget* – and have one meal per day and firewood for the winter. From their kitchen window the old couple could see the grandchildren grow up and feel the security in old age that their toil had entitled them. Following customary tradition in Finland Swede families, Daniel, the only living son, took over the farm that had now grown in magnitude with the purchase of adjoining land as the neighbors Holmquist, Erickson and Tjärnlund relinquished farming.

Anders Daniel Sundquist and Lillian Magdalene Johnson were married 25 October 1930 in a ceremony at the home of her parents Gus and Louise Lange Johnson on Pleasant Ridge near La Conner. Daniel brought his bride Lillian home to the farm.

The life and times of the first generation at the home place came to an end as the next generation took over the farm. John and Ida Maria Sundquist moved 18 December 1930 to the house John and Daniel built at the northeast corner of the farm property. Daughter Esther was at the University of Washington, and Ed Schnebele, who she would later marry, had written 17 December 1930 that he and her sister Alice had gone to Mt. Vernon to check out a new stove and order it right away, as her mother had asked them to do. There was a note of sadness in Esther's writing in 1930 about the new house:

It will never be the real home, for all my life has been centered about that farm dwelling. My life was as we lived it on the old farm place.

What will I do now when we're not living on the farm, there won't be any men to cook for or the big house to keep clean or any garden. Gee! I'm sure going to miss it.

Author Joyce Carol Oates reflected on the place called home: "For what is 'home,' except a place unreasonably loved, indefensibly cherished?"

I described earlier the composition of the Sundquist farmhouse and touched upon its artistic qualities, but it is the physical presence that transforms a house into a symbol for those who lived within and who had a distinct confrontation with place. Behind the symbol lies the other reality: the tenderness of the experience, the emotional impact of a relationship with place that is deeply embedded within the psyche.

Renowned 21st century Finnish architect Juhani Pallasmaa explores the properties, poetics, and phenomenology of lived space:

> "The artistic dimension does not lie in the actual physical embodiment, but in the consciousness of the person experiencing it. The word home makes us suddenly and simultaneously remember all the warmth, protection and love of our entire childhood. The nostalgia for the absent domicile results from the fact that we do not imagine the house, but the home and the life of those who lived within."

Leona returned home from a visit to Finland in 1931 and presented her father with a set of six beautifully bound volumes written in Swedish by Zacharias Topelius, that she had purchased in Finland: *Fältskärns Berättelser av* Z. Topelius, *Illustrerad av* Carl Larsson *och* Albert Edelfelt. Now that her father was retired, he had time to read. "Dad would read those books after dinner sitting in the breakfast nook where the light was good." The set of six beautifully bound books were proudly placed atop the golden oak cabinet that John built, flanked by two sculptural bronze bookends replicating the sculpture *Le Penseur par Rodin*.

Ida Maria was content with her accomplishments. Amid hardships and tragedies overcome, she had fulfilled her American Dream that was for her children. The couple gave thanks for the resources and opportunities that America had bestowed on them

They had accomplished much through hard work, perseverance, and faith along with the extraordinary power of a young Finnish-

American family in a new land working together toward a common good, united in their goal toward success and prosperity. And not to overlook that special inherited determination and inner strength, a Finnish trait called *Sisu*.

On 16 March 1945, the *Mt. Vernon Herald* summarized 50 years, as they were honored on their Golden Anniversary date:

Mr. and Mrs. John Sundquist celebrated their Golden Wedding anniversary, and although Mr. Sundquist was in the hospital suffering from injuries received in a recent fall at his rural home, the occasion was an enjoyable one. During the afternoon neighborhood friends gathered at the Sundquist home to extend their felicitations to Mrs. Sundquist. Presentation of a $50 bill, carrying out the 50th wedding anniversary theme, was made by the Rev. Oliver Nelson in behalf of members of the Salem Lutheran Church. Refreshments served to the guests featured a beautiful anniversary cake, appropriately decorated in gold. Later family members and visitors called on Mr. Sundquist at the hospital, bringing cake and ice cream and flowers.

Mr. and Mrs. Sundquist were married 50 years ago in Telluride, Colorado, and settled on a farm two miles south of Mt. Vernon in 1903. In 1930, when their son, Dan Sundquist was married, they retired and built a new home on the highway on the same property, where they have resided since. Their son now manages the farm.

Family members present for the celebration were their son Daniel and his family; Mrs. Arthur Kulin and son Donald of Pullman, Miss Leona Sundquist of Bellingham and Mrs. Edwin Schnebele of Seattle. A fourth daughter, Miss Alice Sundquist of Washington D.C. was unable to be home for the occasion.

I reflected back to the terse words that I first saw that described my grandmother's emigration to America from Kronoby, Finland:

Ida Maria Anders.dr. Lillbroända, född 1876-02-09 i Överbråtö, Kronoby, död i Amerika. Emigrant. USA & 1893-..-livsöde, inte känt.

245

Ida Maria Andersdotter Lillbroända, born February 9, 1876 in Överbråtö, Kronoby, died in America. Emigrant. USA 1893. Life story not known.

Indeed, there was a life story in America that compelled me to learn more about my grandmother. Perhaps the same words—*livsöde, inte känt*—prompted Leona Sundquist, Ida Maria's daughter, after her visit to Finland in 1931 to write her manuscript: *The Life and Times of the Family of John Leonard and Ida Marie Vikstrom Sundquist As recalled by their Eldest Daughter Leona Marie Sundquist.* The young girl who lived at the end of a little bridge, Lillbroända, in Kronoby, Finland, had emigrated to America, married, and birthed thirteen children. That would be quite enough in an era when women were expected to be supportive housewives, but Ida successfully managed to combine careers and child rearing, from the time she managed the boarding house in Telluride fifty years earlier. I perused my grandmother's astrology sign:

> To be an Aquarius is to be an original. You can't help but
> be true to yourself and your principles, and in the end, you are
> the one who can make a difference, steal the show or change
> the world.

Ida Maria was true to herself and to her principles, and indeed she made a difference in this world. She fulfilled her American dream of education for her family as all her children attended college and several went on to advanced degrees. Because of her encouragement to better oneself, education was solidly woven into the first generation born in America, and by oral tradition, her dream passed on to succeeding generations of the Sundquist family. Together with her husband John for over fifty years, Ida Maria Andersdotter Lillbroända Wikstrom Sundquist left quite a legacy. The cycle continues in America among Ida Maria's descendents, with respect and gratitude for the woman who saw to it that we would be a proud educated American family.

Lilies of the Valley by the back door of the farmhouse and pussy willows along the ditch burst forth as earth's harbingers of spring. The engorged red buds on rhododendron bushes wait to display their brilliance. Spring is the season of rebirth and renewal, and the spring grandmother passed heralded a season of change as the family slipped into new roles.

Daniel and his wife Lillian Johnson Sundquist continued to farm the land that as a young boy, he and his parents had cleared and nurtured. The *Skagit Argus* newspaper reported:

> "The United States government has admitted that Skagit County is the finest farming community in the nation, bar none. An assay of soil was the only soil given a perfect rating in the nation."

The pastoral scene across checkerboard fields of cultivated land is punctuated by vibrant well-kept red barns and white-painted farmhouses embraced by well-tended vegetable and flower gardens, that speak to the pride and vitality of the Sundquist family and other pioneer immigrants who milled the first boards from Douglas fir in the forest and nailed them together not only to create buildings, but with each board and each nail, therein lies a memory and a story. Architecture holds memories within its physical form and stories that bind the present with the past and for future generations to ponder. In poignant contrast, the decrepit abandoned buildings of farmers who had earlier moved on. The old weathered grey barn and milkhouse marked where the Holmquist family once lived, and on the other side of the Sundquist farm, the dark weathered clapboard house, stands in testimony to generations of Lillquists.

Holstein cows raise their heads and gaze, nonchalantly chewing their cud as they silently graze in smooth fields of greens that once gave consternation and blisters to the hardy Nordic people who settled in the Skagit Valley and who pulled and burned stumps left behind after logging. The farmlands are laid out like a soft pieced quilt varying in texture and color and pattern: some squares a solid green blanket of rambling pea vines, some pieces striped with rows of corn, fields of lavender potato blossoms, and bright gold cabbage in bloom. High above the Cascade Mountain Range, snow-covered Mt. Baker's magnificent presence and its glacial glow continues to shine like a beacon of brilliant light.

Shades of grey and green made up the Northwest palette. The light is delicate, luminous, iridescent. A shimmering blue-grey sheen spreads over the valley varying in intensity with the light. There are special places on planet earth. Skagit Valley is one of those places. I have no doubt that Ida Maria and John Sundquist recognized that when they first arrived in the Magic Skagit.

From the time I first returned to the homeplace from the university and still many decades later, I am overcome with love and emotion each time I reach the brow of Conway Hill and the first glimpse of the Skagit Valley below that signals to many of us— Coming Home.

Coming home
the road descends at Conway hill
through dense forests of alder,
tall Douglas fir, graceful hemlock
and majestic Western red cedar.
The vast Skagit Valley comes into view
like a curtain drawn wide open
from the edge of the Cascade Mountains
to the marine-air haze
hovering over saltwater bays.

In the far distance, the San Juan Islands
like a chain of spectrolite gemstones
floating on the silver surface of the Salish Sea.
Orcas Island's Mt. Constitution presides over the archipelago.
On the Skagit flats, checkerboard fields
like a quilt fashioned in shades of gold and green.
And there's a river running through, like a ruffled ribbon
edged in dark green velvet of evergreen trees.
                              —Arlene Sundquist Empie

Ida Maria 1876–1947

Bibliography

Alho, Olli, Editor-in-Chief. *Finland: A cultural encyclopedia.* Finnish Literature Society. Helsinki 1997

Armitage, Susan and Elizabeth Jameson. *The Women's West.* Norman and London: University of Oklahoma Press. 1987.

Bourasaw, Noel. Skagit River online Journal. Article *The New York Times* 1891 by Frank Wilkeson.

Clemensson, Per and Kjell Andersson. *Emigrantforska! Steg för steg.* Stockholm: LTs Förlag. 1996.

Erickson, Vincent O., Editor. *Living in Two Worlds: The Sunnell Family as Seen through the Eyes of Helga Sunnell Erickson Danielson.* March 1976. Fredericton, N.B. Canada. Manuscript in possession of Vincent O. Erickson, Ph.D.

———. *Louisa and Jakob Nyholm foster parents of Hannah Sundquist Nyholm Sunnell Jackson.* Manuscript in possession of Vincent O. Erickson, Ph.D.

"Grosse-Île and Irish Emigration to Canada." National Library News, July/August 1999 Vol. 31, nos. 7-8. SAVOIR FAIRE.

Hand Book of Seward Peninsula and Directory of Nome. E. S. Harrison, Publisher. Nome, Alaska: Nome News Publishing Co. 1903.

Heikkila, Elli, and Elisabeth Uschanov. "The Dynamics of the Finnish Migration to America and the Development of Emigration Databases." Institute of Migration. Finland. 2004.

Luchetti, Cathy, and Carol Olwell. *Women of the West.* New York: W.W. Norton & Company. 1982.

Lönnrot, Elias. *The Kalevala or Poems of the Kaleva District.* Translated by Francis Peabody Magoun, Jr. Cambridge and London: Harvard University Press. 1963.

Marjomaa, Ulpu, Editor. *100 Faces From Finland: A Biographical Kaleidoscope.* Translated by Roderick Fletcher et al. Helsinki: Finnish Literature Society. 2000

Mäkinen, Kirsti. *The Kalevala: Tales of Magic and Adventure.* Translator Kaarina Brooks. Simply Read Books. 2009 Canada. p. 75, rune 11.

McDonald, Lucile. *Where the Washingtonians Lived: Interesting Early Homes and the People Who Built and Lived in Them.* Seattle: Superior Publishing Company. 1969.

Mighetto, Lisa and Marcia Babcock Montgomery. *Hard Drive To The Klondike: Promoting Seattle During the Gold Rush.* National Park Service, Columbia Cascades. A Historic Resource Study for the Seattle Unit of the Klondike Gold Rush National Historical Park. Seattle. 1998.

Myhrman, Anders. *Finlandssvenskar i Amerika.* Helsingfors: Svenska Litteratursällskapet i Finland. 1972.

Ny och Fullständig Förenta Staternas Historia
Olin, K-G. *Vad gjorde farfar I Klippiga bergen? Namnlista.* Jakobstad, Finland: Ab Olimex Oy. 1998.
———. *Klippiga bergen.* Jakobstad, Finland: Ab Olimex Oy. 1998.
———. "Over 200 Swedish Ostrobothnian Immigrants Lived in Telluride of the Gold Rush." *Swedish-Finn Historical Society Newsletter* Vol. 4, No. 2. Seattle. 1995.
Österlund-Pötzsch, Susanne, Doctor in Folkloristics and Carola Ekrem, Doctor in Folkloristics. *Swedish Folklore Studies in Finland 1828-1918.* The History of Learning and Science in Finland 1828-1918. Societas Scientiarum Fennica. Vammala, Finland. 2008.
Österlund-Pötzsch, Susanne. "Swedish Finn Descendants in North America: Creating Cultural Identity – 'American Plus.' Åbo Akademi University, Finland.
Pallasmaa, Juhani. *The Thinking Hand: Existential and Embodied Wisdom in Architecture.* John Wiley & Sons Ltd. West Sussex, England. 2009, p 12.
Silfversten, Carl J. *Finland Swedes in America.* 1931. Translated by Frans E. Strandberg 1995.
Sketches of Finland. Edited by the Finnish Section of the New York World's Fair. OY.F. Tilgmann Ltd. Helsinki 1939.
Smith, Marian L. "Women and Naturalization, (ca. 1802-1940)." *Prologue: Quarterly of the National Archives,* Vol. 30, No. 2 (Summer 1998): 146-153.
Sundquist, Esther. *The Family.* Term Paper Sociology I Section 3, University of Washington. 1932. Manuscript in possession of Edwin Schnebele.
Sundquist, Leona M. *The Life and Times of the Family of John Leonard and Ida Maria Vikstrom Sundquist: As Recalled by Their Eldest Daughter Leona Maria Sundquist.* 1975. Manuscript in possession of author.
Sunnell, Agnes S. *Louisa and Jakob Nyholm.* Manuscript in possession of Vincent O. Erickson, Ph.D.
Sunnell, Bertha. "My Trip to Finland 1928." Edited by Elvera Sunnell. 1974
Söndags Skolbok. Rock Island, Illinois: Lutheran Augustana Book Concern. 1903.
Talmage, Rev. T. DeWitt. *Den Sköna Historien: Gyllne Perlor af Religiösa Tankar.*
Talve, Ilmar. *Finnish Folk Culture. Studia Fennica Ethnologica 4.* Finnish Literature Society. 1997.
United States Department of Interior. *Telluride National Historic Landmark District.* Report prepared 1987 by Christine Whitacre, Front Range Research Associates.
Vincent, Timothy Laitila, and Rick Tapio. *Finnish Genealogical Research.* New Brighton, Minn. Finnish Americana. 1994.
Willis, Margaret, Editor. *Skagit Settlers: Trials and Triumphs 1890-1920.* Skagit County Historical Series No. 4. A Committee of the Skagit Historical Society. Mt. Vernon, Washington. 1975.

Index

Index

Body language: family connection through, 60–61

Books: in Sundquist home, 212–14, 244

Borgå: migrants from, 183

Börje Vestös Cronoby database, 15

Bothnia, Gulf of, 28

Bowers, Esther Sundquist, 61

Brofeldt, Johannes (Juhani Aho): *Juha*, 32

Bullion Tunnel, 118–19

Burrows, Cole, v

Burrows, Kristen, v, 56

Burrows, Leslie Lindskog, v

Burrows, Lilly, v

Cable Act, 228

Campania, SS, 142, 155

Canada, 68, 70, 94; National Archives, 74, 76

Canadian Genealogy Centre, 87

Canadian Library and Archives website, 87

Canadian Pacific Railroad Line, 155–56, 179

Canadian Passenger Arrival list, 92

Carlson, Fred, 113

Carpentry, 157, 172

Cars, 202 (fig.), 219, 229–30 (figs.)

Cattle Boats, 93

Cedardale, 1, 164, 173; Community Hall, 190–92; farmhouses in, 171–72; Finland Swedes in, 182–83

Cedardale Road, 168 (fig.), 188–89

Cederholm, Camilla, 60

Certificates of emigration (*Ämetsbetyg*), 52, 69, 72, 79, 86, 97, 111

Chickens: on Skagit Valley farm, 173–74, 177 (fig.)

Children: emigration of, 94

Christianity, 29. *See also* Lutheran Church

Christmas Eve traditions, 240–42

Church of Latter Day Saints Family History Center: records in, 74, 77, 80, 87

Church records, 140, 175; in Kronoby, 48–51, 53 (fig.), 86, 109; Larsmo, 17; Nykarleby, 79, 111

Citizenship: U.S., 116–17, 123 (fig.), 149–50, 155, 227–28

Clairvoyance, 129–31, 237–38

Coffeetime, 4, 176, 233–34

Clancy, Mike, 5

Collins, Arthur, 118

Colorado, 103–4, 227

Community Hall: Cedardale, 190–92

Confirmation, 51, 86

Conflict of attachment, 139

Continuation War, 42

Corean, SS, 80–81, 148

Crash of 1893, 104

Crusades: in Sweden, 29

Culture, xvii; Finland Swede, 45–46, 111, 240–43; Scandinavian, 35–38, 40–41

Cunard, 73

Dairying, 172–73, 193

Damstrom, Gunnar, xii, xix

Danielson, Helga Sunnell Erickson, 50, 141, 183, 184, 210, 211

Databases: genealogical, 15

Davis, Wade, xvii

Democracy in America (Toqueville), 68–69

Diptheria: quarantine for, 88

Diseases: contagious, 74, 75, 76, 181, 208; quarantine for, 87–88, 91–92

Ditches, 194, 195, 197–98

Dodsworth, Harry, xi

Dominion Line, 73, 92, 93

Downs, John L., 164

Downs, Leonia M., 164

Draft: Finnish military, 148–49; U.S. military, 211

Dumas, Alexander, 61–62

Durose, H. W. "Fred," 220

Eastman, John, 113

Eastman, Mat, 116

Economics: of emigration, 58–59, 68

Index

Arlene Sundquist Empie   Photograph by Kristen Burrows

About the Author

Arlene Sundquist Empie received Bachelor of Arts degree from The Evergreen State College and Certificate for Narrative Nonfiction Writing, University of Washington. She is the author of *Minding a Sacred Place* under pen name Sunnie Empie, which received 2002 Independent Publishers "IPPY" Award for architecture book.

The Legacy of Ida Maria Lillbroända became a personal quest to find her Finnish roots, to learn about her cultural heritage, and not the least, to fall in love with a place called Finland.

> *"Reading and research open horizons not seen before, but only by being in a place can one assimilate the sense of place that is Finland. I search for words that would do justice to the magic of our summer nights in Finland when earth slept, and it seemed that someone forgot to turn out the lights. An experience that will remain with me forever, as I contemplate that haunting, lingering luminous color and sound of the northern night when the sun doesn't set."*

Skagit Valley in the Pacific Northwest is the author's spiritual home. From her writer's studio on an island in the San Juan archipelago, thought and memory meld into twilight moments overlooking the Salish Sea.

Also by the Author

"*Minding a Sacred Place*
features Boulder House, a building
nestled amongst petroglyphs and
Precambrian boulders in the
Sonoran Desert of Arizona."
—*Publishers Weekly*

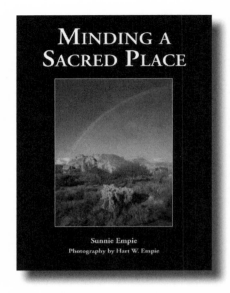

Minding a Sacred Place, an
encounter with sacred space and
ancient iconography that venerates
Nature and the feminine divine.

"The journey in finding kinship with a natural sacred place
is as extreme as is the architecture the extreme in defining
the natural house. To walk here is to experience the pulse of
ancient times. To see a beam of sunlight at solstices and equinox interact with prehistoric imagery carved in stone is not
only spine-tingling, it is a connection to the cosmology of the
first people in the American Southwest. Over twenty bas-relief
vulva-form petroglyphs, representations of the female genita-
lia, repeat the ancient iconography that arose worldwide."

The lavishly illustrated book is a walk through time and a romantic sojourn in the high Sonoran Desert of the American Southwest—
a personal journey with the author Sunnie Empie and photographer
Hart W. Empie.

The Empie Petroglyph Site AZ U: 1: 165 (ASM), National Register of
Historic Places 1998.

Minding a Sacred Place
Narrative nonfiction Architecture/Sacred space
ISBN 1-931025-03-7 $60

Boulder House Publishers
www.boulderhousepublishers.com